NOMINATING
THE PRESIDENT

NOMINATING
THE PRESIDENT

*The Politics of
Convention Choice*

by Gerald Pomper

NORTHWESTERN UNIVERSITY PRESS/1963

54

To Marlene

ACKNOWLEDGMENTS

Any book is a product not only of the author's own efforts, but also of the insights and support he has received from others. Although I am responsible for any deficiencies, I have been assisted, directly or indirectly, by many teachers and colleagues in political science, particularly Stanley Feingold, Mark Ferber, Stanley Kelley, and David Truman. The resources of the New York Public Library and the editorial encouragement of Robert Erwin have been invaluable. Interviews with Governor Robert Meyner and Edward Costikyan were very enlightening. I also have been personally heartened by the encouragement of many students, friends and relatives. Finally, I have been aided by the members of my own family caucus—my favorite sons, Marc and David, and my first lady, Marlene, who has provided unequaled labor, humor, and devotion.

G. P.

CONTENTS

ix

TABLES

Tables—cont'd

NOMINATING
THE PRESIDENT

I INTRODUCTION

"The American President is the most powerful democratic official in the world."

So goes a common statement about American government. Citizens and foreigners alike have accepted the statement and find themselves engaged in the busy game of "President-watching." Catering to this interest, authors have written on topics as diverse as White House menus and the wartime powers of the Chief Executive.

Political analysis of the office, however, has been largely confined to the election rather than the nomination of Presidents. Much has been written about the conduct of campaigns, the issues involved in our national elections, and the behavior of the voters. Yet, the nomination of candidates for President is also of crucial importance. Through the national nominating process, the parties reduce the number of candidates from possibly scores to but two. The voter becomes deeply involved only after his realistic choice has been defined and drastically limited.

This being the case, it is surprising that so little

3

serious attention has been devoted to the method of selecting the national candidates. While the election of the President has been the subject, in part, of four Constitutional amendments, the nominating process is largely unregulated, even by statute, with the exception of some state primary laws. Until recently, academic researchers also have generally neglected the subject. In the past several years, the Brookings Institution has published several works in this field.[1] Together, they now constitute the most extensive analysis of conventions. Many matters, however, still require investigation.

To discuss the nomination of the President requires more than an examination of candidates and national conventions. The conventions themselves deal with other related, but distinct, questions such as the party platform and its internal government. Nominations are also greatly influenced by factors other than convention maneuvering. The personal qualities and policy stands of the candidates, the results of state primaries, and the actions of national interest groups, to cite a few examples, must be taken into account. An examination of the nominating process must be broadly defined. It should also deal not only with analysis of the present system, but also with prediction and recommendation of changes in that system.

One fundamental axiom underlies this study: American national parties are chiefly interested in winning the Presidency. Related to this axiom are three major themes. First, the nominating process is related to the more general features of American politics. The system of nomination is designed to increase the chances of victory within America's unique political institutions. The second theme is the merits and functional quality of the present method. The

[1] These encyclopedic works include Paul David et al., *Presidential Nominating Politics in 1952* (Baltimore: The Johns Hopkins University Press, 1954), 5 vols.; Paul David et al., *The Politics of National Party Conventions* (Washington: The Brookings Institution, 1960); Richard C. Bain, *Convention Decisions and Voting Records* (Washington: The Brookings Institution, 1960).

system is functional because it contributes to the success of these institutions. Third, we will emphasize possible and proposed changes in nominating practices. Such changes are most likely when they contribute to party success.

The American nominating system is unique among national systems for selecting political leaders. A brief comparison with other nations highlights some important differences. In other systems, experience in government and long service to the party is given great consideration. In Great Britain, for example, a long period of apprenticeship is required before a politician is recognized as party leader. Beginning as a back-bencher in Parliament, he will gradually be given responsibility within the party and government, rising to preeminence only after repeated demonstrations of his competence and party standing. Leaders evolve; they are not elected.[2] American Presidential candidates are chosen from far more diverse backgrounds.

In other countries as well, leaders are chosen almost entirely through internal party processes. They are generally selected, in fact if not in form, from and by a small group of party executives. In France, for example, parties as diverse as the Communists and the Radicals are similar in that great powers are held by central committees of some 70 members.[3] Opportunities for dissent and conflict still exist within centralized parties, but they are far more impervious to outside influences than their American counterparts.

Dissent in these nations is often expressed outside of the established party system. Unorthodox individuals may find it necessary to found new political movements, as did Charles de Gaulle, or may not be called to leadership until a crisis situation develops, as in the case of Winston Churchill. The stability of the political order, therefore, is

[2] See Robert T. McKenzie, *British Political Parties* (New York: St. Martin's Press, 1955).
[3] Philip Williams, *Politics in Post-War France* (London: Longmans, Green, 1954), Part II.

often only temporary. American parties have been more successful in holding all types of factions and individuals within their ranks, thereby promoting the equilibrium of national political institutions.

In other nations as well as the United States, party conventions or congresses are prominent features. However, they serve different functions in foreign nations than in America. Abroad, party congresses generally have no real role in the selection of leadership. Nominations are made by other and smaller bodies. Instead, the party conference may deal with policy questions, serve as a guide to the opinions and emotions of the party rank-and-file, or simply provide mass support for the party chieftains. Even in Canada, where conventions do select the leader, the party conference is largely restricted to approving the succession of an heir-apparent when an older leader is replaced.[4] The emphasis in conventions in the United States is on the selection of leadership, while policy discussion and other matters are usually of secondary importance.

The American nominating process is different from that of other nations because American politics generally exhibits certain distinguishing features. Without great elaboration at this point, we may note a number of these important characteristics.

The Constitutional system has had great influence. The major features of federalism and the separation of executive and legislative bodies have promoted a decentralized and uncoordinated politics. The parties do not compete only for national office. Since the prizes of state and local politics are as plentiful and attractive, there is no necessity for cooperation in national elections, even among those who bear the same Democratic or Republican label.[5]

[4] Gwendolyn Carter, "The Commonwealth Overseas: Variations on a British Theme," In Sigmund Neumann, ed. *Modern Political Parties* (Chicago: University of Chicago Press, 1956), pp. 70-74.
[5] For a fuller discussion, see David B. Truman, "Federalism and the Party System," in Arthur MacMahon, ed., *Federalism: Mature and Emergent* (New York: Columbia University Press, 1955), pp. 115-36.

Incohesion is further promoted by the Constitutional separation of President and Congress. Fixed terms of office reinforce tendencies toward independence. Power in American government is not monopolized by either of the two branches and, similarly, power in the national party is not exclusively held by either legislative or executive officials. Each group has its own constituencies, and its own sources of strength. Checks and balances are built into the parties as much as into the formal institutions of government. This distribution of power among many agencies—state, federal, Congressional and Presidential—has also discouraged parties from emphasizing policy objectives. There are simply too many obstacles in American government to make a purely ideological party practicable.

The Presidency itself has provided a centralizing influence on the party system. The power and perquisites of the office have been great enough to provide reason for unification and cooperation among party factions. The unity of the office has also tended to restrain tendencies toward a multi-party system. Moreover, the Presidency has contributed to a peculiar stress on personality in American politics. "It is an entirely personal office. What the President of today decides becomes the issue of tomorrow. He calls the dance."[6] The personal quality of the office has led to a similar stress in nominations. As the office has evolved, the nominating process has changed accordingly. The change from the weak Presidents of the nineteenth century to the strong executives of the twentieth has heavily influenced party designations.[7]

The electoral system has reflected and reinforced many of these influences. The plurality system for electing legislators and the Electoral College for selection of the

[6] Theodore H. White, *The Making of the President 1960* (New York: Atheneum, 1961), p. 365.
[7] See Clinton Rossiter, *The American Presidency,* Rev. ed. (New York: Harcourt Brace, 1960), chaps. III-V for specific effects of Presidential actions.

President have helped to produce a two-party system. These parties have been decentralized, non-ideological, and in competition for many of the same voters.[8] A related influence has been the once-traditional and now Constitutional limitation of the President to two terms. This has widened the opportunities for political advancement, while forcing at least minimum circulation of leadership.

More generally, the nominating system has been affected by the diversity of American society, which has led parties to be coalitions of divergent interests, rather than disciplined organizations. At least until the present, there has been no single policy division on which parties could organize and compete. Voters' loyalties were not only influenced by their economic class, for example. Sectional loyalty has often been more important and has created an entirely different kind of political division. The electorate has also been divided on lines of race, religion, ethnic stock, residence, and other factors. The decentralizing effects of the Constitutional structure have been reinforced by heterogeneity of the population.

American society, moreover, has not paid much deference to the politician. Opportunities for personal achievement outside of politics also have been relatively plentiful in the United States. As a result, it is still probably true that "the proportion of first-rate ability drawn into politics is smaller in America than in most European countries."[9] This limited supply of talent might be expected to lead to a proportionately smaller number of "great men" as Presidential candidates. Another effect has been to encourage the parties to look outside of their own ranks for leadership.

Within the limits of American institutions, the parties

[8] The effect of the electoral system has been best described by E. E. Schattschneider, *Party Government* (New York: Rinehart, 1942), chap. III.

[9] This was suggested by James Lord Bryce, *The American Commonwealth*, 3rd rev. ed (New York: Macmillan, 1914), Vol. II, p. 185.

have evolved a functional nominating system. This system acknowledges the decentralization of national politics. It contributes to the unity and conciliation of a diverse population and many party factions in an effort to win the Presidency. It provides a flexible means for the circulation of leadership and the recruitment of candidates both from within established party circles and from other backgrounds. Most importantly, it promotes an effective democratic choice between competitive party leadership.

The American nominating system, as it now stands, emphasizes certain values and neglects others. National candidates are not chosen because of their individual character and intelligence, or their record of experience in public service, or their adherence to established party doctrine. Possibly, as a result, the office of the Presidency suffers. The nation would certainly benefit if all candidates were intelligent and of high character. Governmental experience and doctrinal consistency might also make for better Presidents, although this conclusion is more doubtful. In any case, the American nominating system will not necessarily or even customarily produce such men.

This system will, however, produce Presidents who are politically talented enough to win a party nomination and sufficiently popular to win an election. Because of their demonstrated political and mass support, such men may be best qualified to lead a government based on popular consent. Candidates will be nominated from a wide variety of backgrounds. They will represent differing policy positions and differing degrees of character, intelligence, and other individual qualities. Personal excellence is not excluded in such a system, but neither is it guaranteed. Given their basic interest in victory, the parties eventually will nominate any type of candidate persistently sought by the electorate. No more should be expected in a democratic political system.

To judge by the record, the nominating process has performed well. American Presidents have generally been able, representative of popular wishes, and adequate to their responsibilities. In a recent poll, 75 historians characterized five Presidents as "great" and another six as "near great." Compared to only two "failures," this is a rather notable record. Moreover, the level of competence of Presidents, as measured by this poll, has been increasing in the twentieth century; the "great" and "near great" Presidents occupied the White House for 35 of 60 years.[10] Some of the credit for this achievement must reasonably be accorded the nominating system, which presented these candidates for public consideration. Defeated Presidential aspirants, the other product of the nominating system, have also included many distinguished individuals, such as Charles Evans Hughes and Adlai Stevenson.[11]

One of the features and merits of the nominating process has been its flexibility. New developments in American political life have brought corresponding change in designating practices. Many of the characteristics of national politics are now being changed, and we can therefore predict and prescribe shifts in the nominating process as well.

Underlying political developments is the growth of a more integrated national society. The pressures of international involvement, population growth, social mobility, and economic growth are lessening the divergencies in American society and producing demands for national action to meet national problems. Sectional and parochial loyalties are being diminished, while ties to national groups and the national government become stronger.

The major political result of these social changes is the continuing shift of power to the national government and, within federal institutions, to the Presidency. American politics is becoming more unified, with the President at the center of the system. The political consequences are more competition between the parties, more cohesion within the

[10] Arthur M. Schlesinger, "Our Presidents: A Rating by 75 Historians," *The New York Times Magazine* (July 29, 1962), pp. 12, 40-41, 43.
[11] See Irving Stone, *They Also Ran* (Garden City: Doubleday, Doran, 1943), for portraits of many of these men.

parties, and more centralization in the nominating process.

Tending in the same direction are developments of new means of mass communication, particularly television. The mass media tend to focus popular interest on the national government in general and the President in particular, thus reinforcing the other centralizing trends. Similar effects follow from the growth of nationwide interest groups whose activities are unlimited by state and local political boundaries.

In these new circumstances, change in the nominating process is inevitable. In the following chapters, we will note many of these changes and investigate their effects. We will not only describe these changes but also evaluate various prescriptions for reform of the nominating process and recommend other innovations. In recommending changes, however, we must recognize that the present nominating system serves many functions, that it is consonant with American institutions and that it has performed well. In this work, we will emphasize the merits, not the defects, of the system. Changes will be proposed not to destroy present practices, but to improve them so as to better realize the main purpose of any nominating system—to organize an effective democratic choice.

The next two chapters will deal with basic preliminary information, the history of Presidential nominations, and the formal mechanics involved in making national party decisions. We then turn to the actual processes involved in party action on platforms, internal government, and the Presidential and Vice-Presidential designations. The eighth chapter comprises an investigation of patterns and trends in party nominations. This in turn raises questions about the future of the nominating process. Therefore, we will examine a number of proposed reforms and then present a series of suggestions for improving this unique American system.

II HISTORY OF
PRESIDENTIAL NOMINATIONS

The history of the nominating process is a reflection of the more general history of American politics. The changes in the forms used to designate Presidential candidates closely parallel more fundamental changes in the method of self-government adopted in the United States.

In particular, the institutions of the nominating process have been conditioned by the two-party system and by popular democracy. The existence of two, and only two, major parties has meant that each group of partisans has a significant chance to gain control of the national government and, thereby, to achieve whatever objectives it may have. Conversely, there is also a distinct possibility that each party may lose the next election and with it the varied rewards of political office.

In this situation the parties have a great incentive to take any action which will increase and consolidate their strength. With a majority always within sight, each major faction will strive to secure that additional support which is necessary for success. Each party seeks to form a coalition of the geographical areas and the major interests of the nation. In seeking this broad support, each party will inevitably include persons and groups with different goals. The likelihood of divergent interests is further increased in a federal system of government, in which states, and therefore state parties, have independent power. To reconcile the differences, some sort of party conference is necessary to provide an opportunity for conciliation, deliberation, and compromise of differences.

If there were no parties or only one party in the United States, as was the case in the early years, there would be only limited pressure for conciliation of differences. If the nation had more than two major parties, a system such as the national party conventions might never have developed. With each party unlikely to win complete control of the government, its members would not feel an urgent need for unity. Rather than reconciling differences through internal deliberation, the various factions within the parties could readily break away and form their own organizations.

Given the imperatives of a two-party system, however, any tendency toward separatism has been severely limited. Schisms have been infrequent in major American parties and a complete rupture has occurred only twice—in the Democratic party in 1860 and the Republican in 1912. In both cases, the inevitable result was electoral defeat for the divided party. By the next national election unity had been achieved again. In striking contrast, the small Marxist movement in the United States is represented by at least four distinct parties. With no chance of victory, these groups are free to indulge in ideological and organizational contests.

The national nominating system has also been greatly conditioned by popular democracy. In the history of the United States, one may observe a continuous increase in the degree of popular participation in politics and popular control of government. The advent of mass democracy first meant popular control of elections through a system of widespread suffrage. A trend toward popular control of nominations followed. The selection of Presidential candidates was first made by small groups of men acting as party leaders, then by a more representative group, the party members in Congress assembled as a party caucus. In time, this system gave way to the national party convention, which provided for more direct popular participation in the selection of Presidential candidates. In later years, and until the present, attempts have been made to increase democratic control through a system of primary elections. The voters were given the power to choose candidates for the Presidency directly, without the intervention of any representative or party body.

In their conventions, the parties have generally sought to meet or anticipate the demands of popular democracy. Procedures have been changed, platforms adopted, and candidates selected in accordance with perceived popular preferences. To be sure, the parties have not been mere puppets of democratic opinion. At times both parties have neglected the wants and needs of the electorate. At other times, popular preferences have been unclear and the parties have led, rather than followed, opinion. However, in a competitive and democratic environment, the party heeding the popular will, when that will is established, is most likely to satisfy its desire for office. It has been to the narrow interest of the parties to further the more general interests of the electorate.

Nominations Before the Conventions

Presidents were elected in the United States for 42 years, or 11 times, before the first nominating conventions were held. It was not until three more elections had passed that the present system was definitely established. Until this time, a variety of methods were used to designate Presidential candidates.

In the first two elections, no nominations were necessary. The members of the Electoral College were allowed to use their independent judgment in selecting a President. Never again were they to be allowed such discretion. The freedom accorded them was not so much a sign of deference to the wisdom of the electors as it was a universal acknowledgment that George Washington would be elected Chief Executive in 1789 and re-elected for a second term. Party loyalty had already begun to effect the election of 1792, however. Small opposing groups of party leaders, led by Alexander Hamilton and Thomas Jefferson, advanced differing candidates for Vice-President. The electoral vote for the second office closely followed party lines, as all Federalists voted for John Adams and all but five Republican electors chose George Clinton.

In the next election, the Federalists again chose their ticket by consultation among the prominent leaders. With Washington's refusal of a third term, John Adams was the logical party choice for President. The Republicans met in the first caucus of Congressional party members to ratify their obvious selection of Jefferson. The diminished discretion of the electors was evident when only four failed to vote for their party's Presidential candidate. Samuel Miles, a Federalist who voted for Jefferson, was denounced for exercising the prerogative granted him by the Constitution. "What!," asked an outraged voter, "Do I chuse Samuel Miles to determine for me whether John Adams or Thomas Jefferson shall be President? No, I chuse him to *act* not to *think*."[1]

In the next election, in 1800, party discipline was almost perfect. Acting in Congressional caucus, the Federalists named Adams again and chose Charles C. Pinckney

[1] Edward Stanwood, *A History of the Presidency*, rev. ed. (Boston: Houghton Mifflin, 1928), Vol. I, p. 51.

of South Carolina as his running mate. All but one of the party's electors chosen that year followed this mandate. In the victorious Republican party, all of the electors chosen, without exception, voted a straight Jefferson-Aaron Burr ticket. Since the electors at that time did not distinguish between their votes for President and Vice-President, the result was a tie vote between the two Republican candidates. The House of Representatives then made the final choice and selected Jefferson.

The evolution of nominating arrangements up to 1800 already evidenced the effects of two-party competition and, to a lesser extent, of popular demands. In order to secure their maximum electoral vote, the parties found it necessary to agree on a complete ticket and thereby to restrict the independence of the electors. With increased popular participation in the voting, it was also necessary that the choice of candidates be made by some representative body rather than by a small number of party leaders. The difficulties of transportation precluded the calling of a special nominating convocation. The Congressional caucus of party members was the most obvious means of meeting these needs for "a body which should impart to its decision sufficient weight to obtain the support of the party throughout the country."[2]

The Congressional caucus was adopted from state legislative caucuses, in which party's representatives met to designate candidates for state-wide offices and then "communicated them to the voters by means of a proclamation, which they signed individually." The first state caucus was held in Rhode Island in 1790 and had been adopted by all states within six years.[3]

Since the method had been proven successful, the Republican party continued to nominate its national candidates in the Congressional caucus. Objections increased,

[2] Charles S. Thompson, *The Rise and Fall of the Congressional Caucus* (New Haven: Yale University, 1902), p. 20.
[3] M. Ostrogorskii, "The Rise and Fall of the Nominating Caucus, Legislative and Congressional," *American Historical Review*, Vol. 5 (January, 1900), pp. 255-59.

however, to the system and its decisions. The selection of James Madison in 1808, his renomination in 1812, and James Monroe's first nomination in 1816 aroused opposition. In 1812, the New York delegation bolted the caucus ticket and supported De Witt Clinton in place of Madison. In 1816, the caucus was the scene of a sharp contest between Monroe and William H. Crawford. At least a quarter of the party members refused to attend each party conclave, and Henry Clay denounced the convening of the 1816 caucus as a "spurious and unhallowed act."[4] No caucus was called in 1820, as there was no opposition to the re-election of Monroe during this "era of good feelings."

The Republican caucus established some practices which have been continued, in one form or another, to the present. From 1804, the caucus was open to the public. Eight years later, a "committee of correspondence," consisting of one member from each state was named to direct the campaign for the caucus choice. In 1816, delegates from the territories were allowed to vote on the same basis as state representatives. All of these practices continue in modern conventions, with the party national committees serving some of the same functions as the committee of correspondence.

The Federalist party used a number of devices in naming its national tickets. Congressional caucuses were used in 1800 and 1804. After that, the party's strength in the national legislature was too small to be representative of the group. Nominations were made basically by small groups of party leaders. In 1808 and 1812, the choice was made at primitive national conventions. The one in 1808 was essentially the first in American politics, although it bears little relationship to the present system. Only half of the states were represented at this meeting, which was closed to persons not specifically invited and to the general public.[5] Similar procedures were followed in 1812. In the following election, the last contested by the Federalists,

---

[4] Thompson, pp. 27-37; Ostrogorskii, pp. 259-64.
[5] S. E. Morison, "The First National Nominating Convention," *American Historical Review*, Vol. 17 (July, 1912), pp. 744-63.

Rufus King was named by the party without any formal action.[6]

Nominating conventions came into increasing use in the first two decades of the nineteenth century. They began to be used for local nominations in the first years of the century. Soon thereafter, county conventions consisting of delegates from local meetings were held, particularly in the Middle Atlantic states. With improvements in highways, it became possible to hold state conventions, particularly in smaller states such as New Jersey and Delaware. As objections were voiced to nominations by state legislative caucuses, the convention system gained support.[7]

The possible uses of conventions were demonstrated by the state meetings and by Federalist nominations. Further demonstration came at the Hartford Convention of 1814, called to protest the conduct of the War of 1812, as well as to assert the power of the New England states and the Federalist party. At the invitation of the Massachusetts legislature, three states and scattered counties in the other states of New England sent delegates. Its organization and procedures presaged many practices of later national conventions. Committees on credentials, rules, and on an official report, or platform, were prototypes of similar groups in modern party conclaves. Except for the lack of a Presidential nomination, the Hartford convention was "a purely partisan meeting, and its report, viewed as a political platform, was intended to promote party unity."[8]

While these embryonic forms of the national convention were gestating, the Congressional caucus was coming under attack. One obvious defect was that the caucus did not include representatives from those areas in which the party had not won legislative seats. In some states, this

[6] For a general review of nominations to this date, see Thomas H. McKee, *The National Conventions and Platforms of All Political Parties*, 6th ed. (Baltimore: Friedenwald, 1906), pp. 2-19.

[7] Eugene H. Roseboom, *A History of Presidential Elections* (New York: Macmillan, 1959), p. 106.

[8] William E. Buckley, *The Hartford Convention* (New Haven: Tercentenary Commission of the State of Connecticut, 1934), p. 28.

problem was met by the holding of a "mixed caucus," in which *ad hoc* delegates were chosen to represent these areas. In other states, the "mixed convention" became established. Under this system, most delegates were chosen specifically as convention delegates, while legislators constituted a lesser proportion. Neither system was adopted for national nominations.

More fundamentally, the caucus system was too centralized. It represented an attempt to assert national control over a political system increasingly dominated by local and regional influences. The system could work when the nation's population was largely confined to the Eastern seaboard, when the eligible voters represented a small proportion of that population, and when the need for party unity in opposition to the Federalists was great and obvious. By 1824, these conditions no longer existed. The Union had expanded to include 24 states, suffrage was being extended to ever-larger numbers, and the Federalist party had disappeared during the period of one-party Republican rule. As a new political system began to evolve, there was a consequent need for a new nominating system.

There were theoretical objections to the caucus system as well. Congressional control of Presidential candidacies was felt to violate the Constitution separation of the executive and legislative branches. The claims of democracy were also being heard in opposition to this quasi-aristocratic method of nomination. "Politicians vied with each other in repeating that the voice of the people is the voice of God . . . The soul of American citizens swelled with pride, with the confidence of the man who is self-sufficing, who knows no superiors. . . . To exercise his proprietary right over the commonwealth, he had no need of another person's intelligence."[9] In the Congressional caucus, party members had no direct voice in the choice of their party's Presidential nominee. In the emerging democracy of America, this system was unacceptable.

In 1824, five men were prominently mentioned as the

[9] Ostrogorskii, p. 271.

Republican party candidate for President. The Congressional caucus collapsed in this year because it was in the interests of all but one, William Crawford, to attack and disregard the decisions of the party meeting.

> On the whole the campaign ... turned upon the question of the Presidential caucus. The Presidential caucus was certainly republican, but it was not exactly democratic ... and, what was even less endurable, it was apparently dedicated to the self-perpetuation of Virginia Presidents.... It was known to be for Crawford, who had been born in Virginia.... The other four candidates were, to be sure, Republicans too, but it was very much to their advantage to give the caucus system a name fully as disagreeable as its sound, and if they were agreed upon nothing else, they were agreed upon the ruin of Crawford.[10]

When the caucus met, it was boycotted by nearly three-fourths of the Republican members of Congress. Amid the derision of the public galleries, this rump meeting named Crawford. The other candidates were nominated principally by action of state legislatures, usually those of their home states. Andrew Jackson and John C. Calhoun were also named as a national ticket by a nominating convention in Pennsylvania.[11] With four different major candidates in contention, none received an electoral majority. The election was forced into the House of Representatives. In this vote, John Quincy Adams was named as President over Jackson. New party lines began to form immediately behind the two leaders.

By 1828, politics had become even more democratic. White manhood suffrage had been established in most states, and all but two now left the choice of Presidential electors

[10] George Dangerfield, *The Era of Good Feelings* (New York: Harcourt, Brace, 1952), p. 310.
[11] Thompson, pp. 37-46.

to the popular vote.[12] In keeping with this trend, no Congressional nominating caucus was held. The obvious Presidential candidates, Adams and Jackson, instead were named by state legislatures and by state conventions. In Pennsylvania, for example, a Democratic legislative caucus issued a call for a state convention. Comprised of delegates chosen at informal local meetings, the convention declared that "the voice of the Democratic party has been unequivocally expressed in favor of that illustrious and patriotic citizen, ANDREW JACKSON OF TENNESSEE, as President, and JOHN C. CALHOUN, of South Carolina, as Vice-President."[13] The convention then went on to choose a ticket of electors pledged to the party candidates, to establish a "committee of correspondence" and to prepare an "address to the people."

This system worked well enough when the opposing candidates were obvious long before the election. It had inherent defects, however. State legislative caucuses were defective in not representing areas within a state or whole states in which the party was a minority. Like the Congressional caucus, they were also apparently undemocratic, since party voters still had no direct part in choosing the nominee. If state conventions were substituted for state legislative nominations, these objections could be overcome. Another defect remained, however. In contrast to the Congressional caucus, nomination by state legislatures or state conventions was too decentralized. Theoretically, each state body might nominate a different candidate, making it impossible to win majority support for any single nominee.

This theoretical problem was a real one in 1824, when the multitude of nominations resulted in the House of Representatives making the final choice of a President. "It was clear that in the future each party, struggling for the great

<hr>

[12] Dangerfield, p. 420.
[13] Democratic Party of Pennsylvania, *Convention Proceedings* (Harrisburg, 1828), p. 1.

national prize of the Presidency ... must choose a single candidate.... Nomination by Congressional caucus was discredited; nomination by state legislatures made for a scattering of strength."[14] As the 1832 campaign approached, the need for some mechanism to promote party strength was evident.

To fit existing conditions, a nominating system was necessary in which all elements of the party could participate, which gave the party rank and file some role, and which could bring a limited degree of unity out of the diversity of American politics. The convention met the needs of the time. "It was representative in character; it divorced nominations from Congressional control and added to the independence of the executive; it permitted an authoritative formulation of a party program; and it concentrated the party's strength behind a single ticket, the product of a compromise of personal rivalries and group or sectional interests."[15]

Once established, the convention was occasionally challenged but never replaced. In its first election in 1836 the Whig party, successor to the National Republicans of 1832, held no convention. Instead, three different tickets were named through the action of state legislatures and conventions. In this way, the Whigs hoped to prevent the Democrats from gaining an electoral majority and to force the election into the House. The strategy failed, and the Whigs adopted the national convention system for the following election. Since then every major party has named its national ticket in convention.

In later years, the conventions were challenged by the system of presidential primaries. In an attempt to further democratize the nominating process, the electorate was allowed to vote directly on its Presidential choice. Beginning with Wisconsin in 1905, 26 states at one time or another

[14] Herbert Agar, The Price of Union (Boston: Houghton Mifflin, 1950), p. 246.
[15] Roseboom, loc. cit.

have provided for direct election of convention delegates
or for expression of popular preference among Presidential
aspirants. These elections have made the nominating process
more open, subject to greater popular influence and more
wearying for those aspiring to the nomination. However,
primaries have not replaced the convention, as many hoped
or feared they would. The Presidential nominating process
remains oriented toward the national party conventions.

Convention Developments

In the years before the Civil War, the conventions
assumed the tasks and adopted much of the procedure
which is still followed at the present time. In 1840, the
Democrats adopted the first true party platform. A model
of brevity, it consisted of nine short resolutions. The Whigs
followed with their own formal program in the following
Presidential election. The platforms replaced the earlier
exhorative "Address to the People," which consisted largely
of praise for the party candidates. Typical of these earlier
appeals for support was the declaration of the New York
Whig party, which praised William Henry Harrison as "the
man of high intellect, the stern patriot, uncontaminated by
the machinery of hackneyed politicians—a man of the school
of Washington."[16] Originally, the platform was adopted
after the nomination of candidates. From the 1852 convention on, however, it became a prior order of business. As
the parties moved toward the ruptures that resulted in the
Civil War, the significance of party policy increased further
and platforms occasioned extensive convention debate.

Another practice adopted early in convention history
was the naming of a national party committee. By 1852,
both major parties had named executive bodies charged
with the duties of conducting the electoral campaign, main-
taining the national party's nominal existence between campaigns, and preparing the next convention. These groups

[16] McKee, p. 37.

were a direct outgrowth of committees of correspondence which earlier had been chosen by the Congressional caucus. The national committees soon assumed the task of selecting the site of the next convention, a power which occasionally proved significant. In later years, they increased their power sufficiently to serve as countervailing powers to the Congressional leadership of the parties. When granted the authority to make preliminary decisions on credentials contests, they became able to affect the most vital decisions of the convention.

Various formal procedures were also established early, among them the selection of convention committees, the allocation of votes in proportion to the electoral votes of the states, and the casting of votes by state delegations, rather than by individuals. These practices largely persist today. In contemporary conventions, however, some states are granted "bonus" votes, and the roll of the states is called alphabetically rather than by geographic region.

In the early conventions, the choice of a Vice-Presidential nominee often presented difficulties. The 1840 Democratic convention adjourned without naming a running mate, and many delegates at other conclaves expressed a willingness to do likewise. By the time of the Civil War, however, the conventions had accepted the task of naming a complete ticket. The Democratic defeat in 1840 demonstrated the need for full party unity. Vacancies in the Presidency caused by the deaths of Harrison and Zachary Taylor also undoubtedly encouraged the party leaders to make a definite choice for Vice-President.

In the early years of convention history there were also occasions for innovation in political practice, as well as in formal procedures. In 1840, the Whigs gave the first demonstration of the vote-trading and manipulation which has become associated with convention decisions. Henry Clay entered the convention as the favored candidate, with Harrison a strong contender. Thurlow Weed, leader of the New York delegation, strongly opposed Clay and advanced the candidacy of Winfield Scott to provide freedom of maneuver for his state party. The Presidential balloting was held off the convention floor in a special committee of delegation leaders. With the aid of this unusual procedure, Weed was able to switch his state's votes to Harrison, who thereby became the nominee and eventually President.

Four years later, the Democrats introduced another political variation when they nominated James Polk, the first "dark horse" in American history. Polk ostensibly was interested only in the nomination for Vice-President, although some had considered him for the head of the ticket. The convention was deadlocked after eight ballots, with Van Buren having gained an absolute majority, but not the required two-thirds vote. This was the classic situation calling for a compromise choice. Having alienated no large faction by his previous actions, Polk was the ideal nominee.

Convention practices were generally settled by the time of the Civil War, although minor changes in the procedural rules and more regular means of selecting delegates continued to be made.[17] The decisions of the delegates, however, continued to show the effects of changes occurring outside of the meeting halls. As the importance of the Presidency increased, for example, the conventions showed greater deference to incumbent Chief Executives and even to defeated nominees of the party. The Republican convention of 1884, which rejected Chester Arthur, was the last to deny renomination to any incumbent President.

In 1892, Democrat Grover Cleveland became the first nominee to be renominated immediately after losing the Presidency. In later conventions, Democrats had eight opportunities to redesignate a defeated leader. They took the opportunity three times—in 1900, 1908 and 1956. Republicans did not avail themselves of seven similar chances until the renomination of Thomas Dewey in 1948.

---

[17] For full details on convention proceedings, see Richard C. Bain, *Convention Decisions and Voting Records* (Washington: The Brookings Institution, 1960), *passim*.

Unusual events have continued to occur within conventions in the twentieth century. In 1904, Democratic nominee Alton Parker took the unusual action of forcing the convention to accept his position on a platform issue—the gold standard—before accepting the party's designation. The Democrats, in 1924, again held a unique convention. This convention was distinguished by its length, as the delegates spent over two weeks and cast 103 ballots before selecting a Presidential candidate. The interminable proceedings provided material for many humorists, particularly Will Rogers, who wrote:

> This thing has got to come to an end. These delegates may not know it but right where they are sitting and sleeping every day is New York's municipal swimming hole. Summer is on us here and you visitors are depriving New York of their annual bath. . . .
>
> The tough part of it is that it is not like the convention you read about in the papers sixty-four years ago that had to move from Charleston to Baltimore They can't move this one. No other town will take it.
>
> A second-hand convention is one of the hardest things to get rid of in the world. . . .
>
> Another reason I know it can't last much longer is that the women who sit in front, on the speaker's platform, are about to run out of different hats to wear. They would rather lose the election than wear the same hat twice.[18]

Like many conventions, this one provided an occasion for the use of new technology. In 1844, Polk had received news of his nomination over the newly-installed telegraph. In 1924, the conventions were carried across the nation by radio. The isolation of the delegates was then ended forever. In 1932, the Democrats were the first to make use of another

[18] Will Rogers, *How We Elect Our Presidents*, Ed. by Donald Day (Boston: Little, Brown, 1952), pp. 34-35.

technological change, the airplane, when Franklin Roosevelt
flew to Chicago to deliver his acceptance address to the
convention personally. A third innovation in party practice
occasioned by technology occurred in 1948, when the party
meetings were first seen over the new medium of television.

With each convention, some new details are added
to the history of American political parties. The conventions
of 1960 were the largest and most closely observed in party
annals. In the future, these conclaves perhaps will appear
to have been the harbingers of further significant changes
in national politics.

The Major Conventions

In one sense, every party convention which has nominated a successful candidate for President has been a
major convention. One might therefore consider more than
half of the party gatherings in American history to be
particularly significant.

Such a view, however, is both too broad and too
narrow. It is too broad because it includes too many conventions. The renomination of Woodrow Wilson in 1916
or the selection of Herbert Hoover in 1928 were not especially notable in themselves, even though these candidates
were successful in the general election. This view is also too
narrow, for it includes only the Presidential nomination
among the accomplishments of the party conventions.

There are other grounds for considering conventions
to be of "major" significance. Unusual events or innovations
in convention practices are among the hallmarks of distinctive party gatherings. Such innovations were discussed in
the previous section. More significantly, some conventions
have resulted in a change in the internal power structure of
the party or have contributed to innovations in the national
two-party system. In particular, the events of four pairs of
conventions may be examined in some detail.

The major national conventions of 1831-2 were significant simply because they were the first. Precedents were established that endure today. Perhaps the most important of these was the allocation of votes among the states on the basis of representation in the Electoral College. In the Democratic convention a vital decision was made when a rule was adopted which required a two-thirds majority vote for nominations. This rule gave the South a veto power on the most vital decision of the party. The importance of the nominating conventions, however, was certainly not understood at the time. In both party conclaves, questions of rules, credentials, officers, and party program were handled rather casually. The very existence of conventions was considered so unexceptional by Senator Thomas Benton that he failed to mention it in his memoirs as one of the significant events of the election year.[19]

Despite this contemporary disregard, the new system of nominations was important in increasing popular control of the political system. Particularly in the party of Jackson, the convention "became the means of implementing the Democratic doctrine of popular sovereignty as well as the instrument for overthrowing the ruling class. . . . Here was a practical application of the party slogan: 'One man is as good as another.' "[20] Even among the more aristrocratic National Republicans the adoption of the convention system marked a trend toward mass participation in politics and popular control of nominations.

At the time, the conventions were more important to party leaders as a means of securing discipline within their organizations. Some kind of coordination was obviously necessary among "those opposed to the re-election of Andrew Jackson." The National Republican party was actually created at the first party convention. Meeting at Baltimore allowed the many opponents to confer with one another, to

---

[19] Thomas Hart Benton, *Thirty Years' View* (New York: Appleton, 1856), Vol. I, pp. 282-83.
[20] Wilfred E. Binkley, *American Political Parties: Their Natural History*, 3rd. ed. (New York: Knopf, 1958), p. 132.

present a unified national ticket and "address to the people," and to establish a rudimentary form of party organization in each state.

In control of the White House and the federal patronage, the Democratic party already had a functioning organization. It too, however, had a problem of discipline. Large elements of the party opposed Jackson's choice for his running mate in 1832, Martin Van Buren. To assure united support of the candidate and to invest this choice with legitimacy, "the Jackson men adopted the nominating convention. They did it in the name of free discussion, but for the sake of party discipline.... Its avowed purpose was to secure a democratic representation of the party will; its real purpose was to make sure that Jackson was obeyed and that Van Buren was nominated for the Vice-Presidency."[21] Indeed, only the question of a running mate caused any disagreement in the 1832 convention. No platform was adopted, and the rules were accepted without open controversy. Even Jackson's nomination was not actually made by the convention, but by state party meetings, with whose decisions the national convention expressed its agreement.[22]

By holding national conventions, the major factions took a significant step toward establishment of a permanent two-party system. Previously, electoral alliances were designed for each Presidential contest, with no assurance of continuity from one four-year period to the next. After the conventions, there was created a continuity of leadership, program, and membership. Party competition and democratic choice were thereby facilitated.

The actions of the 1831-2 conventions also helped to establish the differences between the two parties. These differences originated in the social background and governmental decisions of the Jackson Administration, and were formally recognized by the action of the conventions. Basi-

[21]Agar, p. 247.
[22] National Democratic Party, *Summary of Proceedings of National Convention* (Albany, 1832), pp. 1-8.

cally, the Democratic party was identified with the interests of small property holders, planters, and urban workers, and was opposed to the interests of larger capitalists. This position was made clear in actions such as the repeal of the charter of the Bank of the United States, opposition to protective tariffs, and reduced federal expenditures for internal improvements. "Jacksonian Democracy was an anti-monopoly party, the enemy of special privilege. The whoop and hurrah of the movement afforded a wholesome psychological release of the accumulated resentments of Western small farmers and Eastern urban underlings."[23] The National Republicans, and later the Whigs, became the party of the commercial and manufacturing interests. These differences were to persist for decades.

A basic change in the party system next came with the conventions of 1860. In that year, the Republicans completed the process by which they became the only group which has succeeded in transforming itself from a third to a major party. Four years earlier, the Republicans had engaged in their first national election, campaigning almost exclusively on the issue of the extension of slavery to the territories. In 1860, they widened their appeal and formed a coalition sufficiently strong to win the election and to dominate national politics for nearly three-quarters of a century.

The Republican party gained this dominance by becoming more conservative than it had been in 1856, both in its platform and its candidate. The platform dealt with the slavery question, to be sure, but it also approved of tariff adjustments "to encourage the industrial interests," free farm homesteads, and a program of internal improvements.[24] The dampening of youthful Republican ardor was indicated by a convention vote on the platform, by which the delegates refused to insert the words of the Declaration of Independence, "all men are created equal." Later, however, the

23 Binkley, p. 129.
24 McKee, pp. 114-20.

convention was shamed into endorsing the nation's basic principles.[25]

The choice of Lincoln as the party standard-bearer was made for similar reasons. The delegates sought a candidate "who would not repel the conservative voters of the more conservative northern states. Any aggressive anti-slavery man could have carried Wisconsin or Vermont. What was needed was a man who could carry Pennsylvania, Illinois and Indiana."[26] Affected primarily by a desire to win the Presidency, the Republicans of 1860 put forward a candidate and a platform designed to appeal to farmers and workers, industrialists and abolitionists. They achieved an outstanding success.

In the Democratic party, the 1860 convention marked a process of disruption, rather than consolidation. The division of the party was fostered by a number of factors. One was the two-thirds rule, which made agreement on candidates difficult even under normal circumstances. Another was the conflict between the policy and political demands of delegates from the North and South. Northerners generally favored the candidacy of Senator Stephen Douglas and a platform providing for popular sovereignty on the question of slavery in the territories. If these could not be won, their state parties were assured of defeat. Southerners wished a platform which would specifically guarantee slavery in the territories and a candidate who would support this position. Each group felt compelled to maintain its position. "The Southern leaders were demanding a protection which they knew they could not get. . . . Yet they knew not what else to demand. . . . The clan Douglas had similar emotions, they were tired of minority status and an ineffective position. . . . In other words the shadow of Republican success

---

[25] Allan Nevins, *The Emergence of Lincoln* (New York: Scribner's, 1950), Vol. II, pp. 252-54.
[26] From the *Chicago Tribune*, May 18, 1910, cited Paul M. Angle, "The Republican Convention of 1860," *Chicago History*, Vol. 5 (Spring, 1960), p. 341.

produced an impossible situation in the Democratic party. Its Northern wing was doomed, and the only platforms or candidates which the Southern voters would support could do no more than keep the ruling Democratic party in control in the South."[27]

A third reason for the disruption of the party was the absence of any group with a strong interest in conciliation. In fact, many hoped for disruption. "The Douglas men were not averse to minor schism; . . . it would be easier to roll up a two-thirds vote for their candidate. Many good Unionists in the South believed that two Democratic tickets . . . would throw the election of a President into Congress, and ultimately into the Senate, where the South could choose a trusted son. . . . Far more penetrating was the vision of disunionists like Rhett and Yancey, who saw behind schism their goal of two American republics."[28]

In these circumstances, party unity could not be achieved. After the Southern position on the platform was defeated, delegates from seven Southern states withdrew from the convention, making it impossible to choose a candidate for President. After 57 ballots, the convention was adjourned to Baltimore six weeks later. New delegations were admitted when the convention met again, and new defections occurred. After two additional ballots, Douglas was declared the nominee of the remaining faction of the Democratic party.[29] With the division of the party, Republican victory in 1860 became more certain, and the Democrats were relegated to a minority position for decades. Most significantly, the Civil War drew nearer.

> Alas, that nobody looked further ahead than the next nine months! The cheers that grew thunderous when Glenn of Mississippi predicted a united South before mid-summer were cheers for

[27] Roy Nichols, *The Disruption of American Democracy* (New York: Macmillan, 1948), pp. 321-22.
[28] Nevins, p. 211.
[29] Nichols, pp. 306-20.

the closing of the bright page on which the glories of the old fraternal Union were inscribed. The bright smiles and hand clappings which Charleston ladies bestowed upon the seceding delegates were applause for an irrevocable step toward war; the bouquets which they brought next day to fill the empty seats of the seceders were symbolic of the flowers soon to be cast upon multitudinous Southern graves.[30]

The failure of the Democratic convention of 1860 was undoubtedly the greatest failure of the American nominating system, just as the outcome of the Republican convention of that year was one of its greatest successes. In this year, as in other previous and later years, we can see the close relationship between the national convention and the larger events of American politics.

The Modern Conventions

Nine conventions later, in 1896, another major change took place in the Democratic party and in the national political system. Inspired by the oratory of William Jennings Bryan, progressives and advocates of the free coinage of silver took control of the organization and established a distinctive identity for the Democrats. In the immediate past, the party's programs and candidates had become largely indistinguishable from those of the Republicans. From the time of Bryan's first nomination in 1896, the Democrats were to become identified, even if occasionally incorrectly, as the party more amenable to social change and innovation.

Despite popular mythology, this revolution was not caused simply by Bryan's eloquent "cross of gold" speech. The oration was undoubtedly effective, but hardly decisive:

> Yet what he had to say had been said by him
> in many ways before; it merely had a new setting.
> . . . He had used his 'crown of thorns' and 'cross of

[30] Nevins, p. 223.

gold' phrases in a free-silver speech in the House of
Representatives on December 22, 1894, without at-
tracting comment . . . ; in recent silver debates in
Nebraska he had noted those parts of his speeches
that aroused greatest applause. Thus by frequent
tests of responses he had strung together phrases
that could be depended upon to capture such an
audience as he knew he would have in the convention.[31]

It was evident from earlier actions of the delegates
on convention officers and credentials that the silver forces
controlled the convention. Bryan did not create this sentiment, he only expressed it. More significant than the "cross
of gold" speech, or even the issue of free silver itself, was
the change within the Democratic party. It now became
committed to some form of government intervention in the
economy. It attempted solutions to the problems of disadvantaged groups, particularly small farmers. It became a
less "respectable" party, deserted by "a host of gentlemen of
the old school . . . men who in a changing era made the
Democratic party in the United States the last stronghold
of a political aristocracy."[32] Under Bryan, "the Democracy
broke with part of its past and began to move in a new
direction. . . . His leadership of the Democratic party helped
to force enactment of legislation the previous generation had
felt no need even to consider. . . . The Democratic party
under Bryan became the party of reform."[33]

In 1896, the Republicans were sharply distinguished
from the new Democratic party. The G.O.P. countered the
Bryan appeal with a forthright defense of the gold standard
and with an emphasis on protective tariffs as the means of

[31] Henry L. Stoddard, *Presidential Sweepstakes* (New York: Putnam,
1948), p. 118.
[32] William A. White, *Masks in a Pageant* (New York: Macmillan,
1928), p. 142. For a personal example, see Joseph W. Martin, *My
First Fifty Years in Politics* (New York: McGraw-Hill, 1960), p. 20.
[33] Paul W. Glad, *The Trumpet Soundeth* (Lincoln: University of
Nebraska Press, 1960), pp. 140-41.

assuring prosperity. In the campaign they "looked to the retention of the support of manufacturing interests, the solidification of the loyalties of financial groups, and the recruitment of a substantial vote from industrial labor. . . . The cumulative effect of the planks shaped for specific sectors of the population was a broad appeal to all those of conservative instinct."[34]

The total effect of the conventions' actions was "to set up against a rich man's cure for the business depression a poor man's cure, and thereby to convert a controversy over a technical economic question into a sectional and class conflict."[35] These decisions assured a vigorous and decisive election campaign. More effort, propaganda, and money were devoted to national politics in this year than in any election to this time. The results of the voting were of major significance. A sharp division of the electorate resulted in a clear and undoubted Republican majority. The G.O.P. was thus entrenched as the dominant national party, a position it retained until the period of the New Deal.

The events of 1896 continued to affect the nation's politics for decades. The Republicans remained basically conservative. While Theodore Roosevelt was far different from most of his party's leaders, his rise to power was more the result of accident than of a deliberate change within the party. The real locus of power within the G.O.P. could be seen in convention decisions such as 1912 and 1924. When faced with a definite choice between conservatives and progressives, Republican delegates chose the former—William Howard Taft over Roosevelt in 1912 and Calvin Coolidge over Robert LaFollette in 1924. In the Democratic party, 1896 marked a shift in control toward more progressive groups. In the future, with the single exception of 1904, no member of the more conservative factions of the party

[34] V. O. Key, Jr. *Politics, Parties and Pressure Groups*, 4th ed. (New York: Crowell, 1958), pp. 188-89.
[35] Herbert Croly, *Marcus Alonzo Hanna* (New York: Macmillan, 1923), pp. 204-05,

was able to achieve nomination. When a clear conflict existed, the conventions chose either a liberal leader, such as Woodrow Wilson or Alfred E. Smith, or a compromise choice, such as James Cox or John Davis.

Further changes in the party system have been demonstrated at more recent conventions, but there has not been a single dramatic conclave like that of 1896. Rather, change has occurred over a period encompassing three or four modern conventions. By the end of this period in 1940, the Democrats had replaced the Republicans as the dominant national party. The party itself was transformed from one based on the agrarian interests of the West and South. Instead, its center of political gravity became the urban electorate, union members, and a variety of ethnic and religious minorities. While the Republicans retained their traditional support from the business and financial community, control passed from the state organizations of the Midwest to those of the East. In the process, the policies of the party became more liberal, as it abandoned isolationist foreign policies and even came to accept many of the programs of the Roosevelt New Deal.

In the electorate as a whole, the events of the period from 1928 to 1940 changed American politics from one based essentially on sectional conflict to one based on class and economic differences. The trend in this direction was evident in the 1928 election. Probably the decisive year was 1936. Roosevelt's overwhelming victory in that year was largely due to a consolidation of the urban-worker-minority vote. The coalition formed in that year is still the basis for Democratic pluralities today, and largely accounts for John Kennedy's victory in the last Presidential election.[36]

The changes within the Democratic party began in the 1928 convention, when Smith became the nominee on the first ballot. Blocked four years earlier by Western and Southern delegations, his selection marked the beginnings

[36] See Samuel Lubell, *The Future of American Politics,* rev. ed. (Garden City: Doubleday Anchor, 1956), pp. 34-60.

of a transfer of party control to the urban and northeastern groups. However, the transfer was by no means complete. The party still nominally supported prohibition, for example, although these rising party groups opposed it. In 1932, Franklin Roosevelt's nomination was accomplished largely by the older groups, but the party did come out forthrightly on the question of the repeal of prohibition, while hedging on measures to deal with the depression.

The complete transfer of power in the Democratic party came in the 1936 convention. Roosevelt was of course easily renominated. What was more significant were the other actions of the convention. The platform was a forthright, even eloquent defense of the New Deal and of government intervention to promote social welfare. This theme was supplemented by Roosevelt's acceptance speech, in which he denounced his opponents as "economic royalists." "Roosevelt was looking forward to nothing more than having the opposition of his 'enemies'—the newspapers, the bankers, the businessmen—re-elect him."[37]

The Democratic leader was casting his lot with the urban and liberal section of the party, while limiting the influence of the once-dominant agrarian groups, and other more conservative elements. The meaning of the 1936 convention was fully realized by men such as Smith and Jouett Shouse, who bolted the party and formed the conservative Liberty League to oppose F.D.R.

Small events at the 1936 convention carried the same meaning. The two-thirds rule was abolished. While this action was of no immediate importance, it meant a permanent restriction of the power of the South. Some Southerners were irritated further when the new importance of Negroes to the party was recognized by having the convention addressed by a Negro minister and by Negro Congressman Arthur Mitchell. Senator "Cotton Ed" Smith of South Carolina left the convention in protest. "The death of the

[37] Raymond Moley, *After Seven Years* (New York: Harper, 1939), p. 339.

two-thirds rule and the acceptance of the political equality of Negroes had disenchanted him with the administration and maybe the Democratic party."[38] Southern disenchantment spread at the 1940 convention. There the urban victory was sealed with the designation of Henry Wallace as Vice-President.

The change in the Republican party was somewhat slower and less decisive. It began with Herbert Hoover's nomination in 1928, the first instance of the shift from Midwestern to Eastern control of the party. Since that time, every Republican candidate has been acceptable to, if not actually advanced by, these groups. This is as true of natives of the Plains states, such as Alfred Landon, as of New Yorkers such as Thomas Dewey.

Successive Republican nominations also indicated a trend toward acceptance of more liberal social policies. In their time, even Hoover and Landon were regarded as somewhat to the "left" in their parties. The decisive change, however, is probably most accurately dated at 1940. Four years earlier, the Republican platform had ominously warned: "America is in peril." In 1940, the G.O.P. accepted much of the program of the New Deal. Aid to Britain, social security, social conservation, reciprocal trade and the Wagner Act were endorsed, although with apparent reluctance in some cases.[39]

The choice of a candidate was even more of a break with Republican practice. Wendell Willkie had endorsed almost all of the New Deal measures and had even voted for Roosevelt in the past. "The party of Harding, Coolidge and Hoover, over the objection of its Congressional wing and many local bosses, accepted a former Democrat, a corporation president, and political maverick. . . . The delegates before whom the party was proclaimed to be the 'peace

[38] Edwin P. Hoyt, *Jumbos and Jackasses* (Garden City: Doubleday, 1960), p. 354.
[39] Kirk H. Porter and Donald B. Johnson, *National Party Platforms 1840-1956* (Urbana: University of Illinois Press, 1956), pp. 390-93.

party' nominated the only contender who could be labeled an interventionist, and the convention, which met for the sole purpose of providing alternatives to the New Deal, selected as the titular head of its entire organization, the only man who agreed openly with many of Roosevelt's domestic reforms and much of the President's foreign policy."[40]

The pattern established in the 1928-40 period remains as the basis of present American politics. The Democratic party is generally a more activist group, which bases its support on urban voters and members of the lower income groups. The Republican party is a more conservative group, but its Presidential nominations are invariably garnered by those representing the more liberal elements within the broad range of the G.O.P. In any given election, the party preferences of a majority of voters are likely to favor the Democrats.[41] These are the facts which contemporary conventions must face. In the near future, the nature of American politics may change and new facts will face party delegates. When such change does occur, if the past is any guide, evidence of the new party politics will be made manifest at the national conventions.

Suggestions for Further Reading

Herbert Agar, *The Price of Union* (Boston: Houghton Mifflin, 1950). An interpretation of American political history which finds our decentralized parties an essential means of preserving national stability.

Richard C. Bain, *Convention Decisions and Voting Records* (Washington: The Brookings Institution, 1960). Authoritative account of all major party conventions, including the rollcalls on nominations and other major decisions.

Murat Halstead, *Three Against Lincoln*. Ed. by William Hesseltine (Baton Rouge: Louisiana State University Press, 1960). Originally

[40] Donald B. Johnson, *The Republican Party and Wendell Willkie* (Urbana: University of Illinois Press, 1960), p. 108.

[41] For an interpretation of the 1960 election which substantiates this statement, see V. O. Key, "Interpreting the Election Results," in Paul T. David, ed., *The Presidential Election and Transition 1960-1961* (Washington: The Brookings Institution, 1961), pp. 150-75.

published as *Caucuses of 1860,* this is the best journalistic account of any convention year, written by a perceptive reporter present at the scene.

Edwin P. Hoyt, *Jumbos and Jackasses* (Garden City: Doubleday, 1960). An entertaining, popular history of national elections since the appearance of the Republican party.

Samuel Lubell, *The Future of American Politics,* rev. ed. (Garden City: Doubleday Anchor, 1956). A major analysis of the shift within the Democratic party before and during the New Deal and the rise of the Democrats to majority status.

M. Ostrogorskii, "The Rise and Fall of the Nominating Caucus, Legislative and Congressional," *American Historical Review,* Vol. 5 (January, 1900), pp. 253-283. An excellent account of the history and demise of the caucus system.

Eugene H. Roseboom, *A History of Presidential Elections* (New York: Macmillan, 1959). Including details on both nominations and elections, this is a good general survey of American political history.

Irving Stone, *They Also Ran* (Garden City: Doubleday, Doran, 1943). Portraits and evaluations, generally favorable, of the unsuccessful candidates for the Presidency.

Glydon G. Van Deusen, *Thurlow Weed: Wizard of the Lobby* (Boston: Little, Brown, 1947). The story of one of the most powerful of the old-style convention "bosses," who influenced Whig and Republican nominations from Clay to Grant.

William Allen White, *Masks in a Pageant* (New York: Macmillan, 1928). Portraits of the Presidents and politicans of the late nineteenth and early twentieth centuries, by one who knew many of them personally.

III THE RULES OF THE GAME

The nomination of Presidential candidates is one of the most institutionalized aspects of American national politics. The entire process is conducted through well-established procedures and patterns of behavior. Much of this process, especially that conducted at the national conventions, is an elaborate ritual. Together with elections and the formalities of Presidential inaugurations, it is an American and democratic substitute for the coronation of a king. The nomination represents "the prerecognition of the notables," to be followed by "the tumultous choice of the freemen." [1]

At the nominating conventions, this ritualistic aspect has become increasingly important. Theoretically, the convention is the supreme body of each national party, able at will to change its rules, composition, and leadership. Actually the convention as a whole has limited discretion.

[1] Henry Jones Ford, *The Rise and Growth of American Politics* (New York: Macmillan, 1914), p. 293.

Many of its decisions are made either in accordance with tradition or by smaller groups meeting apart from the convention. We will note the importance of such groups as we trace the actions which culminate in the party nominations.

Selecting the Delegates

In general, the delegates to the national convention are chosen by one of two methods. A majority of the delegates are selected through internal party processes which begin as early as two years before a presidential election. A significant minority of the delegates are named in direct primary elections, held between March and June of the election year. Even when a party body makes the choice of delegates, this body usually bears some responsibility to the electorate, since it is selected directly or indirectly by popular vote.[2]

The party body involved is either a state party committee or a combination of state and Congressional district party conventions. In the Democratic party in Georgia, Arkansas, and Louisiana, the party's state committee selects a complete slate of national convention delegates. In New York and Pennsylvania, the state committee of both parties chooses only the delegates-at-large. In all of these states, the state committee itself is chosen in a popular primary, although interest in its election is not necessarily great.

In all the other states using party processes, delegates are chosen at district and state conventions. There is a great variation, however, in how these conventions in turn are constituted. Members can be elected in the primaries. Alternately, the voters may name members of county committees or conventions, which in turn select representatives

[2] The most complete study is Paul David et al., Presidential Nominating Politics in 1952 (Baltimore: The Johns Hopkins University Press, 1954), 5 vols., particularly Vol. I, pp. 162-73. Further details are presented in Paul David et al., The Politics of National Party Conventions (Washington: The Brookings Institution, 1960), pp. 548-55.

to a state convention. In other areas, delegates to state meetings may be chosen in informal, open party caucuses.

Whatever the particular mechanism involved, the fundamental fact is that the rank-and-file voter is either two or three steps removed from the choice of delegates to the national convention. If two steps removed, he can choose the men who then select the delegates. If three steps removed, he only chooses men who then choose *other* men to name the delegates. The voter's preferences may still be heard, but only through a filter.

The time at which the voter can exercise his influence also varies widely. Some state bodies are chosen in the spring or early summer of Presidential election years. Since the voter's interest in national politics is likely to be aroused by this time, he has a greater opportunity to express his preferences. In other states, however, the choice of party officials is made earlier, and without regard to the Presidential nomination. Popular influence is perhaps least apparent in Arizona. In this state, county committees are chosen in party primaries two years before the Presidential election. This is the voter's last direct participation in the national nominations. Soon after their election, these county committees choose the state party committees. Two years later, the latter groups will name the delegates to the national convention and may even instruct the delegates on the Presidential nomination.

In the remaining states, delegates to the national convention are chosen directly by the voters in a primary election. Under this procedure, the selection of delegates is no longer left principally to the parties, but comes under detailed state regulation. There are great differences among the various state laws and many confusions even in a single state statute. Perhaps the ultimate in chaos came in the 1920 Republican primary in Illinois. In one district, a delegate was elected pledged to the Presidential candidacy of Hiram Johnson. At the same time, a preference poll among voters of the district was won by Leonard Wood, while a state-wide preference poll favored Frank Lowden.[3] Such situations are still possible today.

One means of classifying the primary election systems is to separate preference polls from the election of delegates. In the former, the voters indicate their choice for the Presidential nominee, while the delegates are chosen in another way. Ten states now hold preference polls. In seven of these, the poll is only advisory and does not bind the chosen delegates.

In three states, Oregon, Maryland, and Indiana, the voter's preference is binding on the delegates, even when they are chosen, as in the last two states, in state party conventions. The possible anomalies are obvious. The voters, by expressing their preference, may bind delegates who are personally opposed to the winning candidate. In the 1960 Democratic convention, an Oregon delegate found himself in such a situation of divided loyalty. Bound by the state preference poll to John Kennedy, he personally favored Adlai Stevenson. At the time for decision, he voted for Stevenson and abandoned the mandate for Kennedy.

To be included in a preference poll, a candidate usually must give his consent. Oregon is the only exception. There, the state Secretary of State is authorized to place on the ballot the names of all candidates "generally advocated or recognized." Such individuals can have their names removed only by submitting a sworn affidavit disclaiming all interest in the party nominations.

In 15 states and the District of Columbia, the delegates themselves are chosen by the party rank-and-file in primary elections. No two state systems are precisely the same. Amid the variety, however, there are important distinguishing characteristics. One such feature is the commitment made by delegates to Presidential candidates. In only

[3] Cited by Senator Estes Kefauver, in U. S. Senate, Judiciary Committee, *Nomination and Election of President and Vice-President,* Hearings on S. J. Res. 3 and others, 84th Cong., 1st sess. (1955), p. 355.

TABLE 3-1

PRESIDENTIAL PREFERENCE POLLS AND PRIMARIES

State	Preference Poll	Delegates Elected	Consent of Candidate	Candidate Slates	Size of Constituency	Date 1960	Open or Closed
Ala.	None	Unpledged	Unnecessary	None	District, State	May 3	Closed
Cal.	None	May Pledge	Required	Required	State-wide	June 7	Closed
Fla.	None	May Pledge	Unnecessary	Required	District, State	May 24	Closed
Ill.	Advisory	Unpledged	May Decline	None	District only	April 12	Closed
Ind.	Binding	None	Required	None	District, State	May 3	Closed
Md.	Binding	None	Required	None	State-wide	May 17	Closed
Mass.	Advisory	May Pledge	Required	Allowed	District, State	April 26	Closed
Neb.	Advisory	Unpledged	Required	None	District, State	May 10	Closed
N.H.	Advisory	May Pledge	Optional	Allowed	District, State	March 8	Closed
N.J.	Advisory	May Pledge	Required	Allowed	District, State	April 26	Closed
N.Y.	None	Unpledged	Unnecessary	None	District only	June 7	Closed
Ohio	None	Pledged	Required	None	District, State	May 3	Closed
Ore.	Binding	May Pledge	Unnecessary	Allowed	District, State	May 20	Closed
Pa.	Advisory	Unpledged	May Decline	None	District only	April 26	Closed
S.D.	None	May Pledge	Required	Required	State-wide	June 7	Closed
W.Va.	Advisory	Unpledged	Required	None	District, State	May 10	Closed
Wis.	None	Pledged	Required	Allowed	District, State	April 5	Open
D.C.	None	Unpledged	Unnecessary	None	District-wide	May 3	Closed

two states, Ohio and Wisconsin, are prospective delegates required to pledge themselves to support some particular aspirant. Such an avowal was also required in California through the 1960 election. In another six states, and the District of Columbia, the delegates are not permitted to indicate a preference on the official ballot. In the remaining six states, the delegates are given the option of running pledged or without a stated preference. These and other differences in the state systems are summarized in the following table.[4]

Presidential candidates can usually, but not always, control the frequency with which delegates pledged to their support appear on state ballots. Both of the states requiring prospective delegates to be pledged to a Presidential aspirant also require them to obtain the consent of the candidate. The states in which delegate pledges are optional generally follow the same practice. Consent is not required, however, in Florida and Oregon. In New Hampshire, a candidate must give his consent if a delegate is firmly pledged to him, but this is not necessary if the delegate only declares a "preference" in his favor. Obviously no consent is needed when the delegates are unpledged.

Primary systems also differ in the latitude they allow for the formation of slates. When slates of pledged delegates are not allowed, it is difficult for the voter to make clear his nominating preference. In three states, slates are not only permitted, but are required. In these cases, the voter's choice is simple, campaigning is facilitated, and the meaning of the election becomes relatively easy to interpret.

The size of the voting constituency differs from one state to another. Primary victories may be decided on a

[4] For more detail, see David's 1960 volume, pp. 528-47 and Republican National Committee, Research Division, *The Process of Delegate Selection for the Republican National Convention of 1960* (Washington: mimeo, 1959), pp. 1-24. For the 1964 election, Mississippi has instituted a unique primary election, to be held in September. Voters will then decide whether pledged or unpledged electors will appear on the ballot as Democratic party candidates.

state-wide basis or by both district and state votes. In the Indiana preference poll, for example, a district delegate is bound by the results in his district and the delegates-at-large are governed by the state-wide result. In Maryland, on the other hand, the state-wide result of the preference poll binds all delegates, regardless of the outcome in their individual districts. Obviously, a Presidential aspirant has more to win, or lose, from a winner-take-all system than from one based on the individual districts. Thus, Kennedy in 1960 entered the Maryland contest where he had a good chance of winning all delegates. He shied away from the California contest, where his strength was less, and he risked a complete defeat.

Another major variation is in the composition of the eligible electorate. Most states limit the right to vote in primaries to those registered as party members. However, in Wisconsin, voters may cast ballots in either party contest. This creates the possibility of an invasion, spontaneous or organized, of a party primary by members of the opposition. The participation of Wisconsin Republicans in the 1960 Democratic primary confused the choice between Kennedy and Humphrey there and made the results difficult to interpret. Finally, primaries are held on different dates, generally spread over a three-month period.

From this review, it is obvious that any candidate hoping to advance his Presidential prospects by primary victories faces a complicated and arduous task. Strategy appropriate to one state will be inapplicable in another. New legal problems will be presented constantly. Kennedy, in 1960, began his efforts in New Hampshire which provided for a non-binding preference poll and the selection of delegates pledged to a Presidential candidate. He concluded in Oregon, in which the situation was almost the direct opposite. There the preference poll was binding and the stated position of the elected delegates was inconsequential.

Moreover, the primaries do not always enable voters to express their preferences among Presidential hopefuls.

Present state laws generally allow the aspirants themselves to determine the significance of primaries. Since individuals usually may withdraw from a contest, there is no assurance that the voters will be able to choose among all the major possibilities. Candidates can select their primaries carefully, entering only those where success is likely, while refraining from close contests.

State laws do little to encourage candidates to enter the primaries. In a majority of these states, after entering and winning an election contest, a candidate may find that he has gained no significant support. Advisory preference polls add nothing to the total of pledged delegates. Even binding preference polls, when divorced from the choice of delegates, may be of little benefit. "In time of stress, if the delegates' personal preferences and their instructions are at variance they may either totally ignore their instructions ... or follow their instructions to the letter in voting on nominees but ignore them on other questions which may be vital to the candidate whom they are instructed to support."[5] Considering all of the problems involved, it is not surprising that many possible candidates decline to present themselves to the voters in presidential primaries.

The National Committee

However chosen, the delegates eventually find their way to the national convention. Preparations for the party conclave are managed by the National Committee, consisting of two or three representatives from each state delegation.

The National Committee makes two decisions which are necessarily irrevocable. It decides on the site of the convention and on the apportionment of votes among the states. The choice of a convention city has been deemed important in the past. In 1860, for example, support from the Chicago crowd enhanced Lincoln's nominating drive.

[5] Louise Overacker, *The Presidential Primary* (New York: Macmillan, 1926), p. 64.

In the same year, the efforts of Stephen Douglas were reportedly handicapped by the Charleston location of the Democratic convention. Careful consideration therefore was given to the presumed "neutrality" or central geographical position of a city. Such factors accounted for the early preference for Baltimore as a convention site and the more recent popularity of Chicago.

With the advent of instantaneous communication and rapid transportation, however, the importance of location has been reduced. The National Committee is more likely to consider the advantages of an area as a launching site for the party's Presidential campaign. For this reason, California was chosen by the Republicans in 1956 and the Democrats in 1960. Conversely, the parties have been reluctant to hold their conventions in Miami, for fear of incidents involving racial segregation in that Southern metropolis.

Discretion in the choice of a convention city is also limited by the large size of conventions. Given the thousands of delegates and observers present, a site must be found with a plentitude of hotel accommodations and comparative ease of transportation. The demands of television narrow the choice still further. To obtain the largest audience, conventions tend to be held in the central states. Given this location, voters in all parts of the nation can watch the proceedings at a reasonable evening hour. For these reasons, as well as the traditional ones, the city of Chicago is likely to remain the most favored convention location.

The National Committee also decides on the apportionment of delegates among the states. Originally, in both parties, each state was alloted delegates in proportion to its electoral votes. Under this system, weak state organizations were represented disproportionately. By the turn of the century, the fault had become severe, particularly in the Republican party, where Presidential aspirants competed for the favor of Southern delegates who possessed no popular following, but were able decisively to influence the choice of the convention. In 1912, when President William

Howard Taft relied on it for renomination, the power of this "postmaster vote" became notorious.

The events of 1912 led to reform. In the Republican party, apportionment is now based on a complex formula. Each state receives four votes at-large, plus two for each representative-at-large. An additional six "bonus votes" are granted to any state which voted Republican in the last election for President, governor or senator. An additional delegate is alloted for each Congressional district in which at least 2,000 votes were cast for G.O.P. candidates for President or Congress. A second district delegate is allowed if 10,000 local voters chose the party.[6]

As originally devised, the "bonus" system of apportionment was intended to provide extra delegates only for those states in which the party was genuinely strong. However, the allowances have been increasingly liberalized, so that almost all states are now entitled to a full number of extra delegates. In 1964, if the rules are unchanged, all but three districts in the nation will be entitled to these G.O.P. "bonus" votes.

The Democratic party is more geographically widespread than its opposition. As a result, it has been less troubled with disproportionate convention representation. In recent years, however, the party has given four "bonus" votes to states voting Democratic in Presidential, senatorial or gubernatorial elections. In 1960, the party returned to the original system, allocating 2½ delegates for each electoral vote. The simplicity of this system was disturbed, however, by a provision that no state would receive less representation than it had in the 1956 convention. In addition, each state was to receive one supplementary vote to be cast by its members on the National Committee.[7]

[6] Republican National Committee, p. 1.
[7] For a description of the earlier Democratic system, see U. S. Senate, Library, *Manner of Selecting Delegates to National Political Conventions and the Nomination and Election of Presidential Electors* (1952), pp. 3-4.

Guaranteeing each state the same representation in 1960 as in 1956 had a definite effect on the candidates' strength. If each state had been granted only the basic 2½ delegates for each electoral vote, plus the one vote of the National Committee members, John Kennedy's position in the convention would have been augmented. With the 1956 representation as a minimum, however, his opponents gained votes, although Kennedy still won a clear majority of the total convention votes. Of the votes added to state delegations to equal the 1956 figures, however, he won only 37½ of a total of 96, or less than two-fifths. As can be seen from the following table, the Democratic method of 1960 tends to discriminate against the large urban and industrial states, without necessarily rewarding the strongly Democratic states. Neither Alabama nor Michigan, both Democratic bastions, received additional votes, while Arizona and Mississippi, whose Democratic allegiances are uncertain, did receive bonus representation. The final result of the 1960 convention was not changed by these facts, but it could affect future strategies and decisions.

Evidently the apportionment schemes in both party conventions are not entirely equitable or representative of strength. Various proposals for changing these methods have been suggested. The system of "bonus" votes could be continued, if reformed, so as to constitute a genuine bonus, not an indiscriminate addition to state delegations. Thus additional at-large seats might be granted only to states carried in the Presidential election. These votes need not be equal for each state, but could rather be equal to the state's electoral vote. Alternately, more than one group of bonus delegates could be given a state, which could then get additional recognition for voting for a Republican (or Democratic) senator and governor, as well as President. For the district delegates, the minimums could either be raised, or a third additional delegate provided at a higher level, perhaps as high as 100,000. This would reward only those areas strongly supporting the party.

TABLE 3-2

Apportionment at 1960 democratic Convention*

State	"Normal" Representation	Actual Representation	"Bonus" Votes	Gain for Kennedy	Gain for Others
Ariz.	11	17	6	6	
Ark.	21	27	6		6
Colo.	16	21	5	3	2
Del.	9	11	2		2
Fla.	26	29	3		3
Ga.	31	33	2		2
Idaho	11	13	2	1	1
Ky.	26	31	5	½	4½
Maine	14	15	1	1	
Minn.	29	31	2		2
Miss.	21	23	2		2
Mo.	34	39	5		5
Mont.	11	17	6	3½	2½
Nev.	9	15	6	2	4
N.M.	11	17	6	1½	4½
N.C.	36	37	1		1
Okla.	21	29	8		8
Ore.	16	17	1	1	
R.I.	11	17	6	6	
Tenn.	29	33	4		4
Utah	11	13	2	1½	½
Vir.	31	33	2		2
Wash.	24	27	3	1½	1½
W. Va.	21	25	4	3	1
Wyo.	9	15	6	6	
Totals:	489	585	96	37½	58½

*"Normal" representation is the electoral vote of the state, multiplied by 2½, plus one vote for the National Committee members. The gains for the candidates are calculated by assuming that an aspirant gained proportionally as many votes from the bonus delegates as he won in the entire delegation. Only half and whole votes are included, in accord with the convention voting rules. States without bonus delegates are not included in the table.

The recent Democratic emphasis on the electoral vote could be extended. If each state organization were given three times its electoral vote, there would be no significant need for extra votes to avoid loss of representation. While such action would simplify the apportionment problem, however, it would tend to increase the proportionate strength of weak state organizations, while minimizing the influence of party groups in areas of Democratic strength.

A simple yet far-reaching change would be to base apportionment on the party vote in each state, as is the practice in many state party conventions. If one delegate were awarded for every 25,000 votes, each convention in 1964 would have about 1400 delegates, the same number as recent Republican conclaves. The result of such a change would be a vast increase in the convention power of organizations from states with a high turnout of voters and strong support for the party. In many ways this is the most democratic proposal, since it would establish electoral support as the basic criterion for representation at the party convention. However, because it will adversely affect important factions within both parties, particularly from the South, it is likely to encounter strong opposition.[8]

Aside from the selection of a convention site and the apportionment of delegates, the National Committee makes tentative decisions on the officers and committee chairmen of the convention. The major officers are the temporary chairman, the principal or keynote speaker (the Democrats combine these two positions), and the permanent chairman. There is usually no dispute over these positions, since they are selected after negotiation between the major factions.

The National Committee also tentatively selects chairmen of the four principal convention committees—rules, permanent organization, credentials, and platform or resolutions. Opposition to these selections is unlikely. In most cases, the positions are largely honorary and do not confer substantive power. Moreover, it would be extremely awkward, if not impossible, for the delegates to overturn the National Committee's choice. These convention committees now begin their work weeks and even months before the

[8] See David (1960), pp. 176-92, for a discussion of these alternatives and one of apportionment based on "party strength"—"the electoral vote of each state multiplied by the party percentage in the last election."

party meets. A new chairman could not easily assume the position and complete his assignment in a matter of hours.

The actions of two committees, credentials and platform, as distinct from their personnel, are often contested and reversed by the convention itself. The possibility of such action arises from the different composition of the committees and the entire convention. In the committees, each state is represented equally, regardless of population or party strength. In the convention, these factors are taken into account and result in great variations in the voting strength of state delegations. Because of these disparities, it was possible for the Democratic platform committee in 1948 to recommend a mild civil rights plank, while the convention adopted a "minority" liberal position. Similarly, in the 1952 Republican conference, the credentials committee voted to seat certain Southern delegates favoring Robert Taft for the Presidential nomination. When the matter reached the convention floor, the strength of the Eisenhower forces was brought to bear and the decision was reversed.

Such conflicts between the committees and the convention would be less likely if the committees were made more representative of the actual apportionment of delegates. A state might have one, two, or three committee members, depending on the size of its delegation. Smaller states would still be over-represented, but not to the extent that exists under present arrangements. Alternately, the delegates from each state might be empowered to cast a vote equal to their state's representation in the general convention. A disparity between the convention and the committee votes would probably continue, since not all state delegates are likely to vote as units. However, the difference would be substantially less than exists under the present system.

The Convention Meets

Four years in preparation, the typical national convention today lasts four or five days, usually beginning on a Monday in mid-summer. At a convention many things are happening simultaneously: a party ritual, an appeal to the electorate, a tourists' frolic, a decision on vital issues, a television spectacular, a contest for power, an affirmation of faith. A particular act may have more than a single significance, and different acts are alike in combining serious and ephemeral aspects.

Convention programs are carefully planned. Although the schedule changes from day to day, the parties' aims remain the same: to gain public support, to achieve consensus within the party, and to reach decisions on vital questions of policy and leadership. Even purely ritual observances are designed to serve these ends. Thus, an invocation is offered before each session and a benediction at its close. Spiritual leaders are chosen from all faiths so as to avoid any charges of favoritism and, perhaps most important, any possible loss of votes.[9]

The program of the convention changes from day to day, and each session has its unique attractions. Although the exact timing of events varies, it is possible to describe a "typical" national convention. The first day is marked by the opening ceremonies, formal organization of the convention and the keynote speech. Welcoming speeches are given by the mayor and governor of the host city and state. Because courtesy (and spending by convention delegates) was preferred over partisanship, the Democrats were cordially addressed by the Republican mayor of Los Angeles in 1960 and the compliment was returned to the G.O.P. by the Democratic mayor of Chicago.

The first major appeal to the electorate is made by the keynote speaker. Rarely distinguished in style or content, his address is designed to cheer the partisan delegates

[9] In 1960, for example, prayers were offered before the Democratic convention by leaders of the Catholic, Methodist, Greek Orthodox, Episcopal, Jewish, Congregational, Baptist, Evangelical, Presbyterian, and Mormon faiths. The Republicans found room for most of these and for a Lutheran and Quaker, as well as the same Methodist who blessed the Democratic efforts—Bishop Gerald Kennedy of Los Angeles —*The New York Times*, July 11-15, 25-28, 1960.

while activating whatever support for the party exists among the voters. In describing the 1928 speech of Republican Senator Simeon D. Fess of Ohio, Will Rogers summarized the thesis of most keynote talks:

> A Keynote Speech is Press notices of the Republican Party, written by its own members.
>
> Here are just a few things that I bet you didn't know the Republicans were responsible for: Radio, Telephone, Baths, Automobiles, Savings Accounts, Law Enforcement, Workmen living in houses, and a living wage for Senators.
>
> The Democrats had brought in War, pestilence, debts, Disease, Bo Weevil, Gold Teeth, need of Farm relief, suspenders, floods, famine and Tom Heflin.
>
> He told of so much money that we had saved that I think if he talked another hour he would have paid us a dividend.
>
> Once I thought sure he was referring to 'Our Saviour' till they told me, 'No, it was Coolidge.' The way he rated 'em was Coolidge, The Lord, and then Lincoln.
>
> It was an impromptu address that he had been working on for only six months. He made no attempt at Oratory, he just shouted.[10]

On the second day, while oratory and entertainment continue, some vital decisions also may be made. The permanent chairman is installed at this time and begins his tenure, as might be expected, with a speech. Most of the time will be taken up by committee reports. Those of the credentials and platform committees can be crucial, affecting factional strength, party policy and candidates' ambitions.

The convention nears its vital decisions on the third day. After the last committees have reported, the alphabetical roll of states is called for nominations for President. Considerable negotiation is devoted to deciding who will

[10] Will Rogers, *How We Elect Our Presidents,* ed. by Donald Day (Boston: Little, Brown, 1952), pp. 66-67.

nominate and second the various aspirants. The candidate must seek to meet the claims of a host of ambitious and egocentric politicians while satisfying demands of geographical and group balance among his supporters. He must also avoid unduly straining either the patience of the delegates or the established time limits.

The nominating speech is another of the established convention rituals. The speaker is mandated to ascribe all of the virtues to his candidate, but is not to mention his name until the very end, thus relieving the presumed suspense of his audience. In early conventions, nominating speeches were forbidden or restricted to a single simple sentence. Speakers today seem unable to follow such models of brevity, but the demands of television programming may eliminate some of the most florid appeals.

At the conclusion of the nominating speech, a parade begins. Most of this "spontaneous demonstration" is actually carefully planned in advance, as the candidate's aides provide bands, banners, balloons and buffoonery. No demonstration is known to have changed a delegate's voting preference, and probably no aspirant expects any such change. Until they become repetitive, however, the demonstrations do provide color and excitement for both the delegates and the national audience.

Will Rogers aptly summarized the foolishness involved:

> Thousands of people in a hot stuffy hall up till the early morning hours listening to 'The man I am about to nominate has the qualities of a Jackson, the Statesmanship of a Jefferson and the homely common sense of an Abraham Lincoln.' Then the next one nominated would have all these and then a couple more, maby [sic] the looks of McKinley and the oratory of Bryan. Hours on hours of that, then they would all get up and march around the hall, part would march and part would hiss.[11]

[11] *Ibid.*, p. 127.

Fortunately, the foolishness does not affect convention decisions.

While some delegates are enjoying or enduring these proceedings, others are more fruitfully engaged. Throughout the first three days of the convention, important action takes place off the main floor. Many issues are settled in the committees of the convention. State caucuses are held frequently, to decide the delegation's position on the decisions faced by the convention, particularly the Presidential nomination. Aspirants and their backers devote this time to talks at these caucuses and to individual conferences with delegates. Important leaders will meet frequently, seeking agreement, suggesting compromises and perhaps proposing "deals." Innumerable press conferences, television and radio interviews, and purely social functions are held.

There is an important difference between the overt and open convention, that seen by spectators and the television audience, and the "real" or decision-making convention. The overt convention is noisy, disorganized, apparently irrational and certainly far removed from the model of a deliberative body. However, the decisions of the party are not made in this open and carnival atmosphere. They are made within the smaller state delegations, in conferences of factions and leaders, and in calmer circumstances. The individual delegate is not important as a free agent, deciding alone on his preferences for party policy and leadership. He is important as a member of a state delegation or a party faction. The overt convention is important as a structure, providing a locale and an opportunity for negotiation, maneuvering and the testing of factional strength. While the assembled delegates eventually make the final decisions by their declared votes, the deliberations and the politics leading up to these decisions take place elsewhere.

The structure of the convention is evident in the highlight of the party gathering, the balloting for Presidential candidates. All of the delegates assemble to cast their ballots, but these are actually voted by the delegation as a body, after discussion and decision in caucus, and announced by the delegation chairman. Although delegates can usually vote their individual preference, delegations tend to vote predominantly for one candidate. In some Democratic state groups, agreement is obtained by the "unit rule," whereby the entire state vote is cast for the candidate preferred by a majority. The rule, which may be imposed either by a state convention or by the delegation itself, increases the state's power at the convention, while eliminating the voice of dissident factions in each state.

About half of the state organizations vote without dissent, but the unit rule is not the only explanation of such unanimity. The delegates may simply agree on the same candidate, or may have been pledged by a state primary. In addition, state organizations are bound together by common loyalties, the disciplinary powers of party leaders and the prestige of the "bosses." State parties are often hierarchical bodies, and agreement can be obtained by the exercise of sanctions if it does not come voluntarily.

Frequently no candidate has a majority at the end of the first ballot. Further action will depend on the tactics adopted by the various factions. The established timetable is now forgotten. With the leadership of the party at stake, convenience of the television audience is easily—and rightfully—forgotten. Eventually, one candidate receives an absolute majority of the convention. A leader of the defeated faction will then usually offer a motion to make the nomination unanimous.

The designation of a Vice-Presidential candidate is the principal remaining item of business. His selection is likely to come on the fourth day. The procedure is the same as for the Presidential nomination. Usually, however, there is less excitement since the running mate is selected customarily by the party leaders rather than in an open contest. Action by the convention is more of a formal ratification, rather than a decision of state delegations. Roll calls and balloting may even be dispensed with, and the candidate named by acclamation.

The final day of the convention is one for the completion of party business, the closing of ranks, and the initiation of the election campaign. The delegates now constitute only a cheering section, and major attention is directed toward the national audience. The major and final address is given by the Presidential candidate, a practice initiated by Franklin Roosevelt in 1932. Until that time, in accord with the now-discarded doctrine of "the office seeks the man," potential nominees were expected to be ignorant of convention decisions until notified by an official committee of the convention.

Who will formally introduce the candidate to the convention? This question has assumed some importance in recent years. In 1952, President Harry Truman introduced the Democratic candidate, Adlai Stevenson. In the circumstances, his endorsement had the appearance of the old party leader passing his title on to the new. A similar succession of leadership occurred in 1960, when Stevenson introduced Kennedy, the new Democratic standard-bearer. Stevenson had also been one of the major contenders for the nomination and his introduction therefore was doubly significant. It marked not only the transfer of power but also the unification of the party for the election campaign. Similarly, in the Republican convention, Richard Nixon was introduced by his principal rival, Nelson Rockefeller. A new tradition may be evolving.

After the Presidential candidate's address, the convention is permanently adjourned. In less than a week, it has made decisions that may affect the course of the party and the nation for four years, and perhaps much longer. For the most part, the procedure and order of events is both logical and traditional. There are persistent suggestions, however, for two changes in the order of procedure. One is that the Vice-Presidential candidate be selected before the Presidential nominee. This proposal will be examined in a later chapter. The other suggestion is that the platform be adopted after the candidates are named, so as to allow them to participate in its formulation.

If this change were made, the delegates would probably lose all control over the platform. The Presidential candidate would dominate its formulation, much as he now exercises the decisive role in the selection of his running mate. Opportunities for debate and participation by the delegates, at least within the platform committee and the state delegations, would be severely limited, if not entirely eliminated. The reconciliation of party factions, a basic function of the convention, might be impeded. To be sure, we cannot expect extensive deliberations over policy in the hectic conditions of the conventions. We can expect a degree of compromise, conciliation, and the recognition of divergent interests. The platform is one means to achieve party unity. If it were deferred until after the nominations, there would be less of an attempt to achieve widespread agreement. Consistency between the candidate and the platform is certainly desirable, if it can be accomplished without effects harmful to the parties. It is a moot question, however, whether such consistency is more important than broad party participation in the determination of policy.

Trends and Conclusions

The changes in the nominating process form a major emphasis of succeeding chapters. Three major trends may be noted briefly at this point, the most obvious being the increase in size. At the elephantine 1960 Democratic convention, there were some 3,000 delegates in attendance, as well as thousands of alternates, officials and party figures. This was more than ten times the number present at the original conventions. Republicans have limited their numbers more successfully, only 1300 delegates being present in 1960. In both parties, however, the tendency is to increase convention membership in order to spread party enthusiasm widely.

The large size of the conventions has important effects on their proceedings. More decisions must be made away from the noise and confusion of the convention floor. Delegation leaders gain in power as the need for centralization of authority becomes more apparent. The opportunity for meaningful discussion and face-to-face debate is diminished. These effects were clearly illustrated in the 1960 Democratic convention. Despite its many controversial provisions, the platform was passed without significant objection. Nominating speeches were not heeded. Even the heads of delegations and floor managers for the candidates needed telephones in order to maintain their knowledge of the situation. The size of the convention could well be limited in the future.

In part because of the increase of size, the activities of the conventions have tended to become more formal and ritualistic. As more of the major decisions come to be made outside the meeting hall, little opportunity for spontaneity is left to the body of delegates. All action, from inspirational addresses to the format of nominations, is carefully programmed. The rules and officials of the meetings are already decided in advance. If platforms come to be viewed more as dramatic presentations rather than as matters for party decision, as was the case in 1960, we can expect the convention to exercise less discretion in this instance as well. Even in the nominations themselves, conventions today are less free in their alternatives than in previous years.

The increased formality of convention proceedings is related to a third major trend, the increased importance of audiences outside the convention. These "strangers" now influence the actions of the delegates to a considerable respect. At the same time, the convention program increasingly is designed to appeal to outside audiences, and this emphasis is reinforced by the influence of television and other mass media. In Los Angeles in 1960, Democrats met at the odd hour of 3 P.M. in order to cater to Eastern television viewers. The "favorite son," that unique American candidate, is in danger of extinction because of fears of boring the distant spectators. Even the use of balloons, the manners of delegates, and the placing of delegation standards are regulated to accommodate the cameras.[12] There is some possibility that the convention may become only a ritualistic entertainment, rather than an arena for decision-making.

The increased size, formality, and control of scheduling is not serious in itself. Crucial party decisions usually are not made on the floor in any case, and there is therefore no harm in making the overt convention a larger and more entertaining spectacle. There are two real dangers in these trends, however. First, these changes may come to interfere with the work of the real convention itself. With increased size, for example, it becomes difficult to reach decisions even in state caucuses. As the pressure of television becomes more important, private deliberations may be impeded, as the demands of entertainment take precedence over the more serious business of party negotiation. When communication depends on telephones and radio walkie-talkies, even party leaders may be misinformed, confused, and misled. Rational decisions then become much more difficult to achieve.

Second, there may be occasions, though rarely, when the convention does have to make a decision as a body. Such was the case, for example, with the nomination of the Democratic Vice-Presidential candidate in 1956 or the loyalty oath controversy in the Democratic party in 1952. Reaching a decision would be difficult in any case, given the atmosphere of the convention and the nature of its decision-making processes. The trends toward increased size, formality, and control over scheduling will only increase these difficulties. The convention should be given at least a minimum oppor-

[12] Charles A. Thomson, *Television and Presidential Politics* (Washington: The Brookings Institution, 1956), p. 35.

tunity to function effectively when it is called upon to make vital decisions.

Despite these difficulties, American party conventions continue to perform vital functions, and contribute to the success of American politics. Yet, even as ritual alone, the conventions are an important part of the nation's political life. They provide one of the most dramatic and colorful aspects of the political process. There is need in the United States, as in every nation, for "theatrical" elements of government. As the British commentator Walter Bagehot wrote, public imagination is most likely to be captured by "that which is mystic in its claims; that which is occult in its mode of action; that which is brilliant to the eye; that which is seen vividly for a moment, and then is seen no more; that which is hidden and unhidden; that which is specious, and yet interesting, palpable in its seeming, and yet professing to be more than palpable in its results." [13] In Great Britain, the Crown meets these demands. In America, the conventions partially perform the same role.

Suggestions for Further Reading

Hugh A. Bone, *Party Committees and National Politics* (Seattle: University of Washington Press, 1958). An analysis of the national organs of the two major parties.

Clarence Cannon, *Democratic Manual of the Democratic National Convention* (Washington: Democratic National Committee, 1956). The authoritative manual of parliamentary procedure for national conventions.

Paul T. David *et al.*, *The Politics of National Party Conventions* (Washington: The Brookings Institution, 1960). Deals with all aspects of convention behavior, and provides much detail on primary laws and other methods of selecting delegates.

Maurice Duverger, *Political Parties* (New York: Wiley, 1954). A comparative and comprehensive study of party organization throughout the world.

Abraham Holtzmann, *The Loyalty Pledge Controversy in the Democratic Party* (New Brunswick: Eagleton Institute, 1960). A case

[13] Walter Bagehot, *The English Constitution*, World's Classics ed. (London: Oxford University Press, 1958), p. 7.

study of the attempt to enforce party unity on dissident Southern Democrats.

State University of Iowa, Institute of Public Affairs. *A Report on Presidential Primary Laws* (Iowa City, 1953). A detailed study of the mechanics and details of state primary systems.

Duane Lockard, *New England State Politics* (Princeton: Princeton University Press, 1959). Excellent analysis of party organization in the six states of the region and of experience with state conventions in Massachusetts and Connecticut, in particular.

Joseph W. Martin, *My First Fifty Years in Politics* (New York: McGraw-Hill, 1960). Accounts of politics and conventions by the former Republican leader of the House and permanent chairman of five G.O.P. conventions.

David B. Truman, "Federalism and the Party System," in Arthur W. MacMahon (ed.), *Federalism: Mature and Emergent* (New York: Columbia University Press, 1955), pp. 115-36. A short and incisive analysis of the effect of federalism on American parties.

U. S. Senate, Library, *Manner of Selecting Delegates to National Political Conventions and the Nomination and Election of Presidential Electors* (1952). A factual presentation of the varieties of state practice and the methods of apportioning delegates.

IV ON THE
CONVENTION AGENDA

"We are here to nominate the next President of the United States," proclaim a large number of the speakers at every national convention. Undoubtedly, the nomination of a man who might be President is the most publicized, dramatic and obvious purpose of conventions. But nominating a candidate is not the only purpose, and often it is not the most important.

In some cases, a convention is unnecessary for the purpose of making a nomination. Certainly in those cases where the party renominates an incumbent President or otherwise only ratifies an obvious selection, the delegates are not primarily concerned with deciding upon the party leadership. In nearly half of the major party conventions, the Presidential choice was foreclosed before the first session. Uncontested nominations occurred in the first conventions of both parties, and have continued to the present day. With equal confidence, one may predict that there will be a Democratic convention in 1964 and that John Kennedy will be renominated without opposition. Apparently there are purposes other than the nomination of a Presidential candidate to be served.

Moreover, in the perspective of history, other decisions than the nominations can be seen as more important. The Democratic convention of 1860 and the Republican conclave of 1912 were less significant, for example, for their nominations than for the fact that they resulted in party splits. The result of one division was the Civil War. The other conflict began a social movement which, along with other influences, resulted in the New Deal.

Similarly, the most significant aspect of the conventions of 1852 and 1896—among others—was the platforms adopted in these years. In the former year, both parties, in the last significant attempt to avert conflict over slavery, accepted the 1850 Compromise as "a settlement in principle and substance of the dangerous and exciting questions."[1] In 1896, the party platforms differed completely on the free coinage of silver, the leading issue of the time. Today, the major difference between the two parties is in the greater relative emphasis placed on "sound money" and a "balanced budget" by the Republicans, in contrast to the Democratic stress on the "general welfare" and "spending." While these differences are neither great nor clear, they do represent whatever dividing line exists between the parties. This line was drawn by the platforms of 1896.

The Party Platforms

One of the major non-nominating functions of the convention is the writing of a party platform. However, most commentators and voters tend to deprecate platforms. The criticisms are both familiar and generally unchallenged.

[1] Thomas H. McKee, *The National Conventions and Platforms of All Political Parties*, 6th ed. (Baltimore: Friedenwald, 1906), p. 79. The quotation is from the Whig platform.

Among the major alleged defects of platforms are the following:

(1.) Platform statements are essentially unimportant, ambiguous and often contradictory. "Usually it presents a long list of statements . . . in which everybody can find something to suit him. . . . If there is an urgent problem which demands a straightforward solution, the concocters of the platform endeavor to word it in language which can bear different constructions, to compose a 'straddling' one."[2]

(2.) No differences exist between the platforms of the major parties. They are therefore of no value to the voter in making his choice of party.

(3.) The party principles are not binding on party candidates. "The principal object of the platform is, in the present day, as formerly, to catch votes by trading on the credulity of the electors. . . . As an indication, therefore, of the policy of the future administration elected on this platform, the latter is of no great value."[3]

These criticisms are not entirely valid. Platform provisions often have been meaningful, distinct from the opposition and fulfilled upon the party's election. The critics are partially correct, however, simply because conventions are not legislative conferences, engaged in "discussing political questions and settling a political program."[4] Rather, conventions are party instruments, seeking to choose policies, strategies and candidates which will bring electoral success. Policy statements will only occasionally be important for their own sake. In most cases, the effects on political fortunes will determine whether platforms will be ambiguous or clear, different from or similar to the opposition party, rhetorical affirmations or meaningful pledges.

In the effort to win elections, parties seek to draw

[2] M. Ostrogorskii, *Democracy and the Party System in the United States* (New York: Macmillan, 1910), p. 147.
[3] *Ibid.*, pp. 147-8.
[4] James Bryce, *The American Commonwealth*, 3rd rev. ed. (New York: Macmillan, 1914), Vol. II, p. 224.

support from a great variety of organized and unorganized interests, political factions and divisions of the electorate. The platform is one of the means of obtaining this support. Interest groups make great efforts to secure favorable planks from platform committees. Party factions are willing to engage in long and vigorous convention fights in order to win endorsement of their policy views. Many voters will cast their ballots on the basis of the parties' positions.

With many interested in the platforms, conflicts between groups and individuals of different views are likely. In seeking to appeal to all, platform drafters may resort to ambiguity as the only means of resolving—or at least hiding —the differences. The ultimate in vagueness was probably the Democratic pledge in 1944 to enact "such additional humanitarian, labor, social and farm legislation as time and experience may require, including the amendment or repeal of any law enacted in recent years which has failed to accomplish its purpose."[5]

Ambiguity, however, is not always characteristic of platforms. Conflicts may be fought to a conclusion, rather than suppressed, as in the Democratic civil rights controversy of 1948. Many platforms have included direct and specific statements on major issues. From their first conventions, Republicans opposed the extension of slavery to the territories and favored a protective tariff.[6] Democrats have taken definite positions in favor of unlimited coinage of silver, reduced tariffs, and the repeal of prohibition.

The degree of ambiguity depends on party strategy. Basically, the platform is a campaign document. When the party seeks to appeal to a wide range of interests, vagueness results. When the party feels that its electoral chances will be improved by an uncompromising appeal to one group, platform statements will become clearer. Democratic party history illustrates the matter in two instances. In 1892, the

[5] Kirk H. Porter and Donald B. Johnson, *National Party Platforms 1840-1956* (Urbana: University of Illinois Press, 1956), p. 403.
[6] McKee, p. 114.

party's position on the currency question was ambiguous. The Democrats favored "the use of both gold and silver as the standard money of the country," but also insisted that "the dollar unit of coinage of both metals must be of equal intrinsic and exchangeable value."[7] The party was trying to gain the allegiance of both the silver-producing states of the West and of the financial community of the East. Four years later, the party adopted its famous silver plank, unambiguously demanding "the free and unlimited coinage of both silver and gold at the present legal ratio of 16 to 1, without waiting for the aid or consent of any other nation."[8] Democrats had committed themselves to seeking the support of the West primarily.

Democratic vagueness did not disappear with the advent of William Jennings Bryan. In 1956, the convention was faced with the delicate issue of school desegregation, ordered two years earlier by the U. S. Supreme Court. Avoiding endorsement, or even mention, of the 1954 decision, the party only recognized the Court "as one of the three Constitutional and coordinate branches of the federal government ... the decisions of which are part of the law of the land."[9] Through this language an attempt was made to gain the support of two apparently irreconcilable groups of voters— Negroes and Southern dissidents. This attempt failed and four years later the platform clearly appealed to the former group only. Advanced civil rights proposals were endorsed, including the elimination of literacy tests to ease Negro voting in the South and the initiation of school desegregation throughout the nation in three years.

In summary, ambiguity is not a universal characteristic of party platforms. It occurs as an effort to reconcile the demands of different groups whose support is seen as necessary to the electoral success of the party. When one group is seen as more important to the party than another,

[7] *Ibid.*, p. 265.
[8] *Ibid.*, p. 293.
[9] Porter and Johnson, p. 542.

the platform is likely to be made more specific, reflecting
the wishes of the more favored interest.

In passing, we should also note that vagueness may
be in the national interest. The 1860 Democratic convention
was the last opportunity to prevent the dissolution of the
Union. A majority favored a platform which pledged adherence to the Dred Scott decision, thus admitting slavery
to the territories. The Southern minority insisted, however,
on unequivocal support of slavery. This insistence resulted
in the final division of the party and ultimately of the
nation.[10] The Civil War was precipitated by critics of platform ambiguity.

Platforms are also deprecated because of the alleged
similarity between the party positions. Electoral competition
in a two-party system might be expected to produce parties
which are basically similar in their policies and pledges.
To some extent, this is true of American parties and of their
convention platforms. However, there are important differences between the parties. Both the similarities and differences result from the competition for votes. To the extent
that the parties appeal to the same groups for support, their
platforms will be similar. Insofar as their group appeals are
diverse, platforms will reflect the differences.

In most elections, the parties have disagreed on some
major issues, as shown in the table below, although the
differences did not extend to all issues or even all elections.
From the beginning, the Whig party approved, and the
Democrats opposed, high protective tariffs. These positions
reflected the Whigs' greater strength among Eastern voters
and the Democrats' appeal to the South and West. Similarly,
the new Republican party opposed the extension of slavery
and the Democrats allowed it, the Republicans sought a
gold standard and the Democrats favored the free coinage of
silver.

[10] See Murat Halstead, *Three Against Lincoln*, ed. by William Hesseltine (Baton Rouge: Louisiana State University Press, 1960), pp.
40ff. for a description by an observer of maneuverings there.

TABLE 4-1

MAJOR PARTY PLATFORM PROVISIONS

Year[a]	Whig-Republican Positions	Democratic Positions
1844	Protective tariff	Tariff for revenue
1848	Program of internal improvements	Oppose internal improvements
1852	Criticism of the Mexican War	Praise of the Mexican War
1856	Enforce Compromise of 1850	Enforce Compromise of 1850
	No extension of slavery	Permit slavery in territories
	Oppose Ostend Manifesto	Expansion into Cuba
1860	Oppose all extension of slavery	Judicial control over slavery extension
1864	Unconditional surrender of South	Immediate negotiations to end Civil War
	Anti-slavery amendment	Protection of civil liberties
1868	Radical Reconstruction policy	Immediate restoration of Southern states
1872	Abolish patronage abuses	Civil service reform
	Suppression of Ku Klux Klan	Removal of restrictions on South
1876	Return to specie payment	Return to specie payment
	Honesty in government	Honesty in government
1880	Same as 1876	Same as 1876
1884	Protective tariff	Revenue tariff
1888	Same as 1884	Same as 1884
1892	Protective tariff	Revenue tariff
	Gold standard	Gold standard
1896	Protective tariff	Revenue tariff
	Gold standard	Free coinage of silver
1900	Support expansion of U.S. possessions	Oppose expansionism

Year		
1904	Same as 1900	Same as 1900
1908	Tariff "revision" Uphold use of labor injunctions	Tariff reductions Oppose use of labor injunctions Anti-trust legislation
1912	"Supervise" interstate corporations	Prepare to safeguard "just interests"
1916	"Strict and honest neutrality"	Support League of Nations
1920	Oppose League of Nations	Public electric power development
1924	Economy in government Membership on World Court	Referendum on League of Nations
1928	Vigorous enforcement of prohibition Tariff protection for farmers	"Honest effort" on prohibition Federal farm marketing board
1932	Self-liquidating public works State option on prohibition	Federal aid for relief and public works Repeal of prohibition
1936	Critique of the New Deal	Support, extend the New Deal
1940	State control of welfare programs Aid Britain, within international law	Expansion of welfare programs Aid to Britain, "consistent with law"
1944	Extension of social security Organization of "sovereign nations"	"Additional humanitarian legislation" Postwar United Nations
1948	State control of housing, education Support of Taft-Hartley law	Federal aid to housing, education Repeal Taft-Hartley law
1952	Removal of corrupt, disloyal officials Critique of the Korean War	Protect honest, loyal public servants Seek "fair and effective" Korean peace
1956	Voluntary farm programs Balanced budget, government economy	90%-of-parity farm price supports Federal programs for economic growth
1960	Reliance on private sector of economy Medical care for the needy aged	Stimulate economy to 5% growth rate Medical care under social security

a Both parties did not issue platforms in earlier elections, from 1832 to 1840.

In modern times, the two major parties have divided over such issues as the League of Nations, prohibition, social security, the Taft-Hartley law, and conduct of the Korean War. The Taft-Hartley issue particularly illustrates the importance of platforms as campaign appeals to different groups.

In this case, the party platforms have been consistent, the Republicans supporting the law and Democrats calling for its repeal in each of their platforms since 1948. The maintenance of the Democratic position is notable only if the platform is thought of as an accurate description of future legislation. Certainly by 1956, if not earlier, it was clear that Taft-Hartley would not be revoked. Such action had been attempted immediately after President Truman's surprise victory in the 1948 election and had failed. Since then, labor unions had learned to live with the law and there was no great public interest in its change. Despite these facts, however, the Democrats continued to call for repeal. This was not intended to be a specific promise of action. Rather, it was an attempt to solidify union and worker support behind the Democratic party. Abolishing Taft-Hartley was not significant in itself; it was symbolic of the Democratic party's responsiveness to union needs and wants. The Republican party did not rely substantially on unions for political success. It could, and did, approve of Taft-Hartley's restrictions on labor groups.

While there have been important differences between party platforms, it is also true that they often duplicate one another. Similarity of appeals would mean that both parties are soliciting the same groups. The parties may attempt to promote an inclusive national consensus, as in the support of the 1850 Compromise by both Whigs and Democrats in 1852. In other situations, both parties may seek the support of an exclusive portion of the electorate, while ignoring the claims of others. In the party platforms of the 1870's and 1880's, Republicans and Democrats were equally avid in their support of specie payment of the Civil War debt and honesty in public office. Neither party pledged much effort to deal with the problems of union organization, railroad regulation, or the northern Negro. The major parties both ignored the demands of the economically disadvantaged, while restricting their appeal to an exclusive segment of the population.

The Effect of Platforms

Probably the most accurate criticism of platforms is that party promises are not binding upon the administration of the successful party. In a number of cases, in fact, the party's candidate has repudiated platform planks. In the first instance of this type, the Democrats in 1864 demanded that "immediate efforts be made for a cessation of hostilities" in the Civil War,[11] while the standard bearer, General George McClellan, called for prosecution of the military effort.

Repudiation of the platform is rare, but failure to carry out platform pledges is frequent. Such neglect is most recently illustrated by President Kennedy's failure to seek new civil rights legislation, despite a number of specific and significant proposals in the 1960 Democratic platform. Instead, the Administration has relied on executive actions in behalf of civil rights. A more spectacular example of the disparity between promise and performance came in the first term of Franklin Roosevelt, who had been elected on a platform advocating "an immediate and drastic reduction in governmental expenditures . . . to accomplish a saving of not less than twenty-five per cent in the cost of the federal government" and "maintenance of the national credit by a federal budget annually balanced."[12] The New Deal, of course, resulted in the greatest peacetime spending and budget deficits in all of American history to that time.

Poor performance on the platform is due to many factors. Part of the explanation is due to the nature of platforms as campaign documents. If a group is satisfied by

[11] McKee, p. 122.
[12] Porter and Johnson, p. 331.

inclusion of its demands in the platform alone, there is no need to press for actual accomplishment. However, a party platform cannot consist only of pledges never to be redeemed. Some of the promises must be fulfilled or the party's credit, its voting support, will be dissipated sooner or later. If the Democrats after 1932, for example, did not achieve a reduction in federal expenditures or a balanced budget, they did redeem their pledges of unemployment relief, a public works program, regulation of the stock markets, protection of bank deposits, and the repeal of prohibition. Generally, where planks have specifically dealt with major issues, party performance has been high. This is evident from a reading of the positions included in the previous table.

For more recent evidence, we can take a dozen examples from the Democratic platform of 1948 and the Republican program of 1952. The Truman Administration fulfilled pledges to: (1) establish a United Nations headquarters in the United States; (2) sign a peace treaty with Japan; (3) extend the Marshall Plan; (4) bring Israel into the United Nations; (5) provide federal aid for housing; (6) increase social security benefits; (7) raise the minimum wage; (8) provide fixed farm price supports; (9) repeal margarine taxes; (10) admit displaced persons to the country; (11) extend the reciprocal trade acts; and (12) establish a National Science Foundation. This was certainly a fair performance, even though unredeemed pledges included repeal of the Taft-Hartley Act, federal aid for education, and civil rights legislation.

The first Eisenhower Administration had a similar record. Among the Republican actions promised in the 1952 platform were: (1) support of European integration; (2) conclusion of the Korean war; (3) publication of the Yalta documents; (4) reduction of the civil service; (5) elimination of federal price and wage controls; (6) reduction of corporate taxation; (7) ceding of jurisdiction over offshore oil deposits to the states; (8) restrictions on the TVA; (9)

an increase in the air force budget; (10) extension of social security coverage; (11) opposition to federal educational aid; and (12) enactment of a Korean G.I. Bill of Rights. There were Republican failures, too, including pledges to seek full farm parity prices, amend the Taft-Hartley Act and pass civil rights bills.

Platforms, then, do indicate much about future governmental action. They cannot provide a full blueprint of the future for a number of reasons. For one thing, circumstances may change. Programs promised in the platform may become out of date, or new problems may arise which were unknown during the election campaign. In these circumstances, a party can only indicate its general approach to major problems.

Furthermore, the platform cannot determine future action because of the nature of American politics. The parties are not centralized and disciplined organizations which are able to assume policy positions and then enforce these positions on all members and legislators of the party. Rather, the parties are somewhat disjointed confederations of local and state organizations, which unite intermittently and rather uncomfortably for certain national purposes, particularly the election of a President. Statements of policy adopted in a short meeting of these groups cannot be effectively enforced.

The lack of central control is furthered by the divisions between the President and Congress. The separation of powers between the two branches written into the Constitution has been extended into the electoral process. Party candidates for President and Congress actually conduct separate campaigns. The delegates to a convention can only affect the nomination and election of the President. The platform they approve can only bind the Chief Executive, if anyone. They cannot affect the choice of Congressional candidates, nor bind them to a party position. When elected, the President has no assured method of enforcing the convention's pledges on his party in Congress. Thus, even if a President is chosen who fully agrees with the convention platform, the Congress chosen at the same time may repudiate the party pledges.

We have now examined the major criticisms of party platforms. All of these criticisms are somewhat inaccurate. The cause of these characteristics, where true, is that a platform is intended to win votes. Changes in platform style and content are not made to fit some model of a national town meeting, but made in order to win more votes. American parties are only rarely upholders of great principles or antagonists in debate, but always are vote-getting organizations.

If this is so, must we conclude that the platform has no effect on public policy? Is it only designed, as Ostogorskii maintained, "to catch votes by trading on the credulity of the voters"? While characterizing the platform as a campaign document, we need not see it as only an ephemeral circular. The platform has an effect on future policy, but not as a precise indicator of governmental action.

In most cases, the platform cannot reveal exactly *what* future positions of the party or the government will be. It can indicate *who* will be in control of the party and, if the party wins the elections, of the government. Knowing which individuals and groups are dominant, one has an indication of the trend of policy, although not of precise actions. "The significance of preparing a platform lies primarily in the evidence that the negotiations provide concerning what groups will have access to the developing national party organization. . . . Interest group leaders are aware that the real settlement of the issues they are concerned with, even within the party, will take place later; in the platform they seek tentative assurance of a voice in that settlement."[13]

To return to the question of civil rights, the adoption of the pro-integration platform by the Democrats in 1960 did not guarantee the passage of new legislation to promote school desegregation or to end literacy tests for voting. It

[13] David B. Truman, *The Governmental Process* (New York: Knopf, 1951), p. 285.

did mean that the Administration would be committed to some action on behalf of civil rights. The actions of the Kennedy Administration reveal this commitment, although action has been generally through executive action, rather than the legislation promised in the platform.

In the case of the Taft-Hartley law, the same effect of the platform is apparent. Neither Republican support of the Act, nor Democratic endorsement of repeal, in itself guaranteed that there would be any significant change in the legislation. However, Democratic victory would mean that labor unions would have a greater voice in any new proposals, while Republican success would mean more support for the amendments desired by management groups. Specifically, Democratic proposals for a new labor law in 1949 were written with the aid of the union federations, while the Eisenhower Administration's suggested amendments were arrived at after consultation with a number of lawyers for major corporations.

Even when the issues are not vital and controversial, the platform can give an indication of which groups are influential in the party. The influence of ethnic and religious minorities in the Democratic party can be seen as early as 1856, when the party condemned the Know-Nothing movement as "a political crusade against Catholic and foreign-born."[14] Similarly, Republican platform commitments to party supporters have included the promise of large pensions for Civil War veterans for decades after Appomattox, and a 1952 declaration that the party's aim was to place the national currency "on a fully-convertible gold basis."[15] The promise of pensions had already been fulfilled, while the resumption of the gold standard was hardly to be expected. However, by these pledges, the party showed the importance of the Grand Army of the Republic and of financial conservatives to its electoral success and indicated the likelihood of their influence in a future Republican government.

Platform commitments to specific groups may be of

14 McKee, p. 90.
15 *Ibid.*, p. 501.

importance even when the party candidate is in disagreement with the position. Although McClellan personally repudiated the Democratic plank of 1864 which called for immediate negotiations, his victory would have brought to power a group willing to concede the autonomy, if not actual independence, of the seceding states. As a Union soldier wrote, McClellan's election "would have ended the war . . . by establishing the Confederacy."[16]

The platform, then, is an indication of which groups and interests will be influential should the party win the election. Unsuccessful parties do not face the obligation of redeeming their promises, but these promises do reveal which groups will be dominant within the party in the immediate future and perhaps in a more distant national administration.

Three conventions in the history of the Democratic party demonstrate the significance of platform disputes in determining party control. In 1896, the adoption of a free silver plank evidenced the passing of party power to the Western and Southern state organizations. In 1924, their control was challenged by the nascent groups of the urban Northeast. Conflict occurred on a proposed plank condemning "political secret societies" and pledging "to oppose any effort on the part of the Ku Klux Klan or any organization to interfere with the religious liberty or political freedom of any citizen, or to limit the civic right of any citizen or body of citizens because of religion, birthplace, or racial origin."[17]

Significantly, although no legislation or public policy was proposed, the dispute was still extremely bitter. In the closest vote in convention history, the anti-Klan plank was defeated by ⅘ of a vote, of a total of 1,086 votes. Control of the party was retained by the "Old Guard." This control was later lost, and the passing of power was demonstrated in a

[16] Bruce Catton, *A Stillness at Appomattox* (Garden City: Doubleday, 1954), p. 323.
[17] Richard C. Bain, *Convention Decisions and Voting Records* (Washington: The Brookings Institution, 1960), p. 222.

third platform fight, in 1948. At that time, the northern wing of the party forced acceptance of a liberal minority report on civil rights. What was really at stake was not the wording of a resolution on future legislation, but the control of the party.

In conclusion, the platform is both a campaign document and a policy statement. The platform affects policy indirectly by appealing to certain groups for support in the election, by indicating those interests which will be most influential in the formulation of national governmental policy, and by showing who will control the national party organization in the immediate future. According to an old adage, a party platform is like that of a railroad car—"not to stand on, but to get in on." This is true, but the platform also reveals who will get in and on what type of vehicle they will ride.

conclusion

While the party platform is the main embodiment of party policy, the choice of a candidate also involves a decision on public issues. Conflict may not occur frequently on the platform because the policy choice, in effect, is transferred to the nomination itself. The selection of candidate becomes not only a contest between individuals, but also a selection of policies.

One could hardly doubt in 1952, for example, that General Eisenhower was a more popular personality or more likely to win the Presidency than Senator Robert Taft. Yet, the Senator obtained 500 of 1200 votes on the first ballot. Much of this support came from those who favored his international and domestic policies over those of Eisenhower, and placed more emphasis on the acceptance of those policies than even on victory itself. There was no dispute over the Republican platform in 1952, for the policy question was decided by the Presidential nomination. Similar conflicts have marked other recent G.O.P. conventions.

In the Democratic party, the relationship between candidates and policies has not always been this clear. This is because the more conservative elements of the Democratic party, particularly in the South, usually have not presented a serious contender for the nomination. In 1952 and 1956, however, the choice of Stevenson over Kefauver or Harriman was clearly a decision in favor of a moderate, rather than a militantly liberal, policy in civil rights. Conversely, the choice of Truman in 1948 was an action in favor of strong civil rights action. In this latter case, the relationship is convincingly shown by the correlation between roll call votes on the platform and the nomination.[18] The policy implications of Presidential nominations will be examined in more detail in later chapters.

Rallying and Governing

Writing a platform is one of the convention functions other than the nomination of candidates. A second is the holding of a national campaign rally on behalf of the party and its candidates. In those conventions in which the nominations or the platforms were not in dispute, stimulation of party and popular enthusiasm has been the major objective of the partisan meeting.

Much of the convention atmosphere of disorder, riot, and insensible confusion is due to the efforts of delegates to arouse and maintain their spirits. Many critics of the convention system have argued that a party cannot sensibly choose programs and candidates in such an atmosphere. Condemning the convention as "a colossal travesty of popular institutions," Ostrogorskii described the assembled delegates and spectators as "a raving mob which, under ordinary circumstances, could only be formed if all the inmates of all the lunatic asylums of the country had made their escape at the same time."[19]

These objections are basically irrelevant. Of course

[18] There is a positive correlation of .99 between the vote to adopt the stronger civil rights plank and the first ballot support of Truman. See Bain, p. 276.
[19] Ostrogorskii, pp. 158-59.

rational decisions could not be made in the circus atmosphere prevailing in convention halls. The fact is, however, that the decisions are not made there for the most part, but in calmer and somewhat more judicious surroundings—in caucuses, hotel suites, and even "smoke-filled rooms." The convention is not a circus, but "it is a chess tournament disguised as a circus."[20]

Simultaneously with the serious work of the convention which is being accomplished in these various places, the campaign rally is being conducted on the floor. The division of labor is revealed in an analysis of floor action in the 1952 conventions. Although probably more than the average time was spent in debate and voting that year, the Democrats devoted about a third, and the Republicans a quarter, of their time to actual deliberation and decision-making. The remainder was spent in formalities, speeches and orations. The precise figures are as follows:[21]

	Republican		Democratic	
	Minutes	*%*	*Minutes*	*%*
Formalities	752	32.7	483	17.6
Other Speeches	746	32.4	903	32.8
Ovations	224	9.7	369	13.4
Debate	341	14.8	224	8.2
Voting	240	10.4	773	28.0
Totals:	2303	100.0	2752	100.0

The convention as campaign rally is directed toward two audiences: party workers and the general electorate. In both instances, as in all of the convention, the objective is to arouse sufficient support to bring victory in the forthcoming election. By their participation in the fervor, friendship and partisanship of the convention, party members find their loyalties strengthened and their enthusiasm increased. When they are engaged in the dull and arduous work of the elec-

[20] Alistair Cooke, quoted in Malcolm Moos and Stephen Hess, *Hats in the Ring* (New York: Random House, 1960), p. 161.
[21] Charles A. Thomson, *Television and Presidential Politics* (Washington: The Brookings Institution, 1956), p. 109.

tion campaign, or giving a non-tax-deductible contribution, memories of the convention may provide them with a sense of mission and a personal stake in the outcome. "The value of the convention lies in its permitting the rank and file of the party to participate physically and emotionally in a common enterprise. . . . Here they have their chance to meet, to shout together, to feel together. The relationship of follower and leader is seldom an intellectual bond. A common bond of sympathy, a common symbol, is easily grasped and equally binding."[22]

The continuing increase in the size of the conventions is part of an attempt to extend this bond to as large a number of party members as possible. Other partisans can share the spirit vicariously by following the proceedings through the mass media.

The importance of the convention as an appeal to the general electorate is equally great. Detailed studies of American voting behavior in recent years have revealed two relevant facts. First, the significant effect of a campaign is not to convert voters from one party to another, but to reinforce a partisan committment, or to activate a predisposition to one party. Second, from two-thirds to three-fourths of the voters definitely decide whom they will support by the time the nominations are made, even in elections in which both candidates are designated for the first time.[23]

Insofar as the convention is a campaign rally, it is well designed to take partisan advantage of these facts of voting

[22] Pendleton Herring, *The Politics of Democracy* (New York: Norton, 1940), p. 229.

[23] Bernard Berelson *et al.*, *Voting* (Chicago: University of Chicago Press, 1954), p. 345 in Appendix A. This finding is substantiated for 1940 by Paul Lazarsfeld, Bernard Berelson and Hazel Gaudet, *The People's Choice* (New York: Duell, Sloane and Pearce, 1944); for 1952 in Angus Campbell *et al.*, *The Voter Decides* (Chicago: Row, Peterson, 1954); for 1956 in Angus Campbell *et al.*, *The American Voter* (New York: Wiley, 1960). Evidence for the 1960 election is not yet available, but there is no great reason to expect significantly different results.

behavior. The convention represents a massive assault to win the allegiance of the voters. Orators constantly extol the virtues of their party while denouncing the vices of the other. Popular symbols, memories of past accomplishments, and revered leaders are presented to the electorate. The party platform promises solutions to the problems of the nation, while its candidates are represented as the embodiment of excellence.

The party's opportunity is even more desirable considering the terms on which it is offered. Convention delegates bear their own expenses, while the national organization is paid a substantial sum by the host city. The party's message is distributed throughout the nation without charge by press, radio, television, and motion pictures. This particular party propaganda is probably noticed by more voters than any other electoral appeal. Moreover, the format can be arranged so that candidates for state as well as national office are given a conspicuous forum. In the 1956 Democratic convention, for example, each of 11 platform sections was read by a different speaker, who thereby was given free television time in aid of his political career. As the convention closes, the party's nominees address the electorate for the first time as national candidates while their statements are cheered by an enthusiastic and uncritical audience.

The convention serves well as a campaign rally. Indeed, it may serve too well. There is a danger that the decision-making purposes of a convention will be subordinated to the demands of party managers and television directors for a "good show." There is a further danger that, even in the context of a campaign rally, changes may be forced by a desire to please the mass audience rather than the delegates. Arousing the voters may often be different from arousing partisan convention participants. As a result, efforts may be made to restrain or to manage the delegates. They are increasingly instructed, for example, as to "proper" behavior on the convention floor. In order to provide entertainment for the home audience, the convention members are limited in their freedom to enjoy themselves as they choose. Television may make the conventions more attractive to its viewers, while making them less exciting and personally impressive to the partisans present.

There are indications that the campaign rally is becoming the most important purpose of national conventions. One observer even predicts that in twenty years conventions will be held primarily to ratify previous decisions and "to stage a rally for the benefit of the national television audience."[24] Nominations are contested less often than previously, fewer internal disputes need to be resolved by the convention and even platform fights are becoming less frequent. Since 1928, 19 minority planks have been voted on in conventions, in contrast to 22 in an equally long period before 1928.[25] More decisions are being made outside of the convention.

Of the various functions of the convention, however, the holding of a campaign rally is the most certain to be maintained. Nomination of candidates possibly could be done through national primaries or through a revival of some form of the Congressional caucus. Platforms could probably be written better by a small group meeting at leisure, and the organizational details of the party could be handled by a small, representative committee. A rally, however, in order to be effective requires large numbers, considerable noise and perhaps even a touch of the lunacy observed by Ostrogorskii. These qualities are possessed by the convention. No party wishing to win a national election will abandon the opportunity of arousing its own supporters while reaching an audience of millions.

A final convention function other than the nomina-

[24] William G. Carleton, "The Revolution in the Presidential Nominating Convention," *Political Science Quarterly*, Vol. 72 (June, 1957), p. 237.
[25] Paul T. David *et al.*, *The Politics of National Party Conventions* (Washington: The Brookings Institution, 1960), p. 408.

tions is government of the party. The elements of this task range from details such as the appointment of ceremonial committees to vital decisions on the distribution of power and privilege among party factions. Included in its managerial duties are the election of officers, settlement of disputes among rival state delegations, and the definition of national party membership.

Theoretically, the convention is the supreme governing body of the national party. Aside from the national committee which is formally elected by the convention, there is no other body able to attempt central direction of the party. However, the convention's power is actually not great, for the national organization is sharply limited in its authority. The conventions have full power only over their own procedures and actions. They cannot control the other party agencies—the state and local organizations, representatives in Congress, the executives elected under the party label.

In dealing with these fellow partisans, the national party, as represented by the convention and national committee, has few powers, few opportunities to exert these powers, and few sanctions with which to uphold its decisions. The standards for party membership are defined largely by state law and state parties. Candidates for all offices other than President and Vice-President are nominated and elected independently by their local constituencies. While change is evident, American politics is now highly decentralized.

The composition of the national committee, theoretically the executive agent of the convention, indicates the lack of central power. Each state has approximately equal representation on the body, regardless of the party's electoral strength. If the committee had real power, one would hardly expect the Republican party of Mississippi to have almost the same number of votes as that of Illinois, or the Democratic party of Vermont to be accorded the same representation as that of New York. The committee as a whole exercises little power, although individual members may be influential. They exercise their influence as delegates from their state organizations, the real loci of power, rather than as members of a corporate body with independent authority.

When the party is in control of the White House, Presidential patronage may be distributed through the national committeemen, although this is not obligatory. Even if the procedure is followed, it does not increase the power of the committee, for patronage is distributed through individual members, not through the group as a whole. Moreover, appointments are made in order to increase the President's control of the party, not that of the national committee. When the party is out of power, there are still fewer means of influence available. However, the advent of bodies such as the Democratic Advisory Council, to be discussed later, may represent some change.

Recent attempts in the Democratic party to increase the authority of the national party over state organizations have not succeeded to any great extent. In 1952, to prevent the defection of Southern state parties, the convention adopted a "loyalty pledge" requiring all delegates to declare that they would seek to have the convention nominee placed on their states' ballots. Later, however, the convention voted to seat three delegations which had refused to comply with the requirement. In the next two conventions, no formal loyalty pledge was established. The call for the convention included the hopeful "understanding" that delegates were "bona fide Democrats who have the interests, welfare and success of the Democratic party at heart" and would endeavor to place the Democratic ticket on the ballot in their states.[26] In 1960 this agreement was technically upheld in Alabama and Mississippi, but these strongly Democratic states chose 14 "uncommitted" electors who voted against the party's nominees.

In the governance of the party the convention does not have sovereign power. Because there is no accepted and

[26] Bain, p. 294. Mississippi's new primary law will make it difficult to apply this provision to that state's Democratic delegates in 1964.

institutionalized central authority, the actual form of government will vary from one four-year period to the next. Generally, the patterns of internal party government fall into one of two patterns: hierarchy and bargaining.[27]

Hierarchy, where "leaders exercise a very high degree of unilateral control over non-leaders,"[28] is most evident in the renomination of an incumbent President. The Chief Executive, with the consultation of a few selected leaders, will determine the program, platform, nominations and even timing of the convention and the general course of the national party.

More often, the party is governed by bargaining, or "reciprocal control among leaders."[29] Bargaining is stimulated in conventions by four conditions: non-hierarchical control, interdependence of the bargainers, initial disagreement of the bargainers, and the expectation of gain.[30] Bargaining is necessary because the various political leaders come to a convention with differing preferences on party policy and leadership and because there is no recognized, hierarchical leadership to dictate a decision. Bargaining eventually results in agreement because the factions are hopeful of winning the Presidential election and recognize the need for party unity to accomplish this end.

The result of bargaining can be either the victory of one party faction over others or compromise between them. Republican conclaves for twenty years after the Civil War evidenced a conflict between two major factions, and the frequent triumph of one over the other. Similarly, the 1924 Democratic meeting was a marathon contest between major factions. Competition may take place over the platform, as

[27] Robert Dahl and Charles E. Lindbloom, *Politics, Economics and Welfare* (New York: Harper, 1953), chaps. 6-13. Two other processes—pricing systems and polyarchy, or control of leaders by non-leaders, are not descriptive of party government.
[28] *Ibid.*, p. 227.
[29] *Ibid.*, p. 324.
[30] Nelson Polsby, "Decision-Making at the National Conventions," *Western Political Quarterly*, Vol. 13 (September, 1960), p. 614.

previously discussed, or over party rules and credentials. Most often, the Presidential nomination most clearly reveals who is in control of the party. Especially in years in which the party appears to have little chance of electoral success, the Presidential nomination may be more significant as a contest for party control than as an attempt to gain the White House.

Competition can also result in a bargained compromise between factions. Attempts will be made to conciliate all groups so as to achieve the unity necessary for victory. Conciliation may take place in many ways—through the pre-election distribution of offices, as in the case of Thomas Dewey in 1948, by policy agreement, as in the Eisenhower-Taft post-convention conference of 1952, or through deals in a "smoke-filled room," as in the famous case of Warren Harding's nomination in 1920. William Allen White's description of that convention is an excellent illustration of the convention as a factional conference:

> Daugherty dominated the group which controlled the Southern delegates. That group was necessary to the Senate cabal, and friendly with the oil interests instinctively. . . . The nomination would have to be made when the Senate leaders and the Southern delegates joined forces, and they could not join forces until the oil interests were satisfied. Only one candidate before that convention held the key to the solution. That candidate was Warren Harding.[31]

Later, the remaining factions of the party were appeased by being permitted to have their way in the nomination of Calvin Coolidge for Vice-President.

Through hierarchical control or bargaining, the convention accomplishes the function of party government. Along with the adoption of the platform and the holding of

[31] William Allen White, *Masks in a Pageant* (New York: Macmillan. 1928), p. 405.

a campaign rally, this action is closely related to the nomination of party candidates. This, the central concern of the convention, is to be considered in the following chapters.

Suggestions for Further Reading

Herbert Croly, *Marcus Alonzo Hanna* (New York: Macmillan, 1923). Definitive biography of the man who systematized business influence in the Republican party, while creating a relatively strong national organization.

Alfred de Grazia, *Public and Republic* (New York: Knopf, 1951). An extensive discussion of the theory of representation and legislative mandates.

Seymour E. Harris, *The Economics of the Political Parties* (New York: Macmillan, 1962). Investigates the economic policies of the two major parties and finds significant differences between them.

Bernard Hennessy, *Dollars for Democrats, 1959* (New Brunswick: Eagleton Institute, 1960). Case study of a financial campaign of the Democratic National Committee, which illustrates the nature and limits of its power.

Pendleton Herring, *The Politics of Democracy* (New York: Norton, 1940). A sympathetic observation of American parties and conventions, including their fun and frolics.

Herbert McCloskey *et al.*, "Issue Conflict and Consensus Among Party Leaders and Followers," *American Political Science Review*, Vol. 54 (June, 1960), pp. 406-27. An excellent study, based on detailed questionnaires, of the policy views and differences within the major parties.

Roy F. Nichols, *The Disruption of American Democracy* (New York: Macmillan, 1948). An account of the difficulties and divisions which followed heated debate on platform provisions and party policy by pre-Civil War Democrats.

M. Ostrogorskii, *Democracy and the Party System in the United States* (New York: Macmillan, 1910). A classic, wide-ranging criticism of American political parties in general, as well as convention practices in particular.

Kirk H. Porter and Donald B. Johnson, *National Party Platforms 1840-1956* (Urbana: University of Illinois Press, 1956). The complete text of all party policy statements adopted in national conventions, including those of minor parties.

George F. Whicher (ed.), *William Jennings Bryan and the Campaign of 1896* (Boston: Heath, 1953). A collection of outstanding articles on one of the decisive American elections, one in which a clear difference existed between candidates and policies.

V INFLUENCES
ON THE NOMINATIONS

      Although presidential nominations are formally made by the assembled delegates at the national convention, these party members do not act as independent agents. Delegates come to a national convention as representatives of state organizations bound together by varying degrees of internal cohesion, loyalty and discipline. They are subject to numerous influences, including the power of national party leaders, the desires of interest groups, and the expressed preferences of the general electorate. Presidential aspirants design their strategies to employ these influences for their own benefit.

      Thus, delegates cast their votes in convention amid a variety of restraints on their behavior. Historically, the trend is toward more limitations on the autonomy of the individual delegates and the convention as a whole. New influences have been introduced, limiting the power of the state parties. In addition, more decisions are now being made before the actual opening of the convention, further changing both the form and substance of the nominating process.

In form, a Presidential designation through most of American history was presented as a "call to duty." A candidate would commonly remain at home, ostensibly unaware that some party leaders were seeking his selection. Despite the invention of the telegraph, radio, and telephone, the nominee remained officially unaware of his success until notification by a committee of the convention.

Actually, the tradition was never followed as faithfully as legend suggests. As early as 1844, pre-convention campaigns were conducted by Martin Van Buren and Henry Clay. Though more discreet than candidates today, both traveled extensively seeking party support, and others followed their examples in later years. The real effect of this tradition was to allow considerable freedom to the convention. Since pre-convention campaigning was scorned in theory and restricted in practice, most delegations arrived at the national convention without firm commitments to any candidate. This permitted a maximum of maneuverability and gave the state delegations the fullest power over the nomination.

Most of these practices today, even when still followed, have become no more than rituals. Aspirants now campaign vigorously, traveling throughout the nation before the convention and attempting to win favor at the meeting place itself. Once designated, the candidate is likely to appear immediately before the delegates to accept his nomination.

Past practice has been changed to such an extent that Adlai Stevenson was criticized by many Democrats for not campaigning for the 1960 nomination. Declaring, "If they want me to lead them, I will lead them,"[1] Stevenson was only following the tradition of "the office seeks the man." However, that tradition had been discarded.

[1] On the Columbia Broadcasting System program, "Face the Nation," on July 10, 1960, the day before the convention.

The tradition of restraint could be sustained only if upheld in practice by all candidates, or at least all serious contenders. Should one candidate make an intense pre-convention campaign, he might establish a position so commanding as to make his acceptance by the convention inevitable. Thus Samuel Tilden was able to dominate the 1876 Democratic convention by a vigorous campaign which included the purchase of advertisements in 1,200 newspapers, the distribution of hundreds of thousands of articles, and an intelligence system operating in all sections of the nation.[2]

Violations of the tradition were restrained in the past by the inadequate means available for carrying on a pre-convention campaign. Travel was difficult, means of communication were limited, and popular influence on the nomination was minimal. Today the situation has changed. A candidate can travel between any two states in hours, he can employ a variety of media, and he can gain popular support through opinion polls and primary elections.

These technical and legal innovations have made it easier for candidates to develop support before the convention opens, or even effectively to foreclose the convention's choice for the nomination. To safeguard their own interests, therefore, Presidential hopefuls must use the pre-convention period to develop strength. "He who hesitates is lost" may become an aphorism of nominating politics.

Changes in the form of securing nomination probably contribute to more informed selections, providing "many delegates and managers with a far more complete docket of information, and with more matured attitudes toward personalities and issues developed during the pre-convention period."[3] The preliminary months afford party leaders a relatively long and calm period in which to judge the various aspirants. Popular reaction and preferences may be ap-

[2] Irving Stone, *They Also Ran* (Garden City: Doubleday, Doran, 1943), pp. 203-04.
[3] Charles A. Thomson, *Television and Presidential Politics* (Washington: The Brookings Institution, 1956), p. 23.

praised through appearances on television and success in the primaries. With the candidates present in the convention city, whatever deals may be made will now be participated in by the nominee himself. This should lead to more consistent honoring of promises, even if not necessarily to more honorable promises. Even the new practice of immediately accepting the nomination can contribute to the role of the convention as a campaign rally.

Pre-convention campaigning has also contributed to a change in the substance of the nominating process. New influences can now be brought to bear. The result is to limit the discretion of the delegates and of the party managers who have commonly controlled convention behavior. In past party history, the leaders of the state parties held a monopoly of influence over the nominations, and the method of winning designation was to form a coalition of state political organizations. The convention resembled a diplomatic congress, where the managers of the various aspirants negotiated until an alliance including a majority of delegates was concluded.

Beginning about the turn of the century, the state parties have gradually lost their monopoly position. Convention votes are still cast by state party delegations, but their choices increasingly are conditioned and even controlled by factors beyond their complete control. Party managers still strike the poses of "bosses" and "kingmakers," but they must now take account of three challenges to their position: the prominence of national, rather than state, political leaders, the increased role of nation-wide interest groups, and the development of Presidential primary elections and other expressions of popular preference.

The parties have accepted these new influences in the nominating process. They have done so because they are primarily interested in winning elections. Victory may be brought nearer by the nomination of a well-known national leader, or by the endorsement of an important interest group, or by following the popular preferences revealed in primaries. In order to gain the ultimate end of a Presidential election victory, the parties have accepted restraints on convention freedom.

The National Leadership

National political leaders now exercise greater control over the conventions. Increased power is particularly marked in the case of the most prominent national figure, the President. In the nineteenth century, few Presidents were sure of renomination. While Jackson, Van Buren, Grant, and Cleveland won unanimous renomination, five others were defeated. Four did not seek a second designation, either for personal reasons or because of the strength of the opposition, while two, including Lincoln, had to overcome significant opposition in order to win renomination. (Three Presidents died during their first term.) In all, only three of fifteen incumbent Presidents, not including Cleveland, controlled conventions at which their own renominations were possible.

In the twentieth century, by contrast, not one of nine Presidents has been denied renomination and only one, William Howard Taft in 1912, faced significant opposition. The changing pattern is shown in the table below.

While Presidents have gained in influence, they cannot dictate their party's choice of a successor. Perhaps the only clear case of a President passing on party leadership is that of Andrew Jackson, who accomplished the nomination of Martin Van Buren. Theodore Roosevelt also conferred his mantle on William Howard Taft. However, there is some evidence that his first choice was Secretary of State Elihu Root, but that he was dissuaded from pushing this choice by fear of a convention fight.[4] In another case, Herbert Hoover's nomination as the Republican candidate was approved in 1928 by President Calvin Coolidge. Like most of the actions of "Silent Cal," this approval was tacit rather than explicit.[5]

[4] Henry L. Stoddard, *Presidential Sweepstakes* (New York: Putnam's, 1948), p. 125.
[5] William Allen White, *Masks in a Pageant* (New York: Macmillan, 1928), pp. 455-57.

TABLE 5–1

RENOMINATION OF FIRST-TERM PRESIDENTS

Convention Action	*1832-1896*	*1900-1956*
Renominated Without Contest	Jackson, 1832 Van Buren, 1840 Grant, 1872 Cleveland, 1888	McKinley, 1900 T. Roosevelt, 1904 Wilson, 1916 Coolidge, 1924 Hoover, 1932 F. Roosevelt, 1936 Truman, 1948 Eisenhower, 1956
Renominated After Contest	Lincoln, 1864 Harrison, 1892	Taft, 1912
Did Not Seek Renomination	Polk, 1848 Buchanan, 1860 Hayes, 1880 Cleveland, 1896	
Defeated for Renomination	Tyler, 1844 Fillmore, 1852 Pierce, 1856 Johnson, 1868 Arthur, 1884	

Despite his own claims, President Harry Truman did not control the nomination of Adlai Stevenson in 1952. After Stevenson had disowned Presidential ambitions early in the year, Vice-President Alben Barkley was told that "President Truman had decided to back me for the nomination. . . . Furthermore, he would personally ask his own alternate, Thomas Gavin of Kansas City, to vote for me."[6] Barkley remained Truman's preference at least until the opening session. Interviewed in 1960, Gavin declared that he had been instructed, by means of a sealed message, to vote for Barkley.[7] When the actual balloting occurred, however, Gavin voted for Stevenson. Apparently his instructions had been changed sometime between the opening of the convention and the first nominating ballot, by which time the movement

[6] Alben Barkley, *That Reminds Me* (Garden City: Doubleday, 1954), pp. 230-31. Cf. Harry S Truman, *Memoirs* (New York: Doubleday, 1956), Vol. II, pp. 492-95.
[7] Gavin was interviewed on television immediately after John Kennedy had answered Truman's 1960 challenge that the Senator was too young and inexperienced to be President.

toward Stevenson had become quite forceful. Truman was not leading a surge; he was joining the band wagon.

In the latest succession of party leadership, Richard Nixon had the blessing of President Dwight Eisenhower. However, the General's preference was not expressed until after Nixon was well on the way toward a convention majority. Until then, Eisenhower would say only that there were a large number of acceptable individuals within the Republican party. In addition, the President had tried to discourage Nixon from seeking renomination as Vice-President in 1956, offering him a Cabinet job instead.[8] With Eisenhower in uncertain health, this action was certainly no vote of confidence in the Vice-President. In 1960, Nixon faced no significant opposition at the convention, but his nomination can hardly be said to result from the command of an incumbent President.

Rather than the power to dictate the choice of a successor, Presidents now would seem able to veto an unacceptable nominee. In the nineteenth century, Presidents held no such prerogative. Stephen Douglas and William Jennings Bryan were selected despite the opposition of Presidents Buchanan and Cleveland. In the twentieth century, every party successor has been acceptable to the incumbent President.

One means by which a President has been able to halt unacceptable nominations has been to threaten to run himself. With the passage of the 22nd amendment, limiting the President to two terms, this threat will no longer be effective. Nevertheless, with the increased importance of the national government, the party in power will continue to be identified with the incumbent Chief Executive. It must run on his record with a candidate supporting that record.

Another group of national leaders, defeated candidates for the Presidency, have also gained influence recently.

[8] Sherman Adams, *First-Hand Report* (New York: Harper, 1961), p. 231.

Until 1892, no major party renominated a candidate in the convention following his defeat. While the Whigs did nominate Henry Clay in both 1832 and 1844, they rejected his candidacy in the two intervening elections. The Democrats rejected two active candidates, Van Buren in 1844 and Lewis Cass in 1852.

In eighteen conventions since 1892, defeated candidates have won renomination five times and have exercised considerable influence in the decisions of two other conclaves. Active candidacies for renomination have been rejected only twice. Past experience is tabulated below.

TABLE 5–2

ROLE OF CANDIDATES AFTER ELECTORAL DEFEAT

Candidate Role	1832-1888	1892-1956
Renominated	Clay, 1844	Cleveland, 1892 Bryan, 1900-08 Dewey, 1948 Stevenson, 1956
Influenced Convention		Bryan, 1912 Dewey, 1952
Denied Renomination	Clay, 1836ª-40-48 Van Buren, 1844 Cass, 1852	Smith, 1932 Willkie, 1944

ªThe Whigs held no convention in 1836. Clay was not among the candidates advanced by the state conventions.

Traditionally, defeated "titular leaders" have had more title than power, but the increasing importance of the national party indicates the beginnings of significant change. However, the failure of Thomas Dewey and Adlai Stevenson to be seriously considered for third nominations indicates that the United States has not yet adopted the British practice of retaining the opposition leader after continued defeats.

In the past as well, conventions have limited their choices largely to state leaders. Today, Senators and other individuals less intimately related to local politics are prominent among the candidates. Incumbent Vice-Presidents are now given respectful attention by the conventions, and have a serious chance of receiving the Presidential designation.* Cabinet officials may be considered for nominations even if, like Herbert Hoover, they have no previous political experience. Other national leaders, the parties' spokesmen in the national House of Representatives, are now usually selected as permanent chairmen of the conventions.

Even the National Chairman, in the past only a party functionary, has come to exercise some power. Leonard Hall dominated the arrangements of the 1956 Republican convention. He stifled qualms about a second term for Eisenhower, despite the President's heart attack, and prevented the expression of any significant opposition to the renomination of Nixon. Four years later, in the Democratic party, Paul Butler was accused of "rigging" the convention in favor of the candidacy of John Kennedy. While it may have been inaccurate, this very charge indicates a recent and considerable growth in the Chairman's authority.[9]

Interest Group Influence

The monopoly control over nominations of state parties has also been disrupted by the intervention of nationwide interest groups. Parties seek to enlist a coalition of such groups in their campaigns. The platform is one encouragement to enlistment; the nominees for President and Vice-President are another. To win the nomination, aspirants now must achieve not only a numerical majority of the convention delegates, they must also gain the consent of those interests which are necessary to the party's electoral success.

To a degree, the convention operates according to John Calhoun's proposed system of a "concurrent majority." No decisions should be made, declared the South Carolina

* See Chapter VII for a fuller discussion of the Vice-Presidents.
[9] The increased importance of national leaders is discussed further in Paul T. David et al., The Politics of National Party Conventions (Washington: The Brookings Institution, 1960), chapters 4 and 5.

Senator, until they have been agreed to by both a numerical majority and by each of the interests involved. In effect, a group should hold a veto over any actions affecting it. Convention processes are not as rigid as those counselled by Calhoun. Not all interests are heard, and some may be defeated in a contest with others. Insofar as platforms are specific and meaningful, they constitute the rejection of some group demands and the acceptance of others. Moreover, there is only one Presidential nomination and some are likely to be disappointed when the choice is made. Within these limits, however, the convention will seek to satisfy the interests it regards as important.

Relationships between parties and interest groups existed in the past as well. The present situation is different in that groups are greater in number, more formally organized and more national in scope. Formerly, with a simpler and more localized economy, the number of groups was relatively small, consisting principally of various business interests. Now, there are local, national and international business interests, as well as labor, agricultural, racial, religious, and foreign interests involved in American politics.[10]

Moreover, in the past, interest group involvement was sporadic and dependent largely on individual inclinations. In the case of business, "there had, of course always been corrupt pressure by important capitalists or greedy promoters, swarming about the legislatures; they had always been a Maecenas of politics ready to advance the career of a noted statesman, or make a free gift to his party chest. But there had been no regularity or system."[11]

The important interests of the past were also contained within the state organizations. Since most of their aims could be accomplished through the state and local

[10] See Pendleton Herring, *Group Representation Before Congress* (Baltimore: The Johns Hopkins University Press, 1929), for a description of the proliferation of interest groups involved in lobbying activities.
[11] Matthew Josephson, *The Politicos 1865-1896* (New York: Harcourt, Brace, 1938), pp. 425-26.

governments, they had no need to seek power at a higher level. Important groups worked through the state parties, and occasionally dominated them. For decades, for example, local manufacturers were an integral part of the Pennsylvania Republican party. Thus, in 1888, steel manufacturers were able to veto the Presidential candidacy of Judge Walter Gresham of Indiana.[12] Pennsylvania eventually joined a movement to Benjamin Harrison, after receiving a coded telegram from Andrew Carnegie in Scotland, reading, "Too late. Victor immovable. [Blaine will not run.] Take Trump and Star [Harrison and Phelps]."[13] On the crucial ballot, Pennsylvania gave Harrison 59 of 60 votes, after no more than nine votes on the seven previous tallies.[14]

The influence of interest groups in this period was disorganized and decentralized. With the growth of a national economy and the consequent rise of groups with national interests, fuller integration and organization were needed. Increasingly, the important groups were of such great scope as to be too large for any state party. Their influence instead was exercised more directly in national politics.

Organization of national interest groups was gradually introduced toward the end of the nineteenth century, and most fully developed by Mark Hanna in 1896. On behalf of William McKinley and the Republican party, Hanna systematically collected funds from Eastern financial and Midwestern industrial interests, promising in return that the party would uphold the protective tariff and the gold standard. "It was the first mobilization of class-conscious industrialists. . . . Great manufacturers and their allies in transportation, with their supporters in high finance, had

---

[12] Eugene H. Roseboom, *A History of Presidential Elections* (New York: Macmillan, 1959), pp. 279-80.
[13] Stoddard, p. 90.
[14] Richard C. Bain, *Convention Decisions and Voting Records* (Washington: The Brookings Institution, 1960), Appendix D.

been taking root widely but without premeditated purposes in the administrations of Cleveland and Harrison. But growth came suddenly, and their visions came to flower and fruitage in the Hanna organization of business and politics behind McKinley."[15]

Since Hanna's time, business groups have consciously attempted to influence nominations, particularly in the Republican party, acknowledged by President Eisenhower to be the "party of business."[16] The intervention of business groups is likely to take the form of the giving or withholding of campaign contributions or other assistance, rather than an attempt to choose friendly delegates. Businessmen have not been compelled to intervene overtly in party decisions, for there have been few serious political challenges to their economic position.

The business community had much to do with the surprise nomination of Wendell Willkie in 1940. The Indiana industrialist's campaign was aided by volunteer local clubs, to be sure, but it is doubtful if he could have created a real stir without the financial contributions of businessmen, the free publicity afforded through articles in *Fortune* and the *Saturday Evening Post,* and a host of telegrams to convention delegates from their local business leaders. To some extent, and perhaps decisively, "the financial-industrial clique influenced and financed the amateur enthusiasts."[17]

Again in 1952, business influence was said to be crucial at a Republican conference. Senator Robert Taft attributed his defeat primarily to "underlying causes which had operated steadily for eight months." These included primarily "the power of the New York financial interests and a large number of businessmen subject to New York influence" and the "four-fifths of the influential newspapers in the country [which] were opposed to me continuously and

[15] White, p. 167.
[16] *The New York Times,* July 1, 1962.
[17] Stone, pp. 352-53.

vociferously."[18] Even Nelson Rockefeller, in 1960, found himself opposed by the financial interests of the Republican party and consequently was forced to withdraw his Presidential candidacy.[19]

Other interest groups active at national conventions have included prohibitionists, free traders, suffragettes, veterans, Negroes and farmers. Of these and other interests in the Democratic party, the most apparent cases of group influence have involved organized labor. In 1944, the nomination of Truman for Vice-President was first approved by union leaders before the delegates acted. According to legend, convention managers were told to "Clear it with Sidney," meaning Sidney Hillman, head of the C.I.O.'s Political Action Committee. Even if the exact quotation is only fancy, the fact of a labor veto over the nomination seems established.[20]

By 1952, labor was represented directly by over 100 delegates who caucused as a group.[21] Union leaders were instrumental in blocking the candidacy of Alben Barkley, even against the endorsement of the White House. Barkley publicly attacked the union heads, but withdrew in the face of their opposition.[22] Later in the convention, the union delegates, particularly Walter Reuther, were influential in securing the support of large Northern delegations for Adlai Stevenson.[23]

Labor's influence in the Democratic party is not unchallenged. Other interests, including those of business and of professional politicians, must be satisfied as well.

[18] David, p. 556; *The New York Times,* November 25, 1959.
[19] Theodore H. White, *The Making of the President 1960* (New York: Atheneum, 1961), pp. 72-74.
[20] Irving G. Williams, *The Rise of the Vice-Presidency* (Washington: Public Affairs Press, 1956), pp. 213-17.
[21] David, pp. 341, 517.
[22] Barkley, pp. 236-40.
[23] Paul T. David *et al., Presidential Nominating Politics in 1952* (Baltimore: The Johns Hopkins University Press, 1954), Vol. I, p. 150.

Thus, in 1960, union leaders generally supported John Kennedy as the Presidential nominee. They also sought to prevent Senator Lyndon Johnson from gaining a place on the ticket.[24] Their objections were considered less important, however, than conciliation of Southern delegations.

Interest group influence in the parties is likely to continue and even increase, because the support of these groups is necessary to electoral success. The huge sums of money required in a Presidential election cannot be gained through assessments or contributions from party members; the financial resources of private individuals and groups must be gained. With the decline of traditional local machines, the parties must employ interest groups to provide the manpower for canvassing and staffing the polls. To the extent that issues are important in campaigns, the parties will turn to the interest groups to define and defend their policy positions. Since the parties need the interest groups, they will be required to share with them the power of nominating Presidential candidates.

Primaries and Popular Preferences

A third new influence on nominations is the popularity of the potential candidates, as demonstrated by opinion polls, the mass media and Presidential primaries. Proven popular favor is important because the party is vitally interested in nominating its strongest candidate. As early as 1840, the alleged unpopularity of Henry Clay was partially responsible for his defeat in the Whig party. Polls, mass media, and primaries simply provide a more accurate means of acquiring information which delegates have always sought.

Since the first widespread use of opinion surveys in 1936, it has been possible to determine with some precision the relative esteem of different individuals within the same party and to predict the likely outcome of a contest between

[24] *The New York Times,* July 10, 1960.

two candidates of the major parties. Polls are now taken by the aspirants themselves, party organizations, newspapers, and commercial agencies.

Popular preferences can also be brought to bear through the communications media. A major effect of television and radio is to bring new candidates to the consideration of the party, and to hasten their advance to the front ranks of Presidential aspirants. The rapid rise of such personalities as Wendell Willkie and Estes Kefauver is closely related to the greater role in the nominating process now enjoyed by the mass media and the popular preferences they reflect and create. Along with the other media, "television may widen the choice of available candidates. This may not be apparent at the moments of final choice; the main effect will probably come earlier, during the preparatory period in which the news and public affairs departments of television are bringing before the public politically available and potent personalities."[25]

The Presidential primary is the most publicized and most confusing of the devices for the expression of popular preferences. Its history has been one of exuberant initial growth, until 1916, slow decay until the 1940s, and gradual maturation since that time. The system was first introduced for the 1908 conventions. The Progressive movement of the time sought to reduce the power of party organizations and to simultaneously increase that of the general electorate, by allowing the voters to directly choose delegates to the national conventions.

Support for primaries was engendered by political conditions of the time. Party organizations were marked by corruption, authoritarian leadership and subservience to special interests. At the same time, America generally believed in an optimistic theory of democracy which proclaimed the ability of the citizen to decide on all public issues. Moreover, most states were noncompetitive, one-party areas, leaving the voter without a real choice in parti-

[25] Thomson, pp. 136-37.

san elections. "The cure for the ills of democracy," declared the Progressives, "is more democracy." The results of their efforts were the initiative, referendum and, of interest here, the direct presidential primary.

The spread of the new system was greatly spurred by the defeat of Theodore Roosevelt in the 1912 Republican convention. After winning almost all primaries, Roosevelt was overwhelmed by the "steamroller" of President Taft, driven by the party managers from non-primary states. This experience apparently demonstrated the vices of the old convention system and the democratic virtues of the primaries. The Democratic party, discovering a popular issue, endorsed state primaries in its 1912 platform and President Woodrow Wilson called for a national presidential primary in his first message to Congress.

By 1916, some form of the system was in effect in 25 states,[26] and it was thought the primaries might eventually lead to the total extinction of national conventions. Gradually, the tide ebbed. Only one state enacted a new primary law after 1916, while nine others abolished the system.[27] Party organizations were able to keep control of nominations. From 1912 to 1924, one observer concluded that "presidential primary votes have not controlled the actions of the conventions. In fact the choice of the primaries and the choice of the convention has been the same in only three of eight cases." Of these three, two were of Presidents seeking renomination.[28]

For a time, primaries were of uncertain importance. Victories in these contests served to reinforce the campaigns of Alfred Smith and Alfred Landon but were not of great significance to Franklin Roosevelt or of any importance to Wendell Willkie. The general trend in recent years, however, has been toward an increased role for primaries. This

[26] Louise Overacker, *The Presidential Primary* (New York: Macmillan, 1926), pp. 10-15.
[27] David (1960), p. 528.
[28] Overacker, p. 163.

is clear in a listing of the 26 convention nominees since
1912. As shown in the table below, 15 men were first-time
nominees, of whom seven were aided in their campaigns by
primary victories. Of 11 renominated candidates, five received important support from primary victories.[29]

TABLE 5–3

Presidential Primaries and Convention Nominees

First-Time Nominees (15)		Renominated Candidates (11)	
Aided by Primaries (7)	Unaided by Primaries (8)	Aided by Primaries (5)	Unaided by Primaries (6)
Wilson, 1912	Hughes, 1916	Coolidge, 1924	Taft, 1912
Hoover, 1928	Cox, 1920	Roosevelt, 1940	Wilson, 1916
Smith, 1928	Harding, 1920	Truman, 1948	Hoover, 1932
Landon, 1936	Davis, 1924	Dewey, 1948	Roosevelt, 1936
Dewey, 1944	Roosevelt, 1932	Stevenson, 1956	Roosevelt, 1944
Eisenhower, 1952	Willkie, 1940		Eisenhower, 1956
Kennedy, 1960	Stevenson, 1952		
	Nixon, 1960		

In the first six Presidential elections in which primaries were widespread, from 1912 to 1932, they were
important in winning nominations for only four candidates,
and in three of these elections neither major candidate was
substantially aided by primary victories. In the more recent
seven elections, however, eight candidates have been designated with their aid, and at least one candidate has found
primaries useful in each election year.

The actions of individual candidates also demonstrate that primaries have become more important lately.
In 1940, Robert Taft contested no primary outside of his
own state of Ohio. In 1948, when he was next a candidate,
he entered only a few contests and campaigned modestly.
In 1952, in opposition to Eisenhower, he campaigned widely,
although unsuccessfully. Similarly, Adlai Stevenson won
his first nomination without participation in primaries, but
found it necessary to engage in extensive pre-convention

[29] "Aided by primaries" is necessarily somewhat subjective. It means
more than token or incidental support such as that gained by Nixon
in 1960. Rather, it implies that the primaries were a major element in
the success of the candidates, as in the case of Kennedy in 1960.

efforts to win a second designation. Even incumbent Presidents, controlling the party organization, have found nominating election victories useful. Calvin Coolidge and Harry Truman were able to gain second terms, and Franklin Roosevelt a third, by demonstrating popular support.

The primaries have real significance, then, to judge by recent history. Their significances does not lie, however, in the contests themselves. A candidate cannot win his party's leadership solely through primary victories. In 1960, for example, a Democrat who won every primary contest would gain 384 delegates firmly committed to him, only half of those needed for convention victory. The situation for a Republican candidate would differ only in the exact numbers.

Primaries are also defective in themselves as devices to measure popular opinion. All potential candidates are unlikely to be entered in any given contest, turnout is usually low, and local conditions, including the attitude of the state organization, can result in an unrepresentative vote.

Victories in the primaries, however, can be multiplied into greater success. A triumph in one state contest is apt to lead to a higher standing in public opinion polls.[30] The winner of a primary is also likely to be given more attention in the mass media, by the party organizations and by the general electorate. In seeking committments from other delegates, a candidate can use his primary victory to demonstrate his political appeal. Thus, after winning the Oregon primary in 1948, Dewey also gained the votes of the large Pennsylvania delegation. Similarly, Kennedy's 1960 success in West Virginia assured complete support from New York and other key states, rather than a delegation divided among Kennedy, Stevenson, and Symington supporters.[31] Primary victories in themselves cannot carry a candidate to victory,

[30] David (1960), pp. 312-14.
[31] From an interview with Edward Costikyan, now New York County Democratic Leader. Cf. Robert Bendiner, "The Provincial Politics of the Empire State," *Reporter*, Vol. 22 (May 12, 1960), pp. 21-23.

but they can provide the initial energy to start the band wagon rolling.

Most primary victories also yield the immediate benefit of adding to the number of convention delegates pledged to a candidate. If he cannot win a majority by this method, he can still gain a substantial number that might otherwise be unavailable to him. A candidate refusing to enter primaries is allowing large numbers of delegates to go to his opponents by default. If one candidate chooses to contest the primaries, others will be constrained to follow his example.

Primary victories also serve important functions for the party as a whole, as well as for the candidate. Politicians generally seek a winner, and have a great need for information about the appeal of the various aspirants. They are apt to be more impressed by success in an actual campaign situation than by popularity as measured by a random opinion poll or the unsupported guesses of election observers. A primary victory may also serve to refute a particular argument made against a candidate. In 1960, many Democratic leaders, such as David Lawrence of Pennsylvania, were willing to support Kennedy only after his primary victories had apparently demonstrated that a Catholic candidate would receive Protestant support.[32]

The primaries also simplify the party's task, and define its choice, by eliminating some candidates before the convention meets. In fact, while a series of election victories will not guarantee a nomination, it is almost certain that a series of defeats will remove an aspirant from any serious consideration. In recent years, Wendell Willkie, Estes Kefauver and Hubert Humphrey have abandoned their campaigns after defeats in primary elections.

At the same time, primaries limit the independence of the convention, and thus reduce the authority of state

[32] From an interview with Robert Meyner, former Governor of New Jersey. Cf. "A Kingmaker's Hedge," *Newsweek*, Vol. 55 (May 16, 1960), p. 33.

party leaders and other traditional "kingmakers." With the help of primary victories, a candidate may be able to capture the party's nomination before the convention opens. Even before the advent of primaries, of course, a candidate could follow this course. Primaries are but another means of reducing the convention's independence.

Primaries affect both the candidates and their parties. They also have a more general effect on the nominating process. There are some definite, although not great, differences between candidates who win nomination with the aid of primaries and those who achieve convention success without this help. These differences are detailed in the following table.

First-time nominees assisted by primary victories, to judge by the small number of cases available, are less likely to be professional politicians. They tend to be individuals who achieve success in some non-governmental occupation, and then quickly rise to a position of political prominence. Only Al Smith held more than two public offices on his way to convention success. Their experience in national affairs is even more limited. Of these seven nominees, only Hoover and Kennedy had such training before their Presidential nominations.

Nominees unaided by primaries are a more professional and experienced group. Their assent is slower, typically involving at least three intermediate offices. All but Willkie had at least ten years experience in government, and about half of this was in national politics.

The manner of nomination of these two types of candidates is also different. Primary winners are most likely to be chosen by the party out of power, as happened in eight of the thirteen elections since 1912, and all but one of those since 1936. Moreover, primary winners gain their party's nomination more quickly, typically on the first convention ballot with a large majority of the delegates. Significantly, first-time nominees who win in primaries also are more likely to win in the general elections.

TABLE 5-4

Characteristics of Presidential Nominees, 1912-1960

	First-Time Candidates (15)		Renominated Candidates (11)	
	Aided by Primaries (7)	Unaided by Primaries (8)	Aided by Primaries (5)	Unaided by Primaries (6)
Median Age when Nominated	54	50	56	59
Mean Years in Politics	9	14	22	19
Mean Years in National Politics	3	7	7	13
Occupation before First Nomination: (No.)				
Non-government	1	2	0	1
Federal Govt.	2	3	1	2
State Governor	4	3	4	3
Private Occupation:				
Law	1	5	5	3
Professions	2	0	0	2
Business	2	1	0	0
Journalism	0	2	0	0
Military	1	0	0	1
None (politics)	1	0	0	0
Education:				
Post-College	3	6	4	4
College	3	1	1	2
None-College	1	1	0	0
Region:				
Northeast	5	4	3	4
Middle West	1	3	2	1
Far West	1	1	0	1
No. Prominent in Earlier Conventions	4	5	2	3
No., "out" party	6	5	2	0
Median %, First ballot	66%	17%	75%	99%
Median Victory Ballot	1	5	1	1
No. Winning in General Election	4	2	3	4

The primary winners also show greater variety in their personal backgrounds. They enter Presidential politics from a variety of occupations, while lawyers predominate in the other group. Those employing primaries in their campaigns also extend over a wider age range, from Dewey's 42 to Eisenhower's 62. Those in the non-primary group, by contrast, were all in the age range from 47 to 55 when nominated. The only non-Protestant Presidential candidates are both in the group of primary winners.

Among renominated candidates, there is much less of a difference between those aided and unaided by pre-convention contests. In many respects, the renominated candidates are completely opposite to the first-time primary winners. They have extensive experience in politics, consist only of lawyers, face considerable opposition in the convention itself and win the general election no more frequently than renominated candidates not aided by the primaries.

First-time and renominated primary winners do share one basic characteristic. Both groups employ these contests in order to demonstrate some basic strength or to overcome some apparent weakness. The first-time nominees are not in the mold of the traditional Presidential candidate. They lack some of the attributes of "availability," such as governmental experience, maturity, or a Protestant affiliation. To overcome these deficiencies, they use the primaries to demonstrate their political appeal.

Renominated candidates who employ primaries also do so to overcome a presumed weakness in their candidacies. Dewey and Stevenson had already lost a Presidential election. Coolidge and Truman had become Presidents only through death, while Roosevelt in 1940 was violating the two-term tradition. All needed the extra support engendered by primary victories.

Primaries can be seen to have some definite effects on the entire political system. More information on potential candidates has been provided, not only to the party, but to the general electorate. Through pre-convention campaigns, the voters may be better able to see the differences between them, to learn their policy positions, and to observe them in the crisis situations of the primaries. The statements and conduct of a candidate in the heat of a campaign may have some rough relevance to his capacity to withstand the pressures of the Presidency.

Primaries have also led, to judge by the limited data, to a certain expansion of the pool from which candidates can be recruited. Those outside of the legal profession, or with little political experience, can project themselves into consideration. Defeated candidates have not always been cast aside, but have been given an opportunity to lead their parties again. In increasing the pool of talent from which nominees are chosen, primaries have certainly contributed to the strength of the Presidency.

Yet, primaries have also exhibited some weaknesses. While some additional candidates have been considered, others have probably been excluded by the system of primary election. Success in the primaries requires an appealing personality, a national reputation, great financial resources and prodigious effort. Candidates who are more reluctant, more obscure, poorer, or simply older than others, may be denied nominations. The qualities that make great Presidents are unclear, but it is doubtful that they consist largely of personality, reputation, wealth, and physical vigor.

Moreover, primaries have other effects that are not entirely beneficial to the political system. Factional conflicts are increased in these contests, making it more difficult to unify the party and to present a coherent posture to the electorate. The arts of compromise and moderation, essential to a democratic leader, are de-emphasized. Thus, those who are most successful in primary campaigns may not have some of the basic qualifications for success in office.

Primaries, in short, are a mixed blessing. They make convention decisions more informed, more open and more responsive to popular will, but at the same time, they may eliminate some desirable candidates from consideration, while increasing the difficulties of unifying the national party. These considerations become particularly relevant in discussing a national Presidential primary to replace the party conventions. We will return to this subject in Chapter IX.

Candidate Strategies

Convention nominating decisions are now influenced not only by state party leaders, but also by national figures, significant interest groups, and the primary electorate. Seeking to turn these influences to their own benefit, candidates are likely to follow one of four general strategies. These differ in style and in the relative attention devoted to winning the support of different groups influencing the nomination.

A dominant leader, such as an incumbent first-term President or his chosen successor, follows a simple strategy. His task is not to win a contest for the nomination, but to prevent any contest from developing. His goal is conciliation rather than triumph. Often foregoing a formal announcement of candidacy, he will devote the pre-convention period to consulting with all elements of the party. Primaries may be entered to provide evidence of popular approval, but no real opposition is expected. In this effort, the group with the most influence on the nomination is the national political leadership. Interest groups, state organizations, and party voters are consulted, rather than wooed. This was the course followed by Nixon in 1960.

The most arduous strategy is that of the "popular hero," who tries to create a popular groundswell. Emphasizing the support of the general electorate, he is likely to bypass at least some state party leaders. National figures and interest groups may be consulted, but to a lesser extent than by a dominant leader. Certainly the "popular hero" will engage fully in the primaries, seeking to use election victories as evidence of his wide following. He comes to the convention not to negotiate, but to be accepted as the inevitable choice. Hubert Humphrey most closely resembled this type in 1960.

This strategy is most likely to be followed by party mavericks who attract both the favor of the voters and the personal opposition of professional politicians. Such irregulars as William Borah, Harold Stassen, and Estes Kefauver sought to gain the Presidential nomination by arousing popular support against the opposition of the regular organizations. Although each ran well in the primaries, none approached victory in the convention. Popularity is necessary to success, but it is not alone sufficient.

In sharp contrast is the strategy of the "favorite son." His campaign is directed almost exclusively toward state party leaders. While seeking to win friends, he does not solicit firm committments, hoping to win support after the major contenders have been eliminated in a convention deadlock. He will not enter primaries, unless one is held in his own state. As a result of these tactics, the "favorite son" will have little initial strength at the convention, and his designation cannot be expected until a late ballot. Still, in the uncertainty of conventions, anything is possible—if not the Presidential designation, perhaps that for Vice-President. Governor Robert Meyner of New Jersey was the most prominent of the "favorite sons" of 1960.

The most traditional strategy is that of the major candidate who runs as an "organization man." While welcoming the support of national leaders and party voters, he concentrates his campaign on state party leaders and interest groups. Prospective rewards and punishments are employed to win endorsements. At the least, he seeks assurances that party leaders will give him "second-choice" support if their most favored candidate fails.

Unlike the "popular hero," the "organization man" considers primaries to be only an incidental, although useful, means of gaining the support of state delegations.

Accepting a traditional rule, for example, he will not enter the primary in an opponent's home state. He does not wish to alienate either the native son who might give him "second-choice" support, nor other party organizations that might resent such a breach of party protocol. The "popular hero," on the other hand, does not expect much support from the regular organizations and is willing to rely on his presumed mass following. Thus, in 1948, Harold Stassen challenged Robert Taft in the Ohio Republican primary. Thomas Dewey, adhering to established procedure, refrained from the contest.

Franklin Roosevelt, in his campaign for a first nomination, exemplified the techniques of the "organization man." For years before 1932, the New York Governor corresponded and conversed with party and interest group leaders. As the convention neared, James Farley went on a transcontinental "business trip," seeking to reap the good will Roosevelt had long cultivated. The enterprise involved a good deal of maneuvering between rival factions. For example, in Missouri:[33]

> Farley wrote to the State Chairman of Missouri that he was passing through and would like to talk over state organization with him, not mentioning of course anything about Governor Roosevelt. There has been a split in Missouri between the Reed and the organization factions, with Reed controlling a very large minority. The organization faction arranged a public luncheon to which only organization men were asked. . . . [Farley] not only succeeded in seeing that the Reed people were represented but actually got Reed himself to attend the luncheon. . . . As a result both the Reed and the anti-Reed factions have gotten together for the first time in many years, and both sides are tremendously pleased.

[33] Letter from Louis Howe to Colonel Edward House, in Elliot Roosevelt (ed.), *F. D. R., His Personal Letters, 1928-1945* (New York: Duell, Sloan and Pearce, 1960), Vol. I, pp. 211-12.

Roosevelt entered many primaries, but faced only minor opposition in most cases. When real contests developed, the future President was not too successful, losing to Smith in Massachusetts and Garner in California. However, F.D.R.'s campaign was not based on a popular showing. Most of his support had been gathered in the more traditional forums of party conferences and state conventions. In 1960, Lyndon Johnson and Stuart Symington followed similar, if less successful, strategies.

Recently, the "organization" candidate has adopted some of the techniques of the "popular hero," as seen in the changing strategies of individuals as different as Adlai Stevenson and Robert Taft. The nature of future nominating campaigns may have been indicated by John Kennedy's successful effort in 1960. The Senator entered seven primaries and gained considerable strength from an unbroken series of election victories. At the same time, he followed traditional methods, conferring with leaders of Negro and labor interest groups, and seeking the endorsement of state party leaders.

Kennedy combined the two techniques by using his popularity as a means of gaining organization backing. Choosing friends and enemies carefully, he did not deliberately defy the organizations as a real maverick might. His involvement in the primaries is revealing. Kennedy was willing to oppose Senator Hubert Humphrey or to challenge a minor "favorite son" such as Senator Wayne Morse of Oregon. Yet, he would not challenge a "favorite son" who had the united backing of his state party, such as Senator George Smathers of Florida. In other states, he refrained from participation in the primaries after being assured of strong organizational backing. In this way, Kennedy won all of the Ohio delegation and a substantial part of the California vote and was assured, incorrectly, of some support from New Jersey. His record in the primaries also helped solidify his strength within the vital contingents of Illinois, Michigan, New York, and Pennsylvania. Popular support was blended with organizational techniques to form a majority coalition.

Without his primary victories, Kennedy would not have held the vital support of state leaders. "It was only after he had won confidence from the voters that he had turned East again to the big cities and, with the mandate of the primaries, clubbed the big-city bosses into submission. Only then had they become his allies ... on the Convention floor—and, like defeated chieftains, his most solid allies."[34]

The trend in nominating conventions appears clearly unfavorable to candidates following the pure strategy of the "organization man" or the "favorite son." These candidates rely heavily on winning the support of state political leaders, whose power is declining. They devote less effort to winning the support of those groups whose influence in the nominating process is more recent: national political leaders, national interest groups, and the general electorate. The last true "favorite son" to be nominated was John W. Davis in 1924. The pure strategy of the "organization man" has not succeeded since 1932. Since then, these candidates have become involved in extensive, albeit careful, participation in primary campaigns and other efforts to win popular favor. Over the years, the trend has been toward increasing activity.

The pure strategy of the "popular hero" also has only a limited prospect of success. Such candidates limit their appeal as well, seeking support principally from the general electorate, while neglecting the other influential groups. In the past, this strategy has not been successful, with the possible exception of Willkie's 1940 victory.

In the future, success will follow from the use of strategies directed to the newer groups influential in the nominating process as well as the formerly dominant state organizations. Candidates seeking support from all of these groups have greater freedom to maneuver, and their chances

[34] T. White, p. 166. The information on New Jersey is from Governor Meyner.

of success are correspondingly greater. The strategy of the dominant leader, where there is a dominant leader, will certainly persist. Other types of candidates must broaden their appeal. Principally, they must seek to establish voter support by adopting some of the techniques of the "popular hero." Traditional methods are no longer adequate. Candidates must concern themselves with the party caucus and the party primary, the delegation poll and the opinion poll, the deal in the "smoke-filled room" and the television audience in the family living room.

Suggestions for Further Reading

William B. Brown, *The People's Choice: The Presidential Image in the Campaign Biography* (Baton Rouge: Louisiana State University Press, 1960). Describes how Presidential candidates, or their friends, describe themselves.

Fay Calkins, *The CIO and the Democratic Party* (Chicago: University of Chicago Press, 1952). The relationship of one interest group to a major party is explored, with emphasis on local elections, but with implications for national politics.

Paul T. David *et al.*, *Presidential Nominating Politics in 1952* (Baltimore: The Johns Hopkins University Press, 1954), Vols. II-V. State-by-state account of the nominating strategies followed in both parties in an important year.

Harold F. Gossnell, *Boss Platt and his New York Machine* (Chicago: University of Chicago Press, 1924). An incisive biography of one of the great Republican politicians, one of the last to operate in national conventions completely dominated by state party leaders.

Donald B. Johnson, *The Republican Party and Wendell Willkie* (Urbana: University of Illinois Press, 1960). A biography of one of the most remarkable candidates in American history.

Matthew Josephson, *The Politicos, 1865-1896* (New York: Harcourt Brace, 1938). A leftist interpretation of business influence in American politics in the nineteenth century.

Harold Laski, *The American Presidency* (New York: Harper, 1940). A discussion of Presidential power and the impact of increases in that power on American parties and politics.

Charles A. Thomson, *Television and Presidential Politics* (Washington: The Brookings Institution, 1956). The impact of the new mass medium is discussed, with particular reference to the nominations and election of 1952.

David B. Truman, *The Governmental Process* (New York: Knopf,

1951). The leading analysis of the role of interest groups in American government and politics.

Theodore H. White, *The Making of the President 1960* (New York: Atheneum, 1961). An exciting, insightful, and provoking account of the last election, from the earliest stirrings to the weeks after Election Day.

VI CONVENTIONS AND PRESIDENTIAL CANDIDATES

American politics contains elements of drama, sport, and sorcery. All of these characteristics are evident to a high degree in the culmination of the Presidential nominating process, the national party convention. There, the selection of a potential President is the main order of business and the focus of public interest. In making this decision, the convention delegates consider the performance and person of the various aspirants, decide on issues of party policy involved in the nomination and react to the opposing tactics of the candidates.

"Availability" and "Prominence"

"Who is the man fittest to be adopted as candidate?" This question has been asked by convention delegates before and since the time of James Bryce. In general, the answer is the same one he suggested: "Plainly, it is the man most

122

likely to win. . . . What a party wants is not a good President but a good candidate. The party managers have therefore to look out for the person likely to gain most support, and at the same time excite least opposition."[1]

The traditional standard for judging candidates is "availability." An "available" candidate is one inoffensive to all or most of the party, one who has never fought on behalf of any important cause or against any party faction. "Great men" are not nominated, according to Bryce, because they "make more enemies, and give those enemies more assailable points, than obscure men do. . . . The famous man has probably attacked some leaders in his own party, has supplanted others, has expressed his dislike to the crochet of some active section, has perhaps committed errors which are capable of being magnified into offences."[2]

The general standard of availability has been supplemented by a series of particular tests. A candidate who meets all presumably would be most likely to achieve the nomination—and to win the election. Sidney Hyman lists nine of the conventional criteria:

> 1. He must first have had some official connection with the governmental process in an appointive or elective post.
> 2. Nominating conventions show a clear preference for state Governors.
> 3. A candidate is preferred who comes from a state which has a large electoral vote and which does not have a one-party voting record.
> 4. Candidates have been favored who come from the big Northern states to the exclusion of Southerners.
> 5. Conventions will choose only men who are in fact, or who can be made to appear, hospitable to the claims of many economic interests in the nation.

[1] James Lord Bryce, *The American Commonwealth,* 3rd rev. ed. (New York: Macmillan, 1914), Vol. II, p. 187.
[2] *Ibid.,* Vol. I, p. 78.

6. Presidential candidates, like the English Crown, are expected by nominating conventions to present an idealized version of all that is felicitous in home and family life.
7. In defiance of the fact that the majority of Americans live in great urban centers, candidates are preferred who come from small towns.
8. Candidates are preferred who come from English ethnic stock.
9. Nominating conventions have raised an extra-Constitutional religious test by their decisive preference for Protestant hopefuls.[3]

These tests are not inviolable. If all were applied simultaneously, "the result would be such as to make it virtually impossible for anyone to receive a Presidential nomination. . . . The saving factor in all this is that the rules are never strictly applied all at once every time. In the context of a specific election, they will be rearranged in emphasis—some may even be ignored."[4]

Each of the rules has been violated, both in recent and more distant years. Dwight Eisenhower had no political experience and claimed Texas—a Southern state—as his birthplace, and Kansas—a small, one-party state—as his home. Alfred Smith was Irish, Catholic, and from the largest city in the nation. Grover Cleveland was a bachelor and the reputed father of an illegitimate child.

Despite exceptions, however, "availability" did have real meaning in the past. Given the requisite personal qualities, the ideal and most common candidate was the governor of a state such as New York or Ohio. In 1932, for example, the traditional rules indicated the nomination of Franklin Roosevelt. F. D. R. passed every one of the nine specific tests but, to H. L. Mencken, his designation was an illustration of the absurdity of the standard of "availability":

[3] Sidney Hyman, "Nine Tests for the Presidential Hopeful." *The New York Times Magazine* (January 4, 1959), p. 11.
[4] *Ibid.,* p. 50.

Here was a great party convention, after almost a week of cruel labor, nominating the weakest candidate before it. . . . There was absolutely nothing in his record to make them eager for him. He was not only a man of relatively small experience and achievement in national affairs; he was also one whose competence was plainly in doubt, and whose good faith was far from clear. His only really valuable asset was his name, and even that was associated with the triumphs and glories of the common enemy. . . . Yet here they were giving it to him, and among the parties to the business were a dozen who were patently his superior and of very much larger experience.[5]

To judge by the record of recent years, the tests of "availability" are increasingly invalid. The 1960 election winner, John Kennedy, violated at least five of the specific rules and some of the general criteria as well. The Democratic candidate was neither a Governor, nor from a critical state. In terms of personal background, Kennedy was extremely young, Irish, Catholic, and from the Boston metropolitan area. Having served 14 years in Congress he had voted on hundreds of legislative measures. In so doing, he had aroused opposition among farm groups, some labor unions, conservative and business interests, civil libertarians, Negroes, and Southern segregationists.[6]

Richard Nixon met the traditional tests better than Kennedy. Like him, however, he was young and had no record in state administration. Even more than Kennedy, the Vice-President had aroused considerable opposition. Many were provoked by his voting record in Congress, his zealous partisanship and anti-communism, his finances, and even his personality.

[5] H. L. Mencken, *Making a President* (New York: Knopf, 1932), p. 165.
[6] See James M. Burns, *John Kennedy: A Political Profile* (New York: Harcourt, Brace, 1959), chaps. V-VIII, XI.

Another indication of the lessened importance of "availability" is the renomination of defeated candidates. A renominated candidate cannot meet the tests. He is conspicuous, rather than obscure. He cannot claim to be a likely winner, for he has already been tested in a national election and found wanting. Moreover, he no longer enjoys the ability to avoid a position on public issues. Beginning with his first campaign, he must take a relatively clear stand. In doing so, he inevitably loses some support. Despite these limitations, Thomas Dewey won a second Republican nomination in 1948 and Adlai Stevenson was redesignated by the Democrats in 1956.

We can measure the importance of "availability" more precisely by rating both the convention nominees and their leading opponents on the nine tests suggested by Hyman. If the nominee wins because of "availability," he should score higher than his leading convention opponent. If the nominee scores lower, then "availability" is not controlling. While the exact figures cannot be taken too literally, they do provide an indication of significant trends. Past experience is summarized in the table below. Uncontested nominations or the renomination of incumbents are not included.[7]

In the whole course of American political history,

---

[7] Generally, a candidate was given one "point" for each of the nine tests which he met, although the fifth test, that the candidate be non-controversial, was given special weight. This is the most general and most important of the tests of "availability." The final determinations are necessarily somewhat subjective, but in general agreement with accepted evaluations of the successful and unsuccessful aspirants. In the case of two Vice-Presidents, Coolidge and Truman, who succeeded to the Presidency through death and were later renominated, their "availability" was judged in comparison with their opponents for the first, Vice-Presidential nomination. Theodore Roosevelt was not contested for either his Vice-Presidential or Presidential nomination, and therefore is not included. All other "accidental" Presidents failed to be renominated. Defeated candidates nominated a second time are automatically considered less "available." The biographical information was obtained from the *Dictionary of American Biography* and from Richard C. Bain, *Convention Decisions and Voting Records* (Washington: The Brookings Institution, 1960).

TABLE 6–1

"AVAILABILITY" AND PRESIDENTIAL NOMINEES

Period	More "Available" Candidate Wins	Less "Available" Candidate Wins	Total
	(number of nominations)		
1840-1892	16	5	21
1896-1924	8	3	11
1928-1960	4	6	10
Totals:	28	14	42

"availability" generally has led to success in nominating conventions. This was particularly true in the nineteenth century. Before the beginning of the modern political era in 1896, only Fremont in 1856, Douglas in 1860, Greeley in 1872, Blaine in 1884, and Cleveland in 1892 were able to win nominations despite their lack of "availability." Although previously defeated for the Presidency, Cleveland met the traditional criteria best. Significantly, he was the only nominee in this group to go on to win the general election.

Recently, "availability" has been less necessary. Since 1928, in fact, the historical rules have actually been reversed, as less conformist aspirants have won convention endorsements more often than those meeting the old tests better. Included are Smith in 1928, Willkie in 1940, Dewey in 1948, Eisenhower in 1952, Stevenson in 1956, and Kennedy in 1960.[8] It is interesting to note that a less "available" candidate has been named by the party out of power in five of the last six Presidential contests.

[8] It could be argued that Eisenhower in 1952 was actually more "available" than Taft, his chief opponent, since Taft was a highly controversial figure while Eisenhower was a national hero whose policies were unknown or ambiguous, in the best historical tradition. However, this argument considers only one of the nine criteria. Eisenhower failed on others. He had no direct governmental experience; he was not a state political leader; and he did not come from a large two-party state. Moreover, within the Republican party, he was a controversial figure, since he was the candidate of one of two large antagonistic factions. Eisenhower can only be considered "available" if the criteria are changed sufficiently to constitute entirely different standards.

A similar trend can be seen in the results of the general election, although the evidence is less substantial in this case. We can compare the "availability" rating of the winner and loser in Presidential elections not involving incumbent Chief Executives, as in the table below. Less "available" candidates are more likely to win now than in the past, but there are too few cases, particularly in the twentieth century, in which neither major candidate was the incumbent President. This in itself, however, may provide some inferential evidence of the decline of "availability." Incumbent Presidents cannot enjoy the comfortable anonymity of the traditional candidate. The success of incumbent Presidents in winning renomination and re-election may therefore indicate the reduced potency of traditional standards.

TABLE 6–2

"Availability" and Presidental Elections

	Incumbent Not a Candidate		Incumbent a Candidate		
	More "Available" Candidate Wins	Less "Available" Candidate Wins	Incumbent Wins	Incumbent Loses	Total
Period	(number of elections)		(number of elections)		
1832-1892[a]	8	1	3	3	15
1896-1924	2	1	4	1	8
1928-1960	1	2	5	1	9
Totals:	11	4	12	5	32

1836 is not included, since there was no Whig convention that year.

In the nineteenth century, the only victory of a less available candidate, in a race not involving an incumbent, was that of Zachary Taylor in 1848. Even this case is doubtful. While Taylor did not have the Northern background or governmental experience of his opponent, Lewis Cass, he did have the appeal of a military hero unsullied by factional conflict. By strict accounting, he was less "available" than Cass; in fact, there was little advantage, if any, for the Democrat in this election.

In modern times, three candidates have been elected

over more conforming candidates—Harding in 1920, Eisenhower in 1952, and Kennedy in 1960. Although Harding is a historic symbol of "availability," he actually met these criteria less well than his opponent, James Cox. Harding was a senator, faced the opposition of Republican progressives, and had to meet scurrilous attacks on his morality and parentage. Except for the fact that he was divorced, Cox met all tests.

In place of "availability," Presidential hopefuls are increasingly measured by new criteria, which might be termed those of "prominence." A prominent individual, in these terms, is one who has caught the attention of voters and political leaders by his traits of personality, his performance in some task of public significance, or his identification with important issues and interests. He is a more conspicuous leader, if not necessarily the "great man" favored by Bryce, and less like the colorless, even anonymous, candidates traditionally favored by party conventions. Modifications throughout American politics are forcing this change.

To understand these innovations, we must return to Bryce's argument. He saw two important reasons why the United States elected relatively obscure and undistinguished men to the White House. First, said Bryce,

> a President need not be a man of brilliant intellectual gifts. His main duties are to be prompt and firm in securing the due execution of the laws and maintaining the public peace. . . . Four-fifths of his work is the same in kind as that which devolves on the chairman of a commercial company or the manager of a railway, the work of choosing good subordinates, seeing that they attend to their business, and taking a sound practical view of such administrative questions as require his decision.[9]

Obviously, the role of the President has changed greatly. His administrative job, of primary importance in Bryce's time, is now subordinate to other tasks—the conduct

[9] Bryce, Vol. I, p. 80.

of foreign relations, leadership of national opinion, and management of a complex industrial economy. The traditional criteria do not indicate whether an individual can handle this type of Presidency. Both party leaders and voters must consider new qualities in potential candidates to meet the new challenges of office.

The second reason for the past importance of "availability," according to Bryce, was that "party loyalty and party organization have been hitherto so perfect that any one put forward by the party will get the full party vote if his character is good and his 'record,' as they call it, unstained."[10] Today, party loyalty does not control the Presidential vote. Rather, the Presidency has become a somewhat nonpartisan office, for which a decisive minority of the electorate votes on the basis of the individual character of the candidates.

The separation of the Chief Executive from common party loyalties is indicated by the difference in Congressional and Presidential election results in the last three national elections. In each, the national Congressional Democratic party received five to ten per cent more of the national vote than the Presidential candidate. The vote for Congress was a party vote, by and large; the Presidential vote was influenced to a much greater extent by considerations of personality.

"Availability" applied most completely when the conventions were controlled by state party organizations. They held to the traditional standards for a number of reasons. Such a candidate was most likely to reconcile all elements within the party, and thereby to distribute the rewards of victory most widely. Convention delegates shunned those identified with particular policy positions because they themselves were relatively uninterested in policy questions and did not want to alienate those on either side of an issue. Lacking precise information as to popular preferences, state

[10] *Ibid.*, pp. 77-78.

parties tended to seek the "safe" candidate, again, so as to avoid alienating any group.

As we have seen, however, the state parties no longer control the conventions exclusively. New groups, emphasizing considerations other than the candidate's marital life or administrative record, have entered the nominating process. National party leaders and interest groups are concerned with policy questions and press within the party for the nomination of candidates supporting their views. Considerable information is now gathered on the popular strength of different candidates. The inexact tests of "availability" are replaced by the precise, if sometimes misleading, measurements of an opinion poll or a presidential primary.

The same effect has resulted from increased pre-convention campaigning. It is now possible for a candidate to gather considerable support before the opening of the convention. He may be "unavailable" by the usual standards, but he may still make himself an insistent claimant upon the nomination. Presidential primaries, public opinion polls, and the media of mass communication are available even to the "unavailable." Through their use, a candidate today can force himself on the attention of the convention. In the past, he might have been summarily dismissed.

The rules of "availability" also are no longer politically appropriate. Parties followed these rules in order to increase their vote. Today, their electoral potency has been sharply curtailed. The traditional preference for state governors is illustrative of the change. Governors were able to win Presidential nominations for a number of reasons. They usually controlled their own state delegations to the convention and therefore had firm initial support. The tasks of state executives were relatively easy, allowing them time to campaign, while isolating them from divisive national issues. Governors also benefitted from the apparent analogy between the administrative duties of a state executive and those of a President.

None of these factors is fully operative today. Control of the delegation may be taken from a governor in some states through a presidential primary election. In contrast to past times, a governor's job today is extremely difficult and politically precarious. State governments are now beset by increasing demands for services from a booming population, while residents become proportionately resistant to tax increases to pay for such services. In 1960, the political consequence was that 12 of 27 governors were defeated for re-election. In contrast, only two of 34 Senate seats changed party hands.[11]

While the Governor's job becomes more difficult, much of his experience increasingly seems irrelevant to the Presidency. He has no contact with the problems of foreign policy and national defense, now the chief responsibility of the President. Senators, on the other hand, are relatively familiar with the problems of foreign and defense policy. This familiarity, combined with the greater political security of the upper chamber, is likely to lead to more Presidential candidacies by Senators. The experience of 1960 certainly points in this direction.[12]

Governors, particularly those in the largest states, will also be affected by the widespread growth of two-party competition. When sectional loyalties dominated national politics, only a small number of states were competitive, and nominations tended to be monopolized by political figures in those states, such as the Governors. Today, Presidential victories must be won by a national triumph, not only by success in a few contested areas. Conventions will therefore turn to leaders known and popular in a national constituency, not only in their own bailiwicks. Governors will not often meet these tests, and certainly not only Governors from a few states. As party competition spreads, candidates will

[11] Theodore H. White, *The Making of the President 1960* (New York: Atheneum, 1961), p. 214. In 1962, 10 of 26 incumbent Governors were defeated, in contrast to only 5 of 34 Senators.
[12] This argument is developed further by Louis Harris, "Why the Odds are Against a Governor's Becoming President," *Public Opinion Quarterly*, Vol. 23 (Fall, 1959), pp. 361-70.

be chosen from all areas. Similarly, as the two-party system is extended below the Mason-Dixon line, Southerners will again be considered for the Presidency.

Other rules of "availability" also seem unlikely to endure. With Catholics constituting 20 to 60 per cent of the population in states having 261 electoral votes,[13] the monopoly of Protestant candidates will continue to be broken. Nominations will not be made exclusively of those of English ethnic stock while more than a majority of the voters derive from other origins, nor will small-town residents be able to maintain a prescriptive right to the Presidency while three-quarters of the population lives in cities and suburbs. As the capacity to deal with the ultimate questions of peace and war become the principal test of Presidential ability, less consideration will be given to the state of origin, the domestic economic policy, the political experience, and even the family life of the aspirants.

Even with changed conditions, some of the specific tests of "availability" will still be applied. Candidates who are Catholic, or lack a happy family life, or have no previous experience in government, will find it more difficult than others to win Presidential nominations. As demonstrated by recent experience, however, they will not find it impossible.

In summary, the rules of "availability" are less binding because they are increasingly irrelevant. Their decline is related to the augmented power of the Presidency, the growth of new nominating strategies, and changes in national electoral politics. Future Presidential aspirants must pass the new test of "prominence."

Candidates and Issues

Convention nominations also involve policy considerations. In selecting a candidate, party delegates are also endorsing the policies which he favors. If the party is suc-

---

[13] This figure was presented by John Bailey, now Democratic National Chairman, in his effort to win the Vice-Presidential nomination for Kennedy in 1956. The details are present in White, p. 241.

cessful in the election, the candidate's program is likely to become public policy. Even if unsuccessful, the party will remain identified with these policies for at least four years. The choice of policy implicit in the choice of a candidate therefore is of great importance. These policy decisions may well be more significant than those embodied in the party platform. Words may be ambiguous compromises or forgotten promises. Individuals are less tractable.

Policy considerations enter Presidential nominations in two ways. First, nominees are likely to represent a moderately liberal position on the important issues. Secondly, the parties seek to reach a consensus on vital policy questions, and therefore to name candidates who most fully embody this consensus. These policy implications can be elaborated by examining the Democratic hopefuls of 1960.

All of the four major declared candidates were senators and their voting records are available for comparison. In the following table, the number of roll call agreements among these senators are listed and compared for the sessions of 1957 and 1960. All roll calls during these sessions are included on which more than any three Democrats voted on each side of the issue at hand, and on which all of the four Presidential hopefuls were recorded. The issues involved are also divided into three policy categories: domestic, foreign and civil rights.[14]

On the basis of these figures, a number of conclusions

[14] The data for the roll calls is from *Congressional Quarterly Almanac,* Vol. 13 (1957), pp. 283-315 and Vol. 17 (1960), pp. 472-518. All expressions of a policy position are counted, including pairs, answers to the Congressional Quarterly poll, etc. Included as civil rights votes are proposals in 1957 to increase appropriations for education in the District of Columbia and the 23rd Constitutional amendment, to allow District residents, mostly Negroes, to vote in Presidential elections. The general voting pattern seems to bear out this classification. Not counted are four roll calls in 1957 and 13 in 1960 on which at least one of the four Senators was absent and not recorded. The method employed here is similar to that of David Truman, *The Congressional Party* (New York: Wiley, 1960), pp. 45-48, and C. Herman Pritchett, *Civil Liberties and the Vinson Court* (Chicago: University of Chicago Press, 1954), pp. 177-85.

can be reached. It is apparent that the four Presidential candidates shared a wide measure of agreement. This was particularly true on questions of foreign policy, where the Senators were agreed on the overwhelming majority of roll calls in 1957 and on all in 1960. On other issues, Johnson stood out clearly from his three competitors, disagreeing fairly often with them on both domestic and civil rights questions. There was a similar tendency, although far less apparent, for Humphrey to be somewhat isolated from the group of active Presidential candidates. When the Minnesota Senator dissented, it was in a "liberal" direction—in favor of expanded government housing and farm programs, or against corporation tax relief or restrictions on labor unions. Symington almost never dissented alone. Kennedy's disagreements were generally minor or in favor of economy in some government programs.

TABLE 6–3

POLICY AGREEMENTS AMONG DEMOCRATIC CANDIDATES OF 1960

	All Issues		Domestic		Foreign		Civil Rights	
	'57	'60	'57	'60	'57	'60	'57	'60
Total Roll Calls	57	134	24	74	19	26	14	34
Agreements Between:								
Humphrey-Johnson	38	103	14	55	19	26	5	22
Johnson-Kennedy	40	109	14	61	18	26	8	22
Johnson-Symington	41	112	19	64	17	26	5	22
Kennedy-Symington	46	129	19	69	16	26	11	34
Humphrey-Kennedy	47	123	18	63	18	26	11	34
Humphrey-Symington	50	125	19	65	17	26	14	34
All but Symington	2	0	0	0	2	0	0	0
All but Kennedy	4	2	3	2	1	0	0	0
All but Humphrey	3	5	3	5	0	0	0	0
All but Johnson	11	19	5	7	0	0	6	12
All Four Senators	32	101	11	53	16	26	5	22

The pattern presented by these figures is that of a policy continuum, in which Johnson stands at one end, which in conventional terms is a more conservative position; Humphrey is at the other or liberal pole, while Kennedy and Symington have positions somewhere between, but closer to Humphrey. This describes the position of these four

Senators alone. When we consider all Democrats in the upper body of Congress, the picture is somewhat different. Johnson then represents the center of the senatorial party, while the others are in the liberal group, and Humphrey is the most liberal of these three.

This general arrangement of the four Senators is evidenced by the following table. It shows the number of times each of the four Senators voted with the majority of his party on roll calls in which the party was divided and on which all of the four Presidential candidates were recorded. In both 1957 and 1960, Johnson was most fully in agreement with his party colleagues, while Humphrey was most often in the minority. Further evidence is provided by the "bipartisan opposition score." This measures the percentage of roll calls in which a Senator opposes a majority of both parties. Johnson, occupying a central position, was almost never in the position of going counter to a bipartisan majority. Humphrey, holding to a more extreme position, most frequently took a minority stand. Although the differentials are small, the qualitative differences revealed are reliable. They would be even larger if not for absences.[15]

---

[15] The bipartisanship score is calculated by Congressional Quarterly. However, absences are simply disregarded in this figure. The result is that a Senator absent frequently will have a low bipartisan opposition score, even if he frequently dissents when he is present and voting. Similarly, his bipartisan support score, the reciprocal figure, will also be low if he is frequently absent. This particularly affects Kennedy's score. In both years he was absent far more frequently than any of his Presidential competitors. I have tried to correct the resulting distortion of the Congressional Quarterly figures somewhat by recalculating the percentages on the base of 100. Thus, Kennedy in 1960 has a support score of 22 and an opposition score of 5. On the other 73% of bipartisan roll calls, he was absent. Recalculated, his percentage scores became 82 for bipartisan support and 18 for bipartisan opposition, the figures listed. These figures are still somewhat misleading, however, especially in Kennedy's case. Most of the votes he missed were unanimous or overwhelming votes in which he undoubtedly would have joined the majority if he were present. This would have raised his bipartisan support score and lowered his bipartisan opposition score.

TABLE 6–4

PARTY AND BIPARTISAN VOTES OF DEMOCRATIC CANDIDATES OF 1960

	Johnson	*Symington*	*Kennedy*	*Humphrey*
1957 Votes with Party Majority (57 roll calls)	50	44	41	37
1960 Votes with Party Majority (134 roll calls)	118	108	106	99
Opposed Bipartisan Majority, 1957 (%)	0	7	12	15
Opposed Bipartisan Majority, 1960 (%)	2	17	18	19

There are two notable differences between the voting pattern of the four Senators in 1957 and in 1960. There is much more agreement in the latter year, for one thing. Disagreement on questions of foreign policy was completely ended, and the degree of concurrence on both domestic and civil rights issues increased substantially. Secondly, this agreement is the result of an increased consensus on more liberal policies, favoring greater government intervention and expanded social welfare policies. This is evident in specific votes and also in the Senators' increased "bipartisan opposition" scores. Between 1957 and 1960, each found himself opposed more often to the majority of both parties. As they moved toward a liberal position, they came to be increasingly out of line with the prevailing moderation of the entire Senate.

The experience of 1960 is indicative of the general influence of policy considerations in Presidential nominations. Through pre-convention campaigning, the policy positions assumed by the candidates, and the decisions of the convention, the party reaches a consensus on policy questions. Eventually, the party will probably choose a moderately liberal candidate.

In the pre-convention period, the candidates' positions on issues will be taken into consideration by the party organizations and by the general electorate, the latter particularly in states holding primary contests. Much of the primary campaign period is devoted to the development and reconciliation of the policy differences between aspirants. If issues are not developed in this way, they will still be taken into account by those interest groups and national political leaders able to influence the party convention.

As candidates campaign, they come into closer agreement with one another, as they evaluate the political appeal of different positions, and attempt to capture some of this appeal for their own benefit. The process of policy agreement was evident in both parties in 1960. We have noticed the increased agreement among the four Democratic Senators from 1957 to 1960. By the time the convention opened, there was general agreement on programs "to invest more in education and in roads and dams . . . to insure the fact that our economy grew at least four per cent . . . to give the American people all the brutal truth about our position in the world . . . an outstanding space program . . . conservation bills . . . area redevelopment bills, housing bills, social security measures. . . ."[16] These themes, actually voiced by Johnson and Symington, constituted the major elements of Kennedy's own nominating and election campaigns.

While all Democrats came to endorse similar programs, Kennedy obviously benefitted most from this consensus. The Massachusetts Senator began with the advantage of representing a moderate stand on disruptive issues. On civil rights, for example, Kennedy had taken stands favorable to both Northern and Southern views. Although he generally voted with the liberals, he voted more conservatively with Johnson in 1957 on two important procedural questions and on the vital amendment to the civil rights bill which guaranteed jury trials in most cases involving Negro voting rights.

Beginning as a moderate, Kennedy then captured part of his rivals' strength by appropriating for himself policies

[16] National Broadcasting Company, *Meet the Press* (Washington: Merkle Press, July 10, 1960), pp. 26-33, *passim*.

with which they had become identified and which contributed to their political appeal. In 1960, for example, he always voted with Humphrey and Symington for a strong civil rights position. He moved toward the liberal stance of Humphrey on questions of farm policy and depressed areas legislation. He associated himself with the strong criticisms of Republican foreign policy voiced by Adlai Stevenson, while endorsing the programs of Johnson and Symington for increased defense spending. By the time of the convention, Kennedy's candidacy represented not only a drive for power, but also an individual embodiment of the policy preferences of the Democratic majority.[17]

In the Republican party, while there was little contest for the nomination, the same drive toward policy agreement was evident. A basic reason for Nixon's supremacy in the party was his moderate position between the ultra-conservative faction represented by Senator Barry Goldwater and the more liberal group of Governor Nelson Rockefeller. The Vice-President alone could gain support from these two intra-party groups. In the pre-convention period, he acted to gain more agreement on policy questions, in particular by soliciting Rockefeller's support.

Nixon's position on many public issues was ambiguous, and he had generally refused to take a position on vital questions until after the convention. In order to obtain the crucial backing of Rockefeller, however, Nixon changed his stand and reached a detailed policy accord with the Governor. This agreement committed the Republican candidate to policies of promoting international confederations, stimulation of economic growth, "aggressive action" in civil rights,

[17] One can observe the same process, in an opposite direction, now occurring in the Republican party, as Nelson Rockefeller attempts to represent himself as the embodiment of his party's policies. Originally identified as an extreme liberal, he has moved to more conservative positions on such questions as government spending, medical care for the aged, the division of state and federal responsibilities and defense policy. His chances for the 1964 G.O.P. nomination have been proportionately increased.

contributory medical insurance for the aged, and federal aid to education.[18] Upon the insistence of the Vice-President, many of these points were later included in the Republican platform.

As the nominations of Kennedy and Nixon indicate, conventions favor nominees who, among the possible candidates, represent a moderate position on the important questions of the time. They tend to reject candidates who have taken extreme stands. The preferences for moderates is due simply to the party's desire to win the election. By the choice of a man of the center, the party is best able to maintain its own unity and also to appeal to the largest possible proportion of the general electorate. However, the consensus on policy may not include the entire party or electorate, but only those elements considered significant for victory in the Presidential election.

If the preference for moderates were carried to a logical extreme, one might expect both parties to nominate candidates who stand precisely at dead center on important issues. This outcome is prevented by two factors. First, the two major parties are not identical. There are some real and persistent policy differences between them. Each party seeks the moderate candidate among those seeking its nomination. Since the parties are somewhat distinct, a moderate in the Democratic party will be different from a moderate in the Republican party. In 1960, for example, both Kennedy and Nixon were among the more moderate aspirants in their parties, but there still remained important differences between them.

Second, parties tend to prefer candidates who, while moderate, lean toward the liberal factions and policy positions in their party. This preference is also due to the basic desire of the parties for victory in the Presidential elections. In national contests, the decisive power is held by urban residents and minority groups residing in industrial states.

18 The full text of the agreement is printed in White, pp. 388-90 and *The New York Times*, July 24, 1960.

To gain the votes of these groups and the electoral votes of their states, a liberal candidate advocating liberal policies must be chosen. More than the residents of other states, the majority in the urban and industrial areas favors federal welfare policies, civil rights, government action to stimulate the economy, and the like.

The importance of an appeal to the industrial and relatively liberal states was recognized by all of the candidates in 1960. The four Democratic candidates in the Senate were significantly more liberal in their voting records of 1960 than in 1957. Kennedy actively sought the endorsement of Negroes, labor, and critics of contemporary American foreign policy, for example, but adopted no new policy positions which would please the Southern conservatives of his party. To win the nomination and election, it was far more important for Kennedy to gain the support of the industrial states than to conciliate the South.

Similarly, Nixon went to considerable lengths to gain the support of Rockefeller and the liberals, but he made no concessions to Goldwater and other conservatives. Nixon could afford to disregard Goldwater, for the voters who shared his views were probably less numerous and certainly less strategically situated than those who tended to agree with Rockefeller. In both parties, the nomination went to moderate liberals who assumed even more liberal positions as the campaign developed.

Thus, Presidential candidates must be both "moderates" and "liberals." This apparent contradiction can be resolved by recognizing that each party is actually made up of two coordinate wings: a Presidential party and a Congressional party. The former is the party which campaigns every four years to win the White House. It is largely controlled by the organizations in two-party and industrial states with large blocs of electoral votes. The policies it advocates are liberal, designed to appeal primarily to the voters in these states.

The Congressional party is different. Comprising the

party's national legislative representatives, it is largely dominated by members from the more agricultural and one-party states and districts. Its policies will be more conservative as a result, and designed to appeal to the electorate in these latter areas. Therefore, a given individual may be considered a "liberal" in the Congressional party, but a "moderate" in the Presidential party.

The diagram below indicates the difference. In the Congress, the more conservative elements constitute a substantial segment of the party. Johnson was in the center of the Democratic Congressional group, between Southern conservatives such as Harry Byrd and liberal representatives from the industrial states such as Humphrey.[19] As evidenced by his voting record, Kennedy was clearly associated with the liberal group. In Presidential elections, however, the focus of the party is different. Here, liberals constitute a larger and more important group. From this focus Johnson was closer to the conservative position, and therefore a poor candidate in an election in which the support of liberal groups in the industrial states was decisive. Kennedy and Symington occupied a more central position, while Humphrey remained on the left. On policy grounds, therefore, the convention could best succeed in unifying the party and creating the widest appeal to the voters by nominating either Kennedy or Symington. That they chose the former was due not to policy reasons, but to other considerations, such as Kennedy's pre-convention campaign and his personal appeal.

In summary, policy considerations are closely involved in the choice of a Presidential candidate. In their competition for the party designation, individual aspirants tend to define or reconcile their differences of policy. The actual nomination is likely to be conferred on that individual whose policies will appeal to the largest number of those voters decisive in Presidential elections. The choice will therefore

[19] David B. Truman, *The Congressional Party* (New York: Wiley, 1960), p. 53, provides fuller evidence.

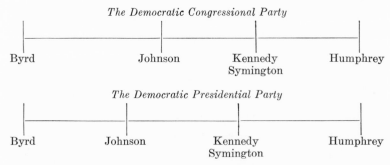

most likely be of one who is a liberal in terms of the Congressional party, and a moderate in terms of the Presidential party.

Convention Tactics

Consideration of individual "availability" or "prominence," as well as of policy issues, occurs in all conventions. At any particular party congress, a third consideration influencing the final choice may be the tactics employed by the various aspirants. To a great extent, techniques will vary with the peculiar circumstances of each convention. There are, however, at least three important tactics which recur frequently. These might be termed "the band wagon," "the test of strength," and "the deal."

There are two general conditions of convention behavior which condition the use and effectiveness of these tactics. First, delegates "behave in a way that will maximize their political power; that is they are politicians. . . . Delegates will trade their votes for access to the candidate they think most likely to win nomination."[20] The various tactics employed are means of convincing delegates that they can best improve their own political fortunes by supporting a particular candidate. Secondly, convention delegates have incomplete information about the strength of the different aspirants and the eventual outcome of the election cam-

[20] Nelson Polsby, "Decision-Making at the National Conventions, *Western Political Quarterly,* Vol. 13 (September, 1960), pp. 609, 615.

144/Nominating the President

paign. Their uncertainty makes it possible for various tactics to succeed. If the delegates had complete information, they would make their decision uninfluenced by the maneuverings of candidates.[21]

In general theoretical terms, "the band wagon" and "the deal" may be thought of as the means by which delegates seek to maximize their political influence, while "the test of strength" is a means of providing fuller information. Candidates and their managers seek to manipulate these tactics for their own advantage.

At the particular moment deemed most advantageous, a candidate will attempt to stimulate a band wagon in his favor, while his opponents work to establish or maintain roadblocks. Delegations wish to be on band wagons because support of the nominee at the convention will be a basic criterion for the later distribution of Presidential favors and patronage. The possibility of a band wagon is increased by the circumstances of the conventions. Dozens of delegations and thousands of individuals are crowded together, subject to a multitude of emotional and confusing pressures. The amount of reliable information available to any particular state or delegate is limited, rumors spread easily, and individuals are likely to act precipitously rather than deliberately.

Given these conditions, it is not surprising that band wagons occur. What is surprising is that few reach their destination unless they are impelled by the objective realities of power within the party. Few conventions have really run wildly out of control. Possibly the only true examples of such abandon have been the nomination of some Vice-Presidential candidates such as Calvin Coolidge in 1920 or Estes Kefauver in 1956.

The Presidential nomination has always had some rational basis. Conventions in which a band wagon has sud-

[21] See Anthony Downs, *An Economic Theory of Democracy* (New York: Harper, 1957), on the general effects of uncertainty and lack of information on politics.

denly materialized and swept through to victory include the Republican meeting or 1880 and the Democratic convention of 1896. In both cases, the Presidential nomination was more than an emotional decision. In 1896, Bryan aroused the convention by his "Cross of Gold" speech, but this alone was not responsible for his nomination. It was clear from the beginning that a pro-silver candidate would be named and equally clear that all of the proposed nominees were unacceptable. Bryan was available, but it took five ballots before the convention accepted him. In 1880, the Republicans were deadlocked for 34 ballots between Ulysses Grant, John Sherman, and James Blaine. The convention was clearly controlled by the combined Sherman and Blaine forces. They finally united on the 36th ballot, nominating James Garfield, Sherman's floor manager.

For a band wagon to succeed, it must move quickly, before delegates have the opportunity to assess different candidates or the opposition has adopted an effective counter-strategy. A candidate must seek a continuous and substantial increase in his vote on each succeeding ballot. Aspirants occasionally have lost strength, only to recoup their losses and go on to win the nomination. More often, once defections begin, disaster is near.

The necessary condition of the band wagon is speed. As Lyndon Johnson described it, the band wagon resembles a "great propoganda effort . . . to stampede folks and to take their integrity away from them and to say that they can't independently exercise their judgment." It may include "various accounts and convention bulletins and newspapers being put out about 'Get on the band wagon now or you'll miss it' . . . and talks about the crash throughs that have been made."[22]

Those opposing a band wagon require delay in order to hold their own ranks and to form an alliance against the leading candidate. In the 1952 Republican convention, typical of many in this regard, Senator Robert Taft claimed "a

[22] *Meet the Press*, pp. 34-35.

tentative agreement on the part of the Warren and Stassen forces to recess the Convention after the first ballot."[23] The respite would have been employed in a final attempt to halt the Eisenhower candidacy.

The techniques used in stopping a band wagon are well established. A typical case was the blocking of William Seward's drive in the 1860 Republican convention. On the evening before the balloting for President, Horace Greeley had telegraphed the *New York Tribune* that "the opposition to Gov. Seward cannot concentrate on any candidate and that he will be nominated."

> But there was much done after midnight and before the convention assembled on Friday morning. There were hundreds of Pennsylvanians, Indianans and Illinoisians who never closed their eyes that night. . . . Henry S. Lane . . . had been toiling with desperation to bring Indiana to go as a unit for Lincoln. And then in connection with others, he had been operating to bring the Vermonters and Virginians to the point of deserting Seward. . . . This was finally done, the fatal break in Seward's strength . . . destroying at once, when it appeared, his power in the New England and the slave state delegations. . . . The Cameron [Pennsylvania] men, discovering there was absolutely no hope for their man, but that either Seward or Lincoln would be nominated, and being a calculating company, were persuaded to throw their strength for Lincoln at such a time as to have credit of his nomination if it were made.[24]

Having halted Seward, the Lincoln group successfully mounted its own band wagon.

A second recurring convention tactic is the test of

[23] Paul T. David *et al.*, *The Politics of National Party Conventions* (Washington: The Brookings Institution, 1960), p. 559. This is from the Taft memorandum also reprinted in *The New York Times*, November 25, 1959.

[24] Murat Halstead, *Three Against Lincoln*, ed. by William Hesseltine (Baton Rouge: Louisiana State University Press, 1960), pp. 161-63.

strength. This comes on a roll call vote on some question other than the nomination. Since these issues usually involve only two alternatives—usually a "yes" or "no" vote on a particular motion—they offer a clear measure of the power of contending coalitions. On the nominating ballots, the issues may be more clouded, since there are usuallly more than two candidates. Thus the test of strength is an excellent means by which a faction can demonstrate latent, but as yet undeclared, support.

The test of strength may be to the benefit of a particular candidate or it may simply demonstrate the power of a majority coalition which has not yet found a standard-bearer. In the 1952 Republican convention, the test vote was designed to reveal latent support for Eisenhower. It came on the issue of the rules for settlement of credentials contests. The Eisenhower forces proposed that no contested delegate be allowed to vote in the convention until his contest was resolved. The Taft group accepted this rule, but proposed an exception in the case of the Louisiana delegation. The test was won by the Eisenhower faction by over 100 votes. Their support from the Minnesota and California delegations was particularly significant, for it indicated that the first ballot strength of two minor candidates—Harold Stassen and Earl Warren—would be more disposed to shift to Eisenhower than to Taft in later tallies.

In the 1880 Republican convention described above, a test vote indicated the existence of a majority coalition, but no specific candidate's prospects were advanced. In that year, the "Half Breed" faction of Blaine and Sherman proved itself to be dominant on a minor procedural motion dealing with the unit rule in state delegations. In the end, this coalition combined to support Garfield.[25]

The test vote can come on any motion before the convention. One of the most frequent issues to arouse factional controversy is the settlement of credentials contests. On such

[25] See Richard C. Bain, *Convention Decisions and Voting Records* (Washington: The Brookings Institution, 1960), pp. 110-11, 116.

votes, as in 1952, a victorious group wins a double triumph: it not only demonstrates its majority strength, but it also gains delegates for the nominating contest from the accepted delegation. Credentials contests have been more frequent in the Republican party, largely because of the fragmentary nature of the G.O.P. in the South. Without a functioning organization in these states, it has been difficult to clearly identify the leaders of Southern Republicans.

Test votes on the platform can also be found, as in the 1948 Democratic convention. The result of the platform vote was to demonstrate the dominance of the liberal wing of the party and to make inevitable the nomination of President Truman for a second term. Even the naming of a permanent chairman, almost invariably a routine matter, became the basis for a factional contest in the 1932 Democratic convention. The forces of Franklin Roosevelt proved their majority support by defeating the choice of the National Committee and placing Senator Thomas Walsh in the chair.

Throughout the history of the Republican party, the relationship of the test of strength and the Presidential nomination has been close. A majority on one vote was designed to lead to a majority on the other. Until 1936, however, the Democratic party required a two-thirds majority for the nomination. With a simple majority insufficient for victory, the test of strength had to be designed more carefully. A candidate would seek an issue which would demonstrate majority endorsement without alienating part of the minority. He would hope thereby to stimulate some delegations to join his camp. Generally, a candidate who received a simple majority would soon gain the necessary two-thirds. There was no guarantee, however, that the movement actually would occur.

A third technique, "the deal," is probably the most notorious of convention tactics, but it hardly deserves its ill fame. Alliance and compromises—other, more neutral names for "deals"—are a necessary part of the process of reaching a majority consensus. Conventions differ in this regard from legislative assemblies only in that the ambitions of men, rather than the provisions of statutes, are the principal objects of compromise. Through deals, a party can be unified before it engages in an exhausting contest with the opposition. The interests of various groups can be reconciled. Policy positions can be agreed upon, thereby making the electoral choice more meaningful to the voters. If competitive political parties are essential to the success of democracy, as the experience of democratic and dictatorial nations alike indicates, then deals too are essential.

The convention system "provides an excellent implement for compromise. . . . Here concessions of many types can be made and victories in various terms are possible. The range of satisfactions is great, and disappointment on one count may be compensated for on another."[26] Some of the materials available for trading are purely token or honorific rewards. For example, to conciliate the Southern wing of the party, the Democrats held their 1928 convention in Houston and named Senator Joseph Robinson of Arkansas as permanent chairman.

The platform represents another means of compromise, as demonstrated by Nixon's 1960 policy pact with Rockefeller, and Stevenson's attempt to gain Southern support in 1956 by endorsing a moderate position on civil rights. The Stevenson forces in 1952 showed that even convention rules can provide the basis for agreement. To gain the approval of the South, they voted to modify the party "loyalty oath," which was resented by the Southern delegations.

More tangible rewards include promises of aid to local tickets, assurances of federal patronage and favors, and even the distribution of Cabinet positions. One aspirant, Abraham Lincoln, telegraphed his campaign manager, David Davis, "I authorize no bargains." Davis demurred, declaring, "We will go ahead as if we hadn't heard from him, and he must ratify it." Lincoln's nomination was accomplished, as

[26] Pendleton Herring, *The Politics of Democracy* (New York: Norton, 1940), p. 230.

Davis won delegates "by paying their price."[27] The deals made were honored, and Lincoln's cabinet included many whose support led to his convention victory.

Certainly the most prominent material for a deal is the Vice-Presidential nomination. Many of those supporting Presidential aspirants hope to gain second place on the ticket. Generally, there is no overt bargain for the position of running mate, however. Individual Vice-Presidential possibilities are only promised consideration when the choice is made. Explicit agreements are both rarely sought and rarely made.

The most famous case in which there was such an arrangement was in the 1932 Democratic convention. Roosevelt had the support of a majority of the delegates but needed the votes pledged to John Garner to gain the necessary two-thirds vote. Garner eventually gave his endorsement to F.D.R. on the fourth ballot, and received the Vice-Presidential designation in exchange. According to one account, the deal was accomplished at a hot dog stand. Senator Tom Connally, Garner's representative, is reported to have concluded the negotiations by saying, "We can iron out the details during the day. And will you pass the mustard?"[28] However, James Farley, Roosevelt's chief strategist, has offered a more prosaic account, while substantiating the existence of an explicit understanding.[29]

Generally, alliances can only be reached between a major and a minor candidate. The ambitions of two major candidates are too different to allow them to conclude a pact. This is why deliberate "stop" movements rarely succeed. Such movements require agreement at a time of great uncertainty and emotional stress between rivals for a single position of political power. In 1920, for example, the two

[27] Carl Sandburg, *Abraham Lincoln: The Prairie Years* (New York: Harcourt, Brace, 1929), p. 506.
[28] Malcom Moos and Stephen Hess, *Hats in the Ring* (New York: Random House, 1960), p. 134.
[29] James A. Farley, *Behind the Ballots* (New York: Harcourt, Brace, 1938), pp. 132-53.

major contestants for the Republican nomination, Leonard Wood and Frank Lowden, spent considerable time and effort trying to devise a common front. They eventually foundered on the vital question of which of them would receive the Presidential nomination and which must be satisfied with the "consolation prize" of the Vice-Presidency.[30]

Candidates seeking to organize a "stop" movement are likely also to have sharp disagreements on policy. Since nominations tend to go to moderate candidates, the other major hopefuls are likely to disagree more on policy between themselves than either of them disagrees with the front-runner. In 1948, Thomas Dewey might have been blocked from the Republican nomination "had not jealousies and mismanagement delayed cooperation until too late. . . . And each candidate probably preferred Dewey to the other."[31] Both Harold Stassen and Robert Taft, Dewey's rivals, were each closer to him in their policy preferences that they were to one another.

Personal conflicts also complicate the making of agreements between major candidates. Through the pre-convention period, they are likely to have had cause to resent their opponents. If they cannot win the nomination for themselves, they are likely to support not their chief rival but some third aspirant "thereby retaining the pleasure of defeating the rival Favorite, while at the same time establishing a claim for themselves and their faction on the aspirant whom they carry."[32]

The obstacles to deals between major and minor candidates are less formidable. There is less emotional involvement, less of a clash of personal ambitions and, possibly, less of a policy difference. Wood and Lowden could not reach a pact in 1920, but Harding and Lowden groups did. The

[30] Henry L. Stoddard, *Presidential Sweepstakes* (New York: Putnam's 1948), pp. 22-23.
[31] Eugene H. Roseboom, *A History of Presidential Elections* (New York: Macmillan, 1959), p. 498.
[32] Bryce, Vol. II, p. 197.

Harding faction agreed to vote for Lowden until Wood was eliminated. If Lowden could not win nomination at that point, they hoped his delegates would turn to Harding. The convention eventually followed the prepared script.[33]

The three major tactics are still employed today. Two others that were frequently used in past conventions are of lesser importance. One is the "steamroller," a hallmark of Republican conventions of the past. The "steamroller" involved a faction gaining control of the National Committee and using this control to recognize contested delegations—particularly from the South—favoring its cause. These delegations then would vote in the convention to retain their seats and to nominate the factional candidate. The steamroller operated most notoriously in the 1912 contest between Taft and Roosevelt. Forty years later, it was finally curbed by a rules change denying contested delegations the right to vote on credentials disputes.

Even without a formal change in the rules, however, credentials contests are becoming less frequent. There has never been any in states choosing delegates in primary elections. In other areas, contests are likely only when the party organization is undeveloped. With both parties now established in almost every state, the choice of delegates should become less subject to challenge. Credentials contests, and the opportunities they offer to the Presidential aspirants, are likely to be confined in the future to the small delegations from the Territories.

Another traditional tactic, that of "packing the galleries," is unlikely to prove particularly useful in the future. To effectively fill the public seats with partisans, a candidate would have to control both the selection of the convention city and the distribution of the tickets. However, the selection of a site is now basically determined by factors such as hotel accomodations and competitive bidding between cities. The distribution of tickets is subject to a variety of

[33] Mark Sullivan, *Our Times* (New York: Scribner's, 1935), Vol. VI, pp. 55-56.

formal rules designed to reward friends of the party and to give all candidates some degree of audience support.

In the past, control of the galleries was reputed to be important. Some attribute Lincoln's nomination in 1860 to the Chicago location of the convention and the consequent bias of the crowd. In 1860, however, the reaction of the galleries was one of the only means by which the delegates could gauge public preferences among the aspirants. There were no mass media, public opinion polls, presidential primaries, or telephones. These are far more reliable means of measuring public sentiment than cheers of a few thousand unrepresentative spectators.

In 1940, Wendell Willkie had the support of the galleries, but it is doubtful if he would have won the Republican nomination without the additional backing given by interest groups and voters absent from the Philadelphia convention. In 1960, Adlai Stevenson's supporters were able to pack the galleries despite the elaborate controls over ticket distribution.[34] Their vigorous support seemed to have no influence on the delegates, who gave the former Governor fewer votes than any other major contender.

With the approval or over the opposition of the immediate audience, the parties choose their leaders. Aspirants are measured by standards of "availability" and "prominence." Policy choices are made. Tactics advance some prospects and detract from others. At the end, the nation has been presented with a potential President.

Suggestions for Further Reading

Russell Baker, "Best Road to the White House—Which?," *The New York Times Magazine* (November 27, 1960), pp. 22, 123-25. A re-examination of the Presidential potential of Governors and Senators in light of the experience of 1960.

James Lord Bryce, *The American Commonwealth*, 3rd rev. ed. (New York: Macmillan, 1914). The classic account of "traditional" American politics, including discussions of "availability," urban machines and party loyalties.

[34] White, p. 165, explains how this was accomplished.

Paul T. David (ed.), *The Presidential Election and Transition, 1960-61* (Washington: The Brookings Institution, 1961). The first two chapters, by David and Paul Tillett, are analyses of the last Presidential conventions.

Paul David *et al.*, *Presidential Nominating Politics in 1952* (Baltimore: The Johns Hopkins University Press, 1954), Vol. I. The "national story" of the 1952 nominations, with emphasis on action at the conventions themselves.

James A. Farley, *Behind the Ballots* (New York: Harcourt, Brace, 1938). The first part of the autobiography of a master politician, including a long account of the preliminaries and convention maneuvering of 1932.

Louis Harris, "Why the Odds are Against a Governor's Becoming President," *Public Opinion Quarterly*, Vol. 23 (Fall, 1959), pp. 361-70. An analysis of the recent reversal of some of the traditional rules of "availability."

Walter Johnson, *How We Drafted Adlai Stevenson* (New York: Knopf, 1955). A leading participant's account of one of the few genuine drafts in American convention history.

Constantin Melnik and Nathan Leites, *The House Without Windows: France Selects a President* (Evanston: Row, Peterson, 1958). A useful comparison and contrast to American methods of selecting national leadership.

Paul Tillett (ed.), *Inside Politics: The National Conventions, 1960* (New Brunswick: Eagleton Institute, 1962). A series of articles by on-the-scene observers of the state delegations and national conventions in 1960, with many insights into the practice of politics.

David B. Truman, *The Congressional Party* (New York: Wiley, 1959). An exhaustive examination of the policy positions and internal blocs of the legislative parties, based on an analysis of the 81st Congress.

VII THE VICE-PRESIDENTIAL NOMINEE

The last substantive business for a national convention is the choice of the party's nominee for Vice-President. His selection contrasts sharply with that of a Presidential candidate. For the latter nomination, aspirants have engaged in lengthy campaigns, the electorate has had some opportunity to consider different possibilities, party organizations have become committed to particular choices, and convention strategies have been developed. For the Vice-Presidency, however, little campaigning is done, public preferences are either unavailable or unsolicited, party leaders have few commitments other than a tepid enthusiasm for a favorite son, and strategy to gain the second position is undeveloped.

The basic cause of this lack of interest has been the nature of the Vice-President's office. In the Constitution, he is given no power other than that of presiding over the Senate. Few legislators have been willing "to trade a vote

155

for a gavel,"[1] and others in positions of power have been equally unwilling to assume an office that is largely cere- monial. Occasionally, Vice-Presidents have been given other tasks to perform, either by the President himself or through legislation. The real power of the office, however, depends greatly on the discretion of the President. The influence of a Vice-President cannot be guaranteed.

John Adams, the first to occupy the office, probably summarized the feelings of many of his successors, when he complained that his position was "the most insignificant office that ever the invention of man contrived or his imagi- nation conceived."[2] In less elegant language, John Nance Garner, elected with Franklin Roosevelt in 1932 and 1936, declared, "the Vice-Presidency isn't worth a pitcher of warm spit."[3] Informed of authoritative opinions of this quality and of the experience supporting them, few have sought the nomination. As a result, convention history includes a much smaller number of contests for the Vice-Presidency than for the major nomination. When contests have occurred, they have been settled quickly. More than three-fourths of all second-place nominations have been decided in one ballot, and none has gone beyond five tallies. Only seven running mates have been both sufficiently interested and influential to secure renomination.

A second reason for the lack of attention paid to the Vice-Presidency has been the nominating process itself. Until shortly before the designation of a running mate, no aspirant need consider the Vice-Presidency. There is always a possi- bility that he will secure the top position. Even an individ- ual with only the slimmest chance can hopefully recall the experience of James K. Polk, the Democratic Presidential

[1] Lyndon Johnson on National Broadcasting Company, *Meet the Press* (Washington: Merkle Press, July 10, 1960), p. 30.
[2] John T. Morse, *John Adams* (Boston: Houghton Mifflin, 1908), p. 251.
[3] Theodore H. White, *The Making of the President 1960* (New York: Atheneum, 1961), p. 176.

nominee of 1844. Polk came to the convention seeking only the Vice-Presidential position. When a deadlock developed, he was chosen as party standard bearer and then elected to the White House.

The probability of such events is low. Nevertheless, the fact that the probability exists at all deters possible candidates, especially those of some repute within the party, from seriously considering the Vice-Presidency until the last minute. The lateness of the decision also makes it psychologically difficult for men who have at least secretly imagined themselves as Presidents to now view themselves in a position of secondary importance.

Under the original Constitution, this problem did not exist. There were no candidates for Vice-President as such. Electoral votes were cast only for the Presidency. The individual receiving the most electoral votes became President, and the runner-up became Vice-President. By this system, distinguished leaders such as John Adams and Thomas Jefferson were chosen as Vice-President. By 1800, however, the party system had come into existence throughout the nation. Jefferson and Aaron Burr, the latter slated for Vice-President by the Republican (now Democratic) party, received an equal electoral vote. As a result, the election was decided by the House of Representatives, which chose Jefferson. Before the next election, the Constitution was changed to provide for separate electoral votes for President and Vice-President. This prevented another tied vote like that of 1800, but the Twelfth Amendment also made it unlikely that leaders of the caliber of Jefferson or Adams would serve as Vice-President in the future.

The combined effect of these factors has been to limit the Vice-Presidential candidacies of the most prominent men in the parties, those who are considered for the Presidential nomination itself. The most noted individuals have been inclined to echo Daniel Webster's refusal to accept the Whig designation as running mate of Zachary Taylor in 1848: "No thank you. I do not propose to be buried until I am really dead and in my coffin."[4] However, the nation's interests have certainly not been served by this attitude. Seven of the thirty-four Presidents of the United States, serving 35 years, became the Chief Executive through death of the elected incumbent. They, like the others nominated for Vice-President, were named to run for an office of little power and with little thought on the part of the delegates of their qualifications to head the government. Their party conventions either did not consider them for the Presidential nomination at all, or else defeated their candidacies. Then, through accident, these men assumed the most powerful political office in the nation, an office which today affects the entire world.

The increased importance of the Presidency has complicated a dilemma inherent in the office of the Vice-President. The convention must find a candidate who is willing to accept a position of secondary importance and who is also able to fulfill the decisive tasks of the Chief Executive, if this should become necessary. It must nominate such a candidate after rejecting—or not even considering—him as its candidate for President. For the most part, conventions have not yet resolved this dilemma.

Candidates and Balances

American parties are primarily concerned with winning elections, not with the problems of government. Therefore, party conventions have been primarily concerned with the political qualifications of Vice-Presidential candidates, not their aptitude for the Presidency. Politically, a Vice-Presidential nominee is most qualified if his designation will contribute to party unity while bringing some additional support to the ticket from the electorate.

Party unity can often be achieved through the conciliation of a faction defeated in the contest for the Presidential nomination or on another issue. In early conven-

[4] Malcolm Moos and Stephen Hess, *Hats in the Ring* (New York: Random House, 1960), p. 157.

tions, the right of the defeated faction to name the Vice-Presidential candidate was openly acknowledged. The Whigs, in 1840, asked Henry Clay, defeated for the major position, to be William Henry Harrison's running mate. When Clay refused, the choice was made of John Tyler, a friend of Clay. In the Democratic convention of 1860, after the South was defeated on every major issue, including platform, credentials and the nomination of Stephen Douglas for President, the Southern state delegations were granted the second-place nomination. A caucus of these delegations chose Benjamin Fitzpatrick of Alabama.[5] The unity move failed, however, when Fitzpatrick declined the nomination and the bulk of the Southerners supported a third party.

Even when the attempt is less overt, conciliation of a party faction is a frequent motive behind the choice of a Vice-Presidential candidate. Southern Democrats in 1948 did not choose the party's running mate themselves, but the naming of Alben Barkley was an attempt to retain their allegiance. Four years earlier, John Bricker was named to Thomas Dewey's Republican ticket in order to conciliate the more conservative Midwest faction of the G.O.P.

Conciliation of a faction may take place before, as well as after, the Presidential nomination. When a "deal" involving the Vice-Presidency is made, differing factions of the party are concluding an alliance which gives each of them some satisfaction. Actually, precise understandings about the Vice-Presidential nomination are far more rare than suggested by legends of the "smoke-filled room." Even in the Republican convention of 1920, when party diplomacy became notorious, the Vice-Presidential nomination was not decided by a trade or a secret caucus, but by an uncontrolled enthusiasm for Calvin Coolidge.

More often, what is given in exchange for support of the Presidential candidate is a more general understanding that some obligation is thereby incurred. There are many

[5] Murat Halstead, *Three Against Lincoln*, Ed. by William Hesseltine (Baton Rouge: Louisiana State University Press, 1960), p. 255.

types of political currency which can be used to repay obligations, only one of which is the Vice-Presidency. A party leader owes debts to many people and groups, but can name only one individual as his running mate. Others must be satisfied with different compensations.

The second political purpose of the Vice-Presidential nomination is to broaden the party's appeal to the electorate. The parties hope that at least marginal support will be provided from certain sections or groups because of the particular attraction of the candidate for Vice-President. Thus, the Democrats in 1952 hoped to recover the electoral votes of four Southern states which they had lost in 1948 by naming Senator John Sparkman of Alabama to the ticket. Four years later, supporters of John Kennedy sought to win the second nomination for him by emphasizing the votes he would gain among Catholics in the metropolitan areas of the Northeast and Midwest.

The Vice-Presidential nomination may also be used to emphasize a particular issue in the election campaign. In 1952, the Republicans sought to exploit the issue of alleged Communist infiltration of the federal civil service. Richard Nixon's designation as Vice-President served to point up the problem, since he had taken a leading role in the investigation of Alger Hiss and had emphasized the question in his election campaigns. When Nixon himself ran for President in 1960, his major campaign appeal was his ability to deal with the international problems facing the nation. He strove to extend this appeal by naming Henry Cabot Lodge, U.S. ambassador to the United Nations, to the ticket.

In an attempt to increase their voting strength, parties have occasionally named a running mate from the opposition. The Whigs in 1840 and the Republicans in 1864 named Democrats as their candidates for Vice-President, the Republicans going so far as temporarily to change their name to the Union party. In both cases, the party won, but the President died and a member of the opposition occupied the White House. Since then, parties have not taken such risks and have restricted both nominations to party loyalists. Other attempts to increase the electoral strength of the party have included the designation of wealthy individuals, newspaper publishers, and those with famous names, such as Franklin Roosevelt in 1920 and Charles Bryan in 1924.

The considerations involved in the choice of a Vice-Presidential nominee could be summarized as an attempt to "balance" the ticket. Many different kinds of equilibrium are involved. In 1940, Republican leader Joseph Martin stressed this factor in urging Wendell Willkie to accept Charles McNary as his running mate, arguing, "While you come from Indiana, you live in New York, and you're identified with the East because of your connection with Commonwealth & Southern. McNary comes from the Far West. You are known as a utilities man; McNary has sided with the public power boys. You're supposed to represent big business interests; McNary was a sponsor of the McNary-Haugen farm bill. You aren't supposed to know much about the legislative process; McNary is a master of it. I think you'd make a perfect team."[6] Democrats in 1928 similarly stressed a balance of policy positions by naming Alfred Smith and Joseph Robinson, who respectively opposed and favored prohibition.

Policy differences between two nominees, or ideological balance, have become less apparent in recent conventions. Not since the 1944 Republican nomination of Thomas Dewey and John Bricker has a national ticket included spokesmen for widely different policies. In 1960, Nixon specifically excluded any running mate opposed to his basic views. Possibly because of the increased strain of the Presidency, nominees for the office seem disinclined to place an ideological opponent in line to succeed to the White House. Interest groups influential in the nomination would

[6] Joseph W. Martin, *My First Fifty Years in Politics* (New York: McGraw-Hill, 1960), p. 160.

certainly object to such procedures. Nor are voters in disagreement with the Presidential candidate likely to vote for him because they agree with the views of his running mate.

Parties also attempt to balance the regional appeal of the two candidates by naming a Vice-Presidential candidate from a section of the nation which is different from the region of the head of the ticket. Although the Constitution only requires that they be from different states, the parties have broadened this provision in an effort to increase their national support. Occasional exceptions include the designation of two Republican Midwesterners, Alfred Landon and Frank Knox in 1936, and two Democrats from the border states, Harry Truman and Alben Barkley, in 1948.

However, the rule still applies, although it has become more difficult to practice. Sectional balance formerly meant one candidate from the Northeast and one from the Midwest. A ticket such as James Cox of Ohio and Franklin Roosevelt of New York, chosen by the Democrats in 1920, was both ideal and typical. The Far West could be disregarded because of its small voting strength, and the South neglected because of its one-party voting record. Now the West has become populous and the South more competitive. Reacting to these changes, the Republicans have named residents of the West Coast to seven of their last nine tickets, and the Democrats have chosen Southerners or border state residents eight times in the same period.

Less obvious than sectional balance is the attempt to balance personal characteristics such as age, size of home town, and occupation. In the future, one may find balance between the religion and sex of the two candidates. Now that a Catholic has been elected President, the parties may believe it advantageous to have a member of that faith on the ticket. The national slate may come to resemble that of the large cities of the Northeast, where a delicate equilibrium is maintained in the nominations of members of different religious and ethnic groups. If a tradition of naming a Catholic to the ticket becomes established, it will be because of the large numbers of Catholics in the nation and their strategic residence in the states with the most electoral votes. For similar reasons, it is not unlikely that a Negro eventually—and probably sooner rather than later—will be named to a national party slate, most likely as Vice-Presidential nominee.

One type of balance the parties have not seriously considered is that of sex. Republican convention delegates have not cast a single vote for a female candidate. Democrats have been slightly more chivalrous, giving as many as 44 votes to a woman for Vice-President, and many Democrats in 1948 seriously considered the designation of Mrs. Franklin Roosevelt to run with President Truman. With women constituting a clear majority of the electorate, it is conceivable that a female candidate will be named to the ticket. However, the number of women prominent in politics is small, and there is no evidence that a female candidacy would attract unusual support from women—or from men.

Whatever particular characteristics will be balanced in the future, the aim will continue to be to arouse the widest possible support. Geography alone is likely to become less important. Instead, emphasis will be placed on the broad group appeals which can be promoted by a Vice-Presidential choice. There will be many possible selections, each in general agreement with the Presidential candidate's policies, each with the necessary personal background. The actual nominee is likely to be the one who brings an increment of support from important groups, whether sectional, economic, or religious.

Methods of Nomination

The running mate is not usually chosen in an open contest, as is the party's Presidential choice. While there have been a number of disputed Vice-Presidential nominations in the past, recent conventions have witnessed a decline in both their number and their duration. In part, this is the result of a greater disposition on the part of the Presidential candidate to participate in the choice of his campaign companion. Few standard bearers are now willing to emulate William Jennings Bryan, who conscientiously refrained from indicating a preference for his running mate in all of his three Presidential campaigns. They are equally unwilling to leave the choice to a caucus of state leaders, as was the practice in many early conventions.

If the Presidential candidate does wish to state a preference, his selection will almost certainly be respected by the convention. Few delegates have come to the conclave with definite preferences, commitments, or even concern for the second position. Even if not satisfied with the designated Vice-Presidential candidate, the party representatives usually would not be willing to oppose the very first decision of their newly-selected leader.

When there has been open opposition to the choice of the party leader, this opposition has been directed as much against the Presidential candidate as against his selected running mate. When some Democrats opposed the nomination of Henry Wallace for Vice-President in 1940, their antagonism was only partially toward the Secretary of Agriculture. They were also contesting the liberal policies favored by President Roosevelt himself and supported by Wallace. F.D.R.'s control of the convention and his demonstrated popularity were too great to allow the dissident delegates to express this antagonism directly. It could be directed with relative safety toward the heir-apparent. In the event, it required the threat of Roosevelt's own withdrawal from the campaign to gain Wallace's designation.[7] Four years later, the opposition to Wallace and his liberal policies was strong enough to force his dismissal from the ticket.

Other incumbent Presidents, including Jackson, Lin-

[7] James M. Burns, *Roosevelt: The Lion and the Fox* (New York: Harcourt, Brace, 1956), pp. 428-30.

coln, Taft, and Hoover, have faced convention challenges to their selected running mates. In effect, the nomination of the Vice-President has served as a safety valve for the delegates when they feel that their control over the Presidential designation has been unduly limited. Two of the most noted convention revolts occurred on the second nomination after party leaders had decided on the Presidential choice among themselves. One instance came in 1900, when the Republicans chose a "damned cowboy," Theodore Roosevelt, over the objections of Mark Hanna, political manager for President William McKinley. The other was in 1920. After the Republican leaders had chosen Warren Harding for President, their presumed preference for Senator Irvine Lenroot was disregarded as two-thirds of the delegates voted for Calvin Coolidge on the first ballot.

For the Presidential candidate, there are probably more risks than advantages in an open contest for the second-place nomination. One committed to an open contest cannot use the lure of the Vice-Presidency to accomplish his own nomination, nor can the designation be used to conciliate a defeated faction. An open contest may simply mean another victory for that group which has already succeeded in naming the party leader. This would serve only to divide the party further, rather than to unify it. Even if the same faction does not win both nominating contests, an open fight for the Vice-Presidency is still likely to exacerbate any splits created or revealed by the major competition.

In an open contest for the second nomination, there is also no assurance that a balanced ticket will result, and the party's strength in the election campaign may therefore be adversely affected. In regard to the Vice-Presidency, the convention is virtually unstructured. No primary contests or other significant measurements of public support are available and few delegates have given any prolonged thought to the question. A free choice in these circumstances cannot be described as truly democratic or representative of the wishes of the party or the electorate. A free choice may only be the expression of a transient mood on the part of the delegates. The result may be unfortunate, bringing the nomination of a candidate who is repugnant to major factions in the party, adds little strength to the ticket, and disagrees with the Presidential candidate on policy questions. There may be further unfortunate results if the ticket is elected. Then the new President will be in a situation where his only elected and non-removable assistant owes no obligation to him for his nomination as Vice-President. He may therefore oppose the President's policies with relative impunity.

The most recent free choice of a running mate came in the Democratic convention of 1956. Adlai Stevenson then favored an open designation for campaign purposes. President Dwight Eisenhower's heart attack had attracted attention to his presumed running mate, Nixon, who was believed to be unpopular. An open contest for the Democratic second spot, it was hoped, would further emphasize the importance of the Vice-Presidency and lose votes for the Republican ticket. The result in the Democratic convention was a chaotic session, at which Estes Kefauver narrowly won the designation. The nomination provided drama, but it also alienated party factions in both the North and South, without demonstrably adding to the electoral strength of the ticket. As a result, Kefauver's selection did not result in conciliation, but in conflict. However, the nominee's views did not differ substantially from Stevenson's, and one would suppose that his mode of selection would not have hampered Stevenson as President.

Today, the usual method of selecting the running mate is by consultation between the Presidential candidate and the leading party figures and interest group leaders. The designation of Nixon by the Republicans in 1952 is fairly typical, although the Presidential candidate then took a rather passive role. General Eisenhower and Herbert Brownell, one of his campaign managers, drew up a list of some seven names, including that of Nixon.

Eisenhower said that he would leave it to Brownell "to get the collective judgment of the leaders of the party" and they were to understand that "Nixon would be very acceptable."

Brownell summoned about two dozen representative Eisenhower leaders to a meeting at the Conrad Hilton Hotel, across the street from the Blackstone where Eisenhower was staying. At the same time proponents of various candidates for the nomination were invited to present their cases.

Paul G. Hoffman, former foreign aid director and a chief organizer of independent Republicans and Democrats for Eisenhower, recalls, "The first person to be discussed was Taft." Several other names also were brought up "and knocked down," he said, "then Nixon's was offered." Everyone in the room had an opportunity to state his opinion. ...

The committee thereupon voted unanimously for Nixon, and Brownell picked up two different telephones to give the news simultaneously to Eisenhower and Nixon.[8]

The real problem of the Vice-Presidential nomination is not the method of nomination, however, but the quality of those selected. The requirements of balance, the limited power of the office, and the timing of selection have not contributed to the choice of men sufficiently prominent to be considered able to fulfill the duties of the Presidency itself. Fortunately, there are signs of improvement.

Modern Changes

Recent developments indicate that the neglect of the Vice-Presidency may be ending. The conventions are considering and nominating men of greater renown, and the office itself is becoming more powerful and more desirable to possible aspirants.

[8] Earl Mazo, *Richard Nixon: A Political and Personal Portrait* (New York: Harper, 1959), p. 96.

The change can be seen by comparing the actions of conventions in the nineteenth and twentieth centuries. One index is the number of Vice-Presidential renominations. Until 1900, neither party had renominated in consecutive conventions either a defeated candidate for the Vice-Presidency or even an incumbent. The Democrats did, however, twice name Thomas Hendricks for the position in the non-consecutive conventions of 1876 and 1884. Hendricks was an unusual nominee, for he had been a major contestant for the Presidential nomination itself.

Particularly indicative of the low estate of the Vice-Presidency was the defeat of incumbents. Three holders of the office were beaten in a contest for renomination. Another four had so little interest in the position or were regarded so lightly by the party representatives that they were dropped without a contest.

In the twentieth century, no defeated candidate for the Vice-Presidency has been nominated to the office again, but incumbents have fared much better. Five holders of the office have been named for a second campaign and one, Democrat Henry Wallace, was defeated in a convention contest. In addition, two Vice-Presidents were named for a second term after they left office. The first Adlai Stevenson was elected in 1892 and then renominated in 1900, and Charles Fairbanks was designated in 1904, when he won office, and again in 1916, when he lost.

The fate of Vice-Presidents who succeed to the White House through the death of the President has been similar. All four "accidental" Presidents before 1900 were denied renomination by their parties. All three since that date have been easily nominated for a term as President of their own.

Another measurement of the greater importance of the Vice-Presidential designation is the use of the nomination as a springboard for a Presidential campaign. In the nineteenth century, not including "accidental" Presidents, four running mates later sought their parties' leadership. Of these four, all Democrats, only Martin Van Buren was successful. In the twentieth century, all of those elected to the second office have later sought the Presidency itself, excluding of course those who died before the opportunity arose. Two running mates, Franklin Roosevelt and Richard Nixon, later gained the leadership of their parties. In each period, one Vice-President later won the Presidential nomination of a minor party.

It appears likely that the ambitions of Vice-Presidential nominees will be attained more frequently in the future. The significant fact is not that more campaigns for the White House are launched by candidates for Vice-President, or that slightly more succeed, but that these campaigns are more impressive efforts than those of the past. Only three Vice-Presidential nominees in the nineteenth century mounted serious efforts: Van Buren, George Pendleton, and Hendricks. In the twentieth century, conventions have considered at least five serious contenders. Aside from Roosevelt and Nixon, formidable campaigns were mounted by Garner, Barkley, and Earl Warren.

The contrast between Van Buren and Nixon, the only incumbent Vice-Presidents to be chosen as party leaders, illustrates the new political importance of the position. Van Buren did not owe his nomination to his national office. He was named for President because he was the chosen successor of Andrew Jackson and because he was the leader of the New York Democratic party, whose support was crucial to election victory.

Nixon, on the other hand, had little political strength outside of the Vice-Presidency. He had no state political base, not even controlling the Republican party in his home state of California. His nomination for President came with the consent, but not through the active efforts of the party leader, General Eisenhower. Nixon used his position as Vice-President to gain political predominance within his party.

Nixon gained pre-eminence by his extensive campaigning for Republican state and Congressional candidates

TABLE 7-1

FUTURE ROLE OF VICE-PRESIDENTIAL CANDIDATES

Renominated	Later Considered for President	Not Further Considered	Defeated for Renomination
Democratic Party			
Hendricks, 1884	Van Buren, 1836*a	Dallas, 1848*	Johnson, 1840*
Stevenson, 1900	Breckinridge, 1860*b	Johnson, 1860	Butler, 1852
Marshall, 1916*	Pendleton, 1868	Blair, 1872	Wallace, 1944*
Garner, 1936*	Hendricks, 1880, 1884	Brown, 1876	
	Kern, 1912	English, 1884	
	Marshall, 1920*	Thurman, 1892	
	Roosevelt, 1932a	Davis, 1908	
	Garner, 1940*	Bryan, 1928	
	Wallace, 1948b	Robinson, 1932	
	Barkley, 1952*	Sparkman, 1956	
		Kefauver, 1960	
Whig and Republican Parties			
Sherman, 1912*	Fairbanks, 1908*	Sergeant, 1836	Dayton, 1860
Fairbanks, 1916	Dawes, 1928*	Frelinghuysen, 1848	Hamlin, 1864*
Curtis, 1932*	Warren, 1952	Wheeler, 1880*	Colfax, 1872*
Nixon, 1956*	Nixon, 1960*a	Morton, 1892*	
		Reid, 1896	
		Knox, 1940	
		Bricker, 1948	

*Incumbent Vice-President
aNominated for President by major party
bNominated for President by third party

TABLE 7–2

TREND OF FUTURE ROLE OF VICE-PRESIDENTIAL CANDIDATES

	1836-1896		1900-1960	
	No.	%	No.	%
Renominated	1	5	7	28
Considered for President	4	19	10	40
Not Further Considered	11	52	7	28
Defeated for Renomination	5	24	1	4
Totals:	21	100%	25	100%

and his reputation as the political expert of the Administration. He further aided his Presidential campaign by newsworthy efforts as a traveling ambassador to South America and the Soviet Union and as a participant in domestic crises, such as the 1959 steel strike.[9] This use of an office which has been considered bereft of power may be a unique case, due to Eisenhower's neglect of partisan activity. However, Nixon's performance has revealed potential power which few previously believed to exist.

The political destiny of Vice-Presidential candidates is summarized in the preceding tables. Those elected to the office who became President on the death of their running mates are not included, nor are those candidates who died before the next party convention. The date given is that of the first convention after the original nomination, or that at which the candidate was renominated or considered for President.

A comparison of the years before and after the turn of the century makes it clear that a Vice-Presidential candidate has a vastly greater chance today than in the past of being renominated as Vice-President and eventually being considered, possibly nominated, for President. This record is undoubtedly one of the reasons why more prominent individuals within the party have been more willing to run for the Vice-Presidency. Nominees are no longer likely to decline a designation, as many have done before the convention voting, and three after their formal nomination.

[9] See Richard Nixon, *Six Crises* (Garden City: Doubleday, 1962).

The last formal declination came in 1924, when Frank Lowden refused a place on the Republican slate. Those invited to run for Vice-President, if not excited by the office itself, are likely to recall the experience of Henry Clay, Daniel Webster, and Hiram Johnson. Each refused second place on the ticket, only to see the election of the slate and the subsequent death of the President.

Rather than restraint, there is now a slight trend toward campaigning for the second-place designation. Aspirants seek support quietly, largely within the party organizations. In the open Vice-Presidential contest among the Democrats in 1956, John Kennedy compressed into a few hours what is usually a longer and less wearying effort.

> In his suite at the Conrad Hilton, Kennedy met late in the evening with aides and family. He had his staff, family, and assorted college and political friends with him. . . . Through the night, Kennedy and his people ransacked the city for delegates, most of whom had gone to bars or to bed. Far off in France, Joseph Kennedy started making phone calls to political leaders. . . .
>
> Meantime, Kennedy workers ranged through Chicago getting placards ready, leaflets printed, noisemakers, buttons, banners. Other vice-presidential aspirants were busy, too; a delegate could hardly cross the street to get a drink without being accosted. . . . But everything was obscure. . . .[10]

One measurement of the new appeal of the Vice-Presidency is the willingness of aspirants defeated for the Presidential nomination to take the second spot on the slate. In the nineteenth century, only two men who received substantial support for their party's leadership were named for Vice-President. These were the indefatigable Hendricks in the Democratic party and John Logan in the Republican camp. In modern times, at least ten major figures—as indi-

[10] James M. Burns, *John Kennedy: A Political Profile* (New York: Harcourt, Brace, 1959), pp. 187-88.

cated either by their voting strength in the convention or their repute in the party—have been named as running mates.[11] The trend began with Fairbanks' designation at the 1916 Republican convention. In the last eight conventions, major party figures have been named five times. The experience of 1960 is especially remarkable. The willingness of the Senate majority leader and the nation's ambassador to the United Nations to run for Vice-President is special testament to the new attractiveness of the position.

The appeal of the office is still unrecognized by many. Harry Truman, who had experienced little power as Vice-President, was surprised when Alben Barkley sought the position in 1948. Exclaiming, "Why didn't you tell me you wanted to be Vice-President?,"[12] Truman quickly approved Barkley's candidacy. The availability of Johnson and Lodge in 1960 was even more startling to most observers. In fact, Johnson's acceptance even surprised some leaders of the Kennedy group.[13]

One reason for this interest in the Vice-Presidency is the greater political influence now inherent in the office. Another reason is the new governmental power which has recently been added to the position. Men originally elected as Vice-President have served as Chief Executive for a third of the twentieth century. In the light of this high mortality rate, both the President and Congress have acted to give more content to the office of "second counsel" than that prescribed by the Constitution. Franklin Roosevelt gave Garner and Wallace extensive legislative and executive responsibilities. Truman, recalling his own lack of preparedness on assuming the highest office, sought to involve Alben Barkley in all major policy decisions. Eisenhower implemented this policy further, giving Nixon such assignments as the chair-

[11] These are: Fairbanks, 1916; Lowden, 1924; Dawes, 1928; Garner, 1932; Knox, 1936; Barkley and Warren, 1948; Kefauver, 1956; Johnson and Lodge, 1960.

[12] Harry S. Truman, *Memoirs* (New York: Doubleday, 1956), Vol. II, p. 190.

[13] White, p. 174.

manship of the Operations Coordinating Board, a committee designed to supervise the execution of security policy. Nixon also traveled widely on "good will" missions throughout the world and dealt with various domestic economic and political questions.

The trend to greater responsibility for the Vice-President has continued in the new Kennedy government. Lyndon Johnson has frequently traveled as an executive "trouble-shooter." He also serves as chairman of administration committees on national space policy and discrimination in government employment.

Presidential initiative has been supplemented by Congressional action. The Vice-President is a statutory member of the National Security Council, the top foreign policy body in the nation. He also has been given special responsibilities in regard to space policy and in case of the disability of the President. All of these changes make the position more attractive and bring more prominent candidates in quest of the office.[14]

Suggestions for the Future

Despite recent improvement, most critics believe "we have little cause for complacency ... in our selection of Vice-Presidential candidates." More general changes in the convention system will be considered in the final chapters. At this point, we may examine some of the proposals for improving the choice of a running mate. "One suggests that the nominee for Vice-President be chosen *before* the Presidential candidate. . . . Other proposals call for the Vice-Presidential nominee to be chosen from the top three contenders for the Presidential nomination; for Presidential and Vice-Presidential candidates to seek the nomination as a team; . . . to decrease the duties of the office, relieving the Vice-President of the responsibility of presiding over the

[14] See Irving G. Williams, *The Rise of the Vice-Presidency* (Washington: Public Affairs Press, 1956).

Senate, allowing him to retain another job (such as senator or governor), with the one Vice-Presidential function being to succeed to the Presidency if it becomes necessary."[15]

The ideal method for nominating the Vice-President would accomplish four objectives. For the party, the choice of a running mate would promote party unity while strengthening the electoral appeal of the ticket. For the nation, the best method would be one that results in the nomination of known men in general agreement with the policy views of the Presidential candidate. In the event of the President's death, there would then be some assurance that the policies on which the ticket was elected would be continued by a competent leader. Using these standards, all of the suggested changes fall short in one way or another.

The last suggested change, to allow the Vice-President to hold another job, would be the most difficult to achieve, for it would require a Constitutional amendment. It would serve the parties' needs, for it would still permit the choice of a running mate to be used to conciliate party factions and to increase the ticket's electoral appeal. It would also serve the public interest by allowing more prominent leaders to accept the designation without forfeiting the office they already hold. There would be two major disadvantages to the plan.

First, it might embarrass the Presidential candidate by virtually requiring him to offer the Vice-Presidential nomination to the leader of an opposition faction. This might lead to divergences in the policy positions of the two nominees, and therefore complicate the course of the national administration if the candidates were elected. If the scheme had been in effect in 1952, for example, General Eisenhower might well have found himself on a slate with Senator Robert Taft. This would certainly have led to awkward problems in the campaign and in the future Republican administration. As it was, Taft's position as Majority Leader of the Senate caused conflict within the

[15] Moos and Hess, p. 169. The authors offer no comments.

councils of the executive branch.[16] If Taft had spoken not only as a legislative leader, but also as a potential President, the adminstration might have found it even more difficult to achieve a coherent set of policies.

The public interest could be adversely affected by this plan in another way. If the Vice-President is also engaged in another full-time job, he will be unable to devote much attention to problems of national executive policy. He will not be intimately familiar with the issues and decisions he will face if he should suddenly become President. Admittedly Vice-Presidents of the past, even though free of other responsibilities, have not been well versed in the problems of the office—Harry Truman, for example, had no knowledge of the atomic bomb when he became President.[17] This lack of preparation, however, is now being remedied by the actions of both Presidents and Congress. It would seem foolish to institute a change which would mean a regression to the inadequacies of the past.

There are equally important, although different, objections to the suggestion that the Vice-President be chosen before the Presidential nominee. However, the sequence is not the decisive question. Because of its importance major interest will continue to be placed on the Presidential nomination, whenever it comes. Choosing the Vice-President first might lead to awkward situations. A coalition which is uncertain of defeating a major aspirant for President might join to nominate him for Vice-President. Then the newly-designated nominee might refuse the invitation. It is hardly fanciful to suggest that, under this plan, Thomas Dewey in 1948 and John Kennedy in 1960 would have been nominated not for President, but for Vice-President.

Party conciliation would not be furthered by the prior selection of the running mate. Open convention contests, with their many defects, would be more common. The group

[16] Robert Donovan, *Eisenhower: The Inside Story* (New York: Harper, 1956), pp. 102-11.
[17] Truman, Vol. I, p. 10.

which loses in the contest for President could no longer be compensated by the second-place designation. Until the main nomination is accomplished, moreover, the composition of the winning and losing coalitions is uncertain. It is therefore impossible to know exactly which group needs to be conciliated. Putting first things first—the Presidential nomination—is a more rational way of reaching decisions.

The objective of this proposal is to provide for more deliberate consideration of the Vice-Presidential nominee by providing for a distinct group of contestants for the office. Actually, separate consideration is now given to the Vice-Presidential candidate—but this is done generally after the major nomination is accomplished, and by the leading party figures rather than the entire convention. If the two nominations were completely separated, as is suggested, the effect would be to remove the major figures of the party from consideration for the Vice-Presidency. An individual would be required to be a candidate for one office or the other. No matter how attractive the Vice-Presidency is made, no ambitious politician is likely to choose that office in preference to the position of Chief Executive. Implementing this proposal would reverse the trend of recent years in which individuals such as Johnson and Lodge would accept second place on the ticket after they were passed over for President. Obviously, this result would not benefit the parties, which would lose the opportunity to increase their electoral appeal by adding a prominent leader to the slate.

The effect on the nation would be equally detrimental. The man in line to succeed to the Presidency would be one who was relatively unknown to the general electorate, and whose talents had been assessed only slightly, even by the leaders of the party. While the "accidental" Presidents have generally performed creditably, and usually far better than was originally expected, the choice of the Vice-President should be more than a random selection.

Some of the same objections hold against the plan to have candidates seek both nominations as a team. Ohio's primary law is modeled somewhat on this idea. In that state, delegate slates must indicate both a first and second choice for President. When major candidates have entered the primary, the second choice for President has actually been a Vice-Presidential choice. However, the listing has had little effect. The "second choice" is usually an Ohio resident placed on the ballot to gain some "favorite son" support for the Presidential aspirant. It obviously does not bind the principal candidate, and has not affected the final choice of a running mate. There is little evidence, moreover, that the voters give any substantial consideration to the second name on the ballot.

If the principle of the Ohio primary were adopted widely, and candidates did run on slates, one effect would again be to bar the most prominent candidates from the Vice-Presidency. A party leader with the possibility of a Presidential nomination before him could hardly be expected to renounce his ambitions to take second place on the ticket of an opponent. The resulting loss of talent in the Vice-Presidency can not be considered in the public interest.

The formation of slates before the convention would probably be a contribution to party conciliation, as the Presidential candidate would be reasonably certain to obtain the necessary balance. It is possible, however, that the wrong group will be conciliated. When the ticket is first established—necessarily, months before the convention—it may appear imperative to reach an agreement with one faction. Later in the campaign, or at the convention itself, a different group or a new issue may have arisen, and the Presidential candidate will have lost a principal tool for the forging of party unity.

At the same time, he may have complicated his future administration, if elected. In seeking the widest possible support before the convention, he may be inclined to select a running mate of opposing policy views. This inclination need not be heeded by a candidate after his nomination, for he has already gained the leadership of his party. Before the nomination, he is more likely to compromise his policies, possibly causing discomfort for himself as President while blurring the principles of the party.

The final suggested change is to choose the Vice-Presidential nominee from the leading defeated aspirants for the Presidential nomination itself. In fact, there is a trend in this direction. It would be risky, however, to make this method mandatory. Let us suppose that the parties always selected the runner-up in the Presidential balloting as their candidates for Vice-President. The result would be that Barry Goldwater would have been the Republicans' choice in 1960, and Robert Taft in 1952. The Democrats would have named Richard Russell for Vice-President in 1948 and Alfred Smith in 1932.[18] While all of these individuals were prominent in their parties, the policy differences between them and the Presidential candidates were too great to enable their parties to present a coherent set of principles. The danger of such a practice is further indicated by the vote in the Democratic convention of 1944. If this rule were in effect then, Harry Byrd would have become President on the death of Franklin Roosevelt, bringing a conservative to the White House after the nation had voted for the liberal leader of the New Deal.

Generally, the plan would mean the selection of prominent individuals. In a convention which supports one Presidential candidate overwhelmingly, however, a mere handful of votes might bring the Vice-Presidency to an individual. By this scheme, Douglas MacArthur would have received the Republican nomination for Vice-President in 1944 although he obtained only one of a thousand convention votes.

For the parties, selection of defeated major candidates would usually be beneficial. Their election prospects are likely to be improved, and the defeated party faction

[18] Of course, Smith would not have been chosen in 1932 in any case because he was from the same state as Roosevelt. However, the point of this example is still valid.

would probably be appeased. It may be better not to rigidly institutionalize such a system. In some cases, a unified campaign by two factional leaders might be awkward. In such cases, conciliation may be better achieved by the selection of some other Vice-Presidential candidate. However, neither Stevenson and Kefauver in 1956, or Kennedy and Johnson in 1960, faced great difficulty in reconciling their differences.

The Vice-Presidential nominations still need improvement. Yet, thus far, the nation has been fortunate in the men who have become "accidental" Presidents. All have performed competently, none has done as poorly as elected Presidents of the caliber of Buchanan and Grant, and at least two—Theodore Roosevelt and Calvin Coolidge—have performed better than the erstwhile heads of the party ticket.

Given present trends, we can be even more confident of the quality of future Vice-Presidents. Without formal changes, the party conventions have tended to name more prominent individuals as running mates. As the power of the office has increased, and its political influence grown, major party figures have been willing to accept nominations to the office. Certain changes may be made to encourage these trends, but the necessity for far-reaching changes is not apparent. As is the case with other facets of the nominating process, the selection of the Vice-Presidential nominee is changing to meet the needs of the present.

Suggestions for Further Reading

Alben Barkley, *That Reminds Me* (Garden City: Doubleday, 1954). Entertaining and informative autobiography of the first of the "new" Vice-Presidents, and a strong contender for the 1952 Democratic Presidential nomination.

Louis C. Hatch. *A History of the Vice-Presidency of the United States* (New York: American Historical Society, 1934). A detailed and scholarly, but dated, study which deals with various aspects of the office, including politics, protocol, and power.

Peter R. Levin, *Seven by Chance: The Accidental Presidents* (New York: Farrar, Straus, 1948). A history and evaluation, generally unfavorable, of those who became President through death.

Richard M. Nixon, *Six Crises* (Garden City: Doubleday, 1962). Revealing study of the restraints on the Vice-President and of the most recent occupant of the office.

Robert V. Remini, *Martin Van Buren and the Making of the Democratic Party* (New York: Columbia University Press, 1959). Principally an account of Van Buren's early political career, this work is an interesting contrast to Nixon's autobiography.

U. S. Senate, Committee on Government Operations, *Administrative Vice-President*, Hearings on Proposal to Create Position of Administrative Vice-President, 84th Cong., 2nd sess. (1956). Discussion of one of the more fashionable ideas on how to upgrade the office of the second national executive.

Edgar W. Waugh. *Second Counsel* (Indianapolis: Bobbs-Merrill, 1956). Discussion of the ascendancy of the Vice-President through election, death, impeachment, and disability, with proposals for making the office more satisfactory.

Irving G. Williams, *The American Vice-Presidency: New Look* (Garden City: Doubleday, 1954). A short study of the recent increase in the importance of the Vice-Presidential office.

Irving G. Williams, *The Rise of the Vice-Presidency* (Washington: Public Affairs Press, 1956). A more thorough and definitive study by the same author, examining the historical, political, and governmental sources of the modern Vice-Presidency.

Klyde Young and Lamar Middleton, *Heirs-Apparent: The Vice-Presidents of the United States* (New York: Prentice-Hall, 1948). Brief biographies of the 34 Vice-Presidents up to 1948, but with little attempt at comparison or comment.

VIII PATTERNS AND TRENDS IN NOMINATIONS

Every nominating campaign and every national convention has its unique events and its unique place in history. After 65 major party conventions, however, individual events tend to fall into patterns. History does not repeat itself in exactly the same way, but there are recurring similarities between party conclaves in the more distant and recent past.

In reviewing the Presidential nominations, each designation can be classified in one of four categories. The criterion for classifying a particular nomination is the degree of discretion actually available to and employed by the party delegates. In order of increasing discretion, the four categories are:

1. No real choice is available. The convention only ratifies the selection of an obvious leader. His nomination is accomplished on the first ballot with the support of more than two-thirds of the delegates.

2. Limited, but significant, choice is available. The convention chooses a leading party figure against strong competition. The designation again is made on the first ballot, but with more than a third of the delegates in opposition.

3. The convention is able to choose among major candidates, eventually selecting an important party figure after the first ballot. Thus real power is held by the body of delegates. Major aspirants are defined as those who receive at least a fifth of the convention votes on the first ballot.

4. Exercising the fullest freedom of choice, the party representatives select a minor candidate. With less than a fifth of the first ballot votes, the minor candidate obviously is selected after the initial roll call of the states.

Patterns of Nominations

In the first case, typified by nearly half of the conventions, the delegates had no real influence over the Presidential nomination. Pre-convention campaigning, popular preferences, decision of the party leadership, or a combination of these factors, had reduced the role of the delegates to an endorsement of the undoubted party leader.

Most commonly, this situation occurs when an incumbent President wishes his party's nomination for re-election. Since 1884, when Chester Arthur was denied the Republican designation, every President has been given the opportunity for a second term by his party. In all of American history, only five incumbents have both sought and lost this chance.

Of those rejected, only Franklin Pierce had been elected Chief Executive. The others had been chosen as Vice-President, occupying the White House upon the death of the popular choice for President. In modern times, the political power of the President has become great enough to assure the renomination even of these "accidental" party leaders. All three of these Presidents in the twentieth century—Theodore Roosevelt, Calvin Coolidge and Harry Truman—won renomination without significant opposition. The President's political potency is also indicated by the fact that no modern Chief Executive has declined to run for a second term. In earlier years some left the White House voluntarily after four years, thereby averting conflict and possible defeat over a renomination.

Candidates other than an incumbent President can also reduce the convention to the powerless role of a ratifying body. The very first major party convention, of the National Republicans, met only to ratify the selection of Henry Clay. With the increased importance of pre-convention campaigning and the development of nominating strategies, the possibility is greater today that a candidate will arrive at the convention with his nomination already assured. Thus, combining appeals to the electorate with consultation among state party organizations, Thomas Dewey and Richard Nixon were able, respectively, to capture the Republican designations of 1944 and 1960. Neither expended any considerable effort at the convention site.

The convention's discretion can also be limited through the actions of an outgoing President. While he cannot dictate his party's nomination of a successor, he is able to exercise influence. Use of this influence limits the freedom of the delegates to some extent. In the nominations of Martin Van Buren and William Howard Taft, the delegates' freedom was effectively ended. In these latter two situations, as in the renomination of an incumbent President, the delegates are not independently choosing a standard bearer, but are ratifying a decision which has already been made by others elsewhere. The thirty nominations of this type are listed in Table 8-1.

Whigs and Republicans, it can be seen, more frequently hold conventions only to ratify a nomination than do Democrats. Exactly half of the former party's 32 conventions have been ratification ceremonies, while 14 of 33 Democratic gatherings fall into this category. Whigs and Republicans have been particularly disposed to submit to

leaders other than the President, naming nine such dominant figures, in contrast to the Democrats' total of six.

This difference between the parties has become even

TABLE 8–1

CONVENTIONS RATIFYING NOMINATIONS[1]

Year	Candidate	Total Votes	Candidate Votes	Per Cent
		Democratic Party		
1832	Jackson*	283	283[a]	100%
1836	Van Buren	265	265	100
1840	Van Buren*	245	245[a]	100
1864	McClellan	226	174	77
1872	Greeley	732	686	93
1888	Cleveland*	822	822[a]	100
1892	Cleveland	910	617	68
1900	Bryan	936	936	100
1908	Bryan	1002	889	89
1916	Wilson*	1092	1092[a]	100
1936	Roosevelt*	1100	1100[a]	100
1940	Roosevelt*	1100	946	86
1944	Roosevelt*	1176	1086	92
1948	Truman*	1234	926	75
		Whig and Republican Parties		
1832	Clay	[b]	[b]	100
1844	Clay	275	275	100
1864	Lincoln*	519	494	93
1868	Grant	650	650	100
1872	Grant*	752	752	100
1896	McKinley	924	662	73
1900	McKinley*	926	926	100
1904	Roosevelt*	994	994	100
1908	Taft	980	702	72
1924	Coolidge*	1109	1065	96
1928	Hoover	1089	837	77
1932	Hoover*	1154	1127	98
1936	Landon	1003	984	98
1944	Dewey	1059	1056	100
1956	Eisenhower*	1323	1323	100
1960	Nixon	1331	1321	99

*Incumbent President
[a]Nomination by acclamation
[b]Exact number of votes is not available

[1] The basic figures for all tables in this chapter are from Richard C.
Bain *Convention Decisions and Voting Records* (Washington: The
Brookings Institution, 1960), Appendix D. All percentages and fractional votes are rounded to the nearest whole number. Where there
are switches on the first ballot, the vote given is that before switches.

more marked in recent years. Since 1928, except for incumbent Presidents, the Democrats have not passively ratified the nomination of any party figure. They rejected the opportunity to do so on five occasions. The Republicans had the same opportunity seven times, and ratified the nominations of new leaders at four conventions.

In contrast, the Democrats have been more willing to renominate incumbent Presidents. Only once has the party rejected an active candidacy of the Chief Executive. Whigs and Republicans have rebuffed incumbent Presidents four times. In modern times, however, this particular difference between the parties has ended, as both have docilely designated elected leaders for a second term.

In the second type of convention, the delegates have more, but still limited, choice in their Presidential nomination. The eventual candidate establishes a commanding lead before the convention meets, but he is not certain of actually receiving the necessary majority. This situation existed in the last three conventions of the party out of power. Dwight Eisenhower in 1952, Adlai Stevenson in 1956, and John Kennedy in 1960 earned their nominations principally through their efforts among party organizations and interest groups and their successes in primary elections. By the time the conventions opened, they had almost won their parties' nominations—almost, but not quite. Eisenhower still needed victory in the contest over the credentials of Southern delegations. Stevenson faced a possible platform fight and the opposition of former President Harry Truman. Kennedy had to concern himself both with Truman's opposition and the threat of a sudden stampede to another candidate, particularly Stevenson.

In explaining the decisions of such conventions, we must avoid, as Senator Taft warned in explaining Eisenhower's victory, "a tendency to lay too much stress on particular circumstances at the Convention and exaggerate the importance of events which made headlines at the moment."[2] The foundation of victory had been built before the delegates met. Yet, convention incidents did have some importance. The independence of the party delegations was limited, but real.

The eight cases in which the conventions exercised such limited discretion are listed in Table 8-2. The vote of the leading opponent is included to indicate the closeness of the contest. As can be seen from these votes, a basic strength of the leading candidate is the dispersion of his opposition. Only in the 1952 Republican convention was a contest between just two closely matched contenders decided on the first ballot. The 1912 convention of the G.O.P. was similar in some respects. In the other years, the front-runner was opposed by a number of aspirants. For reasons already discussed, it is difficult for major candidates to form alliances. Given a strong initial lead, therefore, the leading candidate can hope for a first ballot victory. Close contests in the future may be indicated by the declining first ballot percentages of the winning candidates.

TABLE 8-2

CONVENTIONS WITH LIMITED DISCRETION

Year	Candidate	Total Votes	Candidate Votes	Per Cent	Leading Opponent
		Democratic Party			
1904	Parker	1000	658	66%	Hearst—200
1928	Smith	1100	725	66	Hull—71
1956	Stevenson	1372	906	66	Harriman—210
1960	Kennedy	1521	806	53	Johnson—409
		Republican Party			
1856	Fremont	567	359	64	McLean—190
1892	Harrison	906	535	59	Blaine—182
1912	Taft	1078	556	52	Roosevelt—107
1952	Eisenhower	1206	595	49	Taft—500

The table also shows the effect of the two-thirds rule, operative in Democratic conventions before 1936. Un-

[2] Paul T. David *et al.*, *The Politics of National Party Conventions* (Washington: The Brookings Institution, 1960), p. 556, and *The New York Times*, November 25, 1959.

til then, Republicans held more conventions of limited discretion than Democrats. Under the old rule, only Alton
Parker and Alfred Smith were able to win first-ballot Democratic nominations against substantial opposition. Each was
only ten votes short of the required two-thirds vote on the
first ballot and achieved the nomination upon a switch of
votes. Other leading candidates have had to wait until a
later ballot before achieving the nomination, or have been
defeated, despite their initial support by an absolute majority. Without this rule, Stephen Douglas and Franklin
Roosevelt would have been named on the first ballot. James
Polk and Woodrow Wilson would never have been nominated at all. Instead, Martin Van Buren and Champ Clark
would have been the party's candidates, respectively, in
1844 and 1912. Each had an early simple majority, but
never received the necessary two-thirds vote. Since the abolition of the rule, two of three "free" Democratic conventions
have been cases of limited delegate choice.

The convention exercises real discretion in the nominations classified in the last two categories, and the selection
of a nominee is actually, as well as formally, within its
power. In the first instance, the delegates eventually approve one of the major contenders for the nomination after
considering other possibilities. Sixteen conventions—nine
Democratic and seven Whig and Republican—have nominated one of the initial leaders. Usually the task is accomplished fairly quickly. Of the major aspirants nominated for
President, fully three-fourths have been selected by the
fourth ballot. Only one Whig and three Democrats among
leading candidates have been able to achieve success on a
later vote. The differences between the parties again are
due to the old two-thirds rule, which encouraged lengthy
negotiations by reducing the pressure of incipient band
wagons.

With the abolition of the rule, and the development
of pre-convention strategies, major candidates must succeed
early in convention voting. Since Wilson's nomination, no

major candidate has required more than four ballots for victory. The last two nominations of this type were those of Dewey in 1948 and Stevenson in 1952. Each came to the convention with firm initial strength. Each was quickly judged superior to other aspirants in terms of personal attributes, policy positions, political or popular support. The opposition then was eliminated and their nominations achieved in short order. Of course, Stevenson was not a candidate in the usual sense, and he all but refused to be considered at all. However, he was a very distinct possibility to the delegates.[3]

The major candidates, their initial strength and that of their chief opponents are listed in the following table. Most successful major candidates have led the field on the first ballot. In five instances, however, the initial lead of an

TABLE 8–3

CONVENTIONS NOMINATING MAJOR CANDIDATES

Year	Candidate	Total Votes	First Votes	Per Cent	Last Ballot	Leading Opponent
		Democratic Party				
1848	Cass	254	125	43%	4	Buchanan—55
1856	Buchanan	296	136	46	17	Pierce—123
1860	Douglas	303	146	48	59	Hunter—42
1876	Tilden	738	405	57	2	Hendricks—141
1880	Hancock	738	171	23	2	Bayard—154
1884	Cleveland	820	392	48	2	Bayard—170
1912	Wilson	1094	324	30	46	Clark—441
1932	Roosevelt	1154	666	58	4	Smith—202
1952	Stevenson	1230	273	22	3	Kefauver—340
		Whig and Republican Parties				
1840	Harrison	254	91	36	2	Clay—102
1848	Taylor	280	111	39	4	Clay—97
1852	Scott	296	132	45	53	Fillmore—133
1860	Lincoln	466	102	22	3	Seward—174
1884	Blaine	820	335	41	4	Arthur—278
1916	Hughes	987	254	25	3	Weeks—105
1948	Dewey	1094	434	40	3	Taft—224

[3] See Walter Johnson, *How We Drafted Adlai Stevenson* (New York: Knopf, 1955) and Paul T. David *et al.*, *Presidential Nominating Politics in 1952* (Baltimore: The Johns Hopkins University Press, 1954), Vol. I, pp. 106-10, 117-19, 150-55, for somewhat different accounts of the nomination of the Illinois Governor.

opponent has been overcome and the candidate has then gone on to win the nomination. There is no direct relationship between the winner's percentage on the first ballot and the number of tallies necessary to reach a winning majority. Hancock, for example, first received less than a quarter of the total votes, but obtained the required two-thirds vote on the second ballot. On the other hand, Franklin Roosevelt had the largest initial vote of any candidate in this group, but his nomination was delayed until the fourth count. Moreover, of the four candidates who required more than four ballots to win the nomination, all but Wilson had at least 45 per cent of the first ballot vote. When the opposition is united, it can compel the leader to undergo a long contest.

In the final type of convention, a minor candidate is chosen as the party nominee. In this case, the delegates exercise the most discretion, as they abandon the commitments and preferences developed in the pre-convention period. The major candidates must first be eliminated. The party then selects an individual of lesser prominence, usually a compromise between the various factions which have been unable to gain victory for their own favorites. In the designation of minor candidates, there has been little difference between the parties. Of the 11 nominations in this category, six have been of Democrats and five Republicans.

As might be expected, the convention does not move to support these candidates until relatively late in the balloting. The average designation of a minor candidate comes on the tenth tally. The earliest such success was that of William Jennings Bryan on the fifth Democratic ballot of 1896; the longest deliberations involved the compromise choice of John W. Davis by the Democrats in 1924 after 103 votes. The effect of the two-thirds rule is seen again when one compares the length of time necessary for the two parties to agree on a minor aspirant as party leader. Only once has the G.O.P. needed more than ten ballots, while four Democratic conventions have gone beyond—indeed, far beyond—this point before all factions could agree on a satis-

TABLE 8-4

CONVENTIONS NOMINATING MINOR CANDIDATES

Year	Candidate	Total Votes	First Votes	Per Cent	Last Ballot	First Leader
		Democratic Party				
1844	Polk	266	0	0%	9	Van Buren—146
1852	Pierce	288	0	0	49	Cass—116
1868	Seymour	317	0	0	22	Pendleton—105
1896	Bryan	930	137	15	5	Bland—235
1920	Cox	1094	134	12	44	McAdoo—266
1924	Davis	1098	31	3	103	McAdoo—432
		Republican Party				
1876	Hayes	756	61	8	7	Blaine—285
1880	Garfield	756	0	0	36	Grant—304
1888	Harrison	820	85	10	8	Sherman—229
1920	Harding	984	66	7	10	Wood—288
1940	Willkie	1000	105	11	6	Dewey—360

factory candidate. The minor candidates, along with the first ballot leaders, are listed in Table 8-4.

In contrast to the major candidates, there is some definite, although not exact, relationship between the first ballot strength of the minor aspirant and the number of ballots necessary to achieve his designation. All of the candidates in this group who had no votes or only infinitesimal support on the initial tally were nominated on or after the tenth ballot, with the single exception of Polk. Conversely, again with a single exception of Cox, all candidates with the backing of at least a tenth of the delegates on the first ballot have won the nomination relatively quickly—by the eighth roll call.

The process by which these candidates are chosen was described by Harry Daugherty when he predicted the nomination of Harding at the Republican convention in 1920:

> Well, there will be no nomination on the early ballots. After the other candidates have failed, after they have gone their limit, the leaders, worn out and wishing to do the very best thing, will get together in some hotel room about 2:11 in the morning. Some fifteen men, bleary-eyed with lack of

sleep, and perspiring profusely with the excessive heat, will sit down around a big table. I will be with them and will present the name of Senator Harding. When the time comes, Harding will be selected, because he fits in perfectly with every need of the party and nation. He is the logical choice, and the leaders will determine to throw their support to him.[4]

As Daugherty implied, there is more involved in the minor candidate's nomination than simple exhaustion. Usually, his selection also involves some bridging or moderation of policy differences, and a relative truce in the efforts of powerful factions to gain control of the party. This compromise on substantive differences is shown by the Republican nomination of Benjamin Harrison in 1888, which followed a series of convention conflicts. "Both sides, trusting Benjamin Harrison, the meticulous, dignified, quiet, little Senator from Indiana, a brigadier general of the Civil War with a spotless record, named him in a sort of truce of God; between on the one hand, the growing power of the Mugwumps, who stood for civil service, ballot reform, a scientific tariff, hard money, with only such good times as justice would guarantee; and, on the other hand, the saber-rattling, free-and-easy advocates of manifest destiny and an open treasury."[5] Not surprisingly, the seven minor candidates who were obviously compromise choices also received the least support on the first ballot.

Not all minor candidates, however, have been compromises. Bryan's victory was clearly a triumph for the Populist and Western wing of the party, for which he had spoken in his "Cross of Gold" oration. Similarly, Willkie's nomination in 1940 was a victory for the Eastern and internationalist faction of the Republican party. In these cases,

[4] Mark Sullivan, Our Times (New York: Scribner's, 1935), Vol. VI, p. 37.
[5] William Allen White, Masks in a Pageant (New York: Macmillan, 1928), p. 77.

the convention chose a minor candidate not as a compromise, but as the new spokesman for a dominant faction.

The minor candidate is not the same as that peculiar type of nominee, the "dark horse." While every "dark horse" is a minor candidate, as defined above, the reverse is not necessarily true. The authentic "dark horse" is not only minor, but is not seriously thought of as a candidate until his name is surprisingly presented to the convention. Opinions differ as to how many such creatures there have been in American party history.[6] Of the 11 minor candidates, probably Bryan, Cox, and Willkie should not be included. All had campaigned for the nomination before the convention met, and their names were familiar enough to the delegates to gain for each of them more than a tenth of the first ballot vote. These three, at best, should be considered "grey horses." There may even be doubt that Harding and Harrison should be included in the select company, since their availability for the nomination was well-known to the delegates.

The Trend of Nominations

We have now reviewed four different types of conventions, classified according to the degree of discretion the delegates are able to exercise in the choice of Presidential candidates. Possibly the most significant trend in the party conclaves is the diminishing degree of discretion available.

An increasing proportion of conventions are held to ratify an obvious nomination, or to provide a first-ballot vic-

---

[6] Sidney Hyman, "Size-up of the Dark Horse Species," *The New York Times Magazine* (November 6, 1955), p. 9, says that "oral tradition" includes five "dark horses"—Polk, Pierce, Hayes, Garfield, and Davis. He also included Harding and Willkie. Paul David and his collaborators in their 1960 volume, p. 119, drop Willkie from this list and add Seymour. Charles E. Merriam and Harold F. Gosnell, *The American Party System*, rev. ed. (New York: Macmillan, 1937), p. 286, also add Harrison and Bryan. All are agreed that Cox was not a "dark horse."

tory for the contested front-runner. On the other hand, conventions which have gone beyond one ballot before choosing a major contender, or which have elevated a minor candidate to the position of party leader, have become less frequent. The following table summarizes the situation for both parties, using the 1896 conventions as the dividing line. This date is selected because the present party system is generally acknowledged as originating in that year. There were 31 major party conventions before 1896 (the Whigs did not meet in 1836, thereby causing the odd number), and there have been 34 since. Also included are the differences between the "in-party," controlling the White House, and the opposition "out-party."

TABLE 8–5

PATTERNS OF NOMINATIONS

Convention Type	Democratic	Whig-Republican	Total	In-Party	Out-Party
Ratification					
Until 1892	7	5	12	8	4
From 1896	7	11	18	13	5
First Ballot					
Until 1892	0	2	2	1	1
From 1896	4	2	6	1	5
Major Candidate					
Until 1892	6	5	11	5	6
From 1896	3	2	5	1	4
Minor Candidate					
Until 1892	3	3	6	2	4
From 1896	3	2	5	2	3
Totals:	33	32	65	33	32

In both parties, whether in or out of the White House, the trend is the same. Simple ratification is likely in Republican and "in-party" conventions. Contested first ballot nominations are more common among the disputatious "out-party" and Democratic organizations. In either case, the freedom of the delegates is curtailed. Reduced opportunities for independent convention action are particularly apparent in the case of nominations of major candidates after the first ballot. This decline is especially notable at "in-party" conclaves since 1896, where only one major aspirant has had to go beyond the first ballot to achieve success. Even the single exception, that of Stevenson in 1952, might not have existed if the Illinois Governor had expressed a willingness to run earlier. We may summarize these figures by comparing the first two kinds of conventions with the latter two. While party leaders and delegates could be said to exercise wide discretion in 55 per cent of the conventions held before 1896, this has been true in only 30 per cent of the succeeding party conclaves.

Reduced freedom for the delegates is further reflected in the number of ballots necessary for nomination. Before 1896, 14 conventions selected a Presidential candidate on the first ballot. Since then, 24 nominees have been chosen on the initial tally. The number of conventions requiring two to four counts has been reduced from eight to four, and a proportional decline has occured in conclaves calling the roll of the state more than ten times. In both periods, three conventions have required from five to ten ballots. The average (median) number of ballots has declined from two in the first period to one in the modern political era.

If this trend were to continue, the importance of the convention as a decision-making body might soon be at an end. We could then agree with William Carleton, who argues: "Delegates to national conventions, even the biggest of the 'big shots,' are in the process of being reduced to popular rubber stamps, very much as presidential electors were reduced to nullities during the first decade of our present federal Constitution."[7]

Statistical evidence, however, does not fully support this contention. If we examine the conventions since the watershed year of 1928, it is apparent that there has been some continuation of the trend previously noted. Since 1928, only 22 per cent of the conventions—compared to 55 per cent before 1896 and 30 per cent in the whole modern era—

[7] William G. Carleton, "The Revolution in the Presidential Nominating Convention," *Political Science Quarterly*, Vol. 72 (June, 1957), p. 224.

have been able to do more than ratify or decide a first-ballot nomination, and only one minor aspirant, Wendell Willkie, has been chosen. Since 1928, Willkie's nomination is the only one to go beyond the fourth ballot, and only one other went that far. The changes are summarized in table 8-6.

TABLE 8-6

TREND OF NOMINATIONS

| Convention Type | To 1892 | | 1896-1960 | | 1928-1960 | |
	No.	%	No.	%	No.	%
Ratification	12	39	18	53	10	56
First Ballot	2	6	6	17	4	22
Major Candidate	11	36	5	15	3	16
Minor Candidate	6	19	5	15	1	6
Totals:	31	100%	34	100%	18	100%

Although there is evidence of further decline in the independence of the convention, there is no proof that the delegates are being reduced to "rubber stamps." The percentage of conventions meeting only to ratify nominations has increased little since 1928. In fact, since the Civil War, this percentage has changed only slightly in any given period. While the proportion of contested first ballot nominations has risen, so has that of major candidates after the first ballot.

While the choice of a major candidate is still open to the convention, that of a minor candidate seems closed. The selection of Wendell Willkie, the only minor candidate to win a convention majority since 1924, is indeed the exception that proves the rule. For Willkie followed none of the accepted rules for a minor candidate. He was not a compromise choice in a deadlocked convention. He did not campaign quietly for second-choice backing from supporters of the major aspirants. He was not an inconspicuous figure waiting unobtrusively for the party leaders to turn to him in a moment of need. Rather the opposite. He was the candidate of an identifiable faction within the Republican party, who conducted an unprecedented campaign to gain popular support and force his nomination on a reluctant convention. Violating past tradition, he came to Philadelphia, the convention site, and openly solicited the votes of the delegates.[8] Through this unconventional campaign, he won 105 votes on the first ballot. If he had entered primary contests or had approached the state organizations more directly, he would certainly have entered the contest as a leading contender. In all respects but his first ballot strength, he was a major candidate.

The conclusion seems clear. "The days of the favorite son, the dark horse, the stalking horse, the smoke-filled conference room, the senatorial and congressional cabal, and the decisive trading of votes by local bigwigs are numbered, if indeed they are not already finished."[9] Conventions will reach their decisions quickly, avoiding prolonged contests and exhausted nominations of unknown but inoffensive compromise choices. The party's designation will go to an aspirant who has already established himself as a major possibility among the electorate and the party leaders. The convention's decision will be largely one of choosing from a number of major hopefuls—but, in many years, this will still be a decision for the convention to make.

The changing role of the conventions is shown by the Vice-Presidential nominations, as well as those for the top position on the ticket. In analyzing the designations for Vice-President, we cannot use the same classifications as for President, because there is little campaigning for the position of running mate, and thus no real candidacies are established before the convention meets. The field has not been limited for the delegates by organizational commitments, primary contests, and the like. The discretion of the convention can still be restricted, however, by decisions of the Presidential candidate or a small group of party leaders.

The freedom allowed to the convention as a whole

[8] Malcolm Moos, *The Republicans* (New York: Random House, 1956), pp. 409-12.
[9] Carleton, p. 224.

can be gauged by the extent of agreement on the Vice-President's selection. If the choice is concluded on one ballot without a third of the delegates in opposition, it is apparent that no opportunity for a real contest existed. Opposition of at least a third to the designated running mate, on the other hand, would indicate that the choice had not been a mere formality. The figures for the three time periods previously considered are presented below.

TABLE 8–7

TREND OF UNCONTESTED VICE-PRESIDENTIAL NOMINATIONS

| | To 1892 | | 1896-1960 | | 1928-1960 | |
	No.	%	No.	%	No.	%
Democrats	9	60	9	54	6	67
Republicans	6	40	13	79	8	89
In-Party	6	40	11	66	6	67
Out-Party	9	60	11	66	8	89
Totals[a]:	15	50%	22	66%	14	78%

[a]Because the Democrats made no nomination in 1840, there is one less candidate for Vice-President than for President. Percentages represent the proportion of all Vice-Presidential selections for the particular group in the given period.

Democrats tend to be somewhat more in conflict over the Vice-Presidential nomination than the Republicans. In part, the difference is explained by the two-thirds rule, which applied to both spots on the ticket. However, Democratic contests have continued since the abolition of the rule, occurring twice under President Franklin Roosevelt and in 1956, on the occasion of Stevenson's second nomination. Contests are also more frequent in the party controlling the White House. Presumably, eagerness to capture the Administration brings greater cohesion to the "out-party."

Certainly the most obvious conclusion that can be drawn from these figures, however, is that the nomination of a Vice-Presidential candidate is less often the prerogative of the entire convention. Until 1928, there were contests over the second spot in half of the conventions. Since then, there have been open contests in less than a quarter. Moreover, although lengthy balloting on the question has always been rare, only two conventions since 1928 have required more than one tally to reach a decision.

While retaining some influence on the Presidential nomination, the general body of delegates seems to have little to do with the choice of the Vice-President at the present time. However, the institution of the convention, as distinguished from the individuals attending it, remains important in the choice of a running mate. The convention, as an institution, provides an opportunity for party leaders to consult on the choice of a nominee for Vice-President, to form a majority coalition with the second-place nomination as one of the links in the alliance, and to reconcile the preferences of the party's new standard-bearer with the needs and demands of the professional organizations.

The continuing importance of the Vice-Presidential nomination as a means of achieving consensus can be shown by comparing convention action on Presidential and Vice-Presidential candidacies. An uncontested nomination for Vice-President indicates that an arrangement has been made beforehand. If the nomination is used to promote consensus, such an arrangement would be most likely in a convention which nominates a major candidate after the first ballot. In this situation, the major candidate needs some extra support in order to win the party leadership. Offering the Vice-Presidential designation to some group, and thereby avoiding a contest, can provide this extra support. One would expect to find more contests for the position in conventions ratifying a Presidential nomination. Assured of victory, the party leader has not had to bargain for support and therefore is not required to dictate a selection. Somewhere in between would be candidates winning a contested first ballot nomination over substantial opposition and minor candidates. These aspirants may or may not be required to select a Vice-Presidential candidate before the convention votes.

Table 8-8 indicates that the expected pattern exists

TABLE 8-8

UNCONTESTED VICE-PRESIDENTIAL NOMINATIONS,
BY CONVENTION TYPE

Convention Type	To 1892		1896-1960		1928-1960	
	No.	%	No.	%	No.	%
Ratification	4	36	12	67	7	70
First Ballot	1	50	3	50	3	75
Major Candidate	7	64	4	80	3	100
Minor Candidate	3	50	3	60	1	100
Totals[a]:	15	50%	22	66%	14	78%

[a]The ratification of Van Buren's nomination in 1840 is omitted because no Vice-Presidential candidate was named. Percentages represent the proportion of all Vice-Presidential nominations for the particular type in the given period.

in all of the three time periods. Over the years, regardless of the way in which they have selected their Presidential candidate, the conventions have tended to name their Vice-Presidential nominee without a contest. However, this tendency is more marked in those conventions where the Presidential candidate has found it more difficult to secure his victory. When a candidate does not secure victory on the first ballot, he is more willing to bargin the Vice-Presidency for additional support. Candidates whose Presidential nominations are simply ratified by the convention have less reason to foreclose a contest for their running mates.

The trend in nominations for both spots on the ticket indicates less discretion and power for the convention as a whole. In neither case, however, is there any evidence that the convention no longer serves a purpose. For President, the convention is now largely limited to a choice between major candidates—but it still retains that choice. For Vice-President, the delegates as a body have even less discretion, but the institution of the convention provides a mechanism by which consensus on the running mate and within the party as a whole can be achieved.

Causes of Change

The changes in the role of the convention are due to a large number of causes, some of which we have already noted and may now review. Certainly one major cause has been the growth of the Presidency as a position of party leadership. The great increase in the number of "ratification" conventions in the twentieth century is almost entirely the result of the renomination of incumbent Presidents. Control of the party by the President is related to developments in both the governmental and political position of the Chief Executive. Within American government, the President's power has increased with the industrialization of the United States, the rise of the nation to international power, and the growth of domestic social conflicts requiring coordinated and rapid action. At the same time, the democratization of national politics, the invention of means of mass communication, and the development of Presidential prerogatives have increased the influence of the Chief Executive on his party. Even when personally disposed to limit executive power, modern Presidents have found themselves with more means of control than those available to the most aggressive of their nineteenth-century predecessors.[10]

Repudiation of a first-term President would be difficult today because the program of the party and that of the President increasingly are identified as the same by the electorate. In 1868, the Republican platform berated Andrew Johnson, elected on the party ticket as one "who has acted treacherously to the people who elected him and the cause he was pledged to support; ... [and] who has employed his executive powers to render insecure the property, the peace, the liberty and life of citizens."[11] In 1896, the Democrats refused to approve a resolution praising the conduct of the Cleveland Administration. Since then, no party has publicly opposed the policies of a President elected under its name.

When necessary, Presidents have used their various powers to prevent any challenge to their party leadership.

[10] See Clinton Rossiter, *The American Presidency,* rev. ed. (New York): Harcourt, Brace, 1960), chaps. I, III, V.
[11] Thomas H. McKee, *The National Conventions and Platforms of all Political Parties* (Baltimore: Friedenwald, 1906), p. 138.

Theodore Roosevelt brought public pressure to bear and secured an endorsement from the Republican state convention in Ohio, the base of his likely rival in the next national convention, Mark Hanna. Taft employed federal patronage to win the support of Southern delegates in 1912, while Calvin Coolidge and Franklin Roosevelt entered a variety of primaries to reinforce their respective claims for renomination. By 1948, when Harry Truman successfully sought renomination, Presidential control of the party was so complete that his antagonists were forced to form new parties in order to make their dissatisfaction effective.

Presidential control is the most apparent element in a general development toward more centralized and national leadership within the parties. One result of this development is that major candidates, representative of a more national constituency than those of previous years, are nominated more often. The titular leader of the opposition party does not disappear from active political life, but is more likely to continue to influence his party and perhaps lead it again in the next election. Similarly, the Vice-Presidency has become a position of significance.

The influence of the general electorate on Presidential nominations, which has been augmented recently, tends to increase the opportunities for major candidates. The names and accomplishments of such leaders are likely to be relatively familiar to the electorate. Those of minor candidates, of sectional leaders, and particularly of "dark horses" will not be, and these men will be unable to gather the popular support which is increasingly crucial for convention victories.

Insofar as policy considerations enter the nominations, the trend is also toward the choice of national candidates and to more centralized leadership of the parties. The President, by the very nature of his office, concentrates the attention of the party on national issues and defines the attitude of the party on these issues. Interest groups are involved in the Presidential nomination because of the effect of the conventions' decisions on their aims. These groups are unlikely to support a candidate simply because he meets the essentially parochial tests of "availability." They seek nominees who are sympathetic to their aims.

National leaders and major candidates have taken some positions on issues, and they can be appraised with some degree of objectivity. The growing favor of titular leaders may be partially due to the fact that they have already stated their views in the course of a campaign. For similar reasons, Vice-Presidential candidates are less likely to represent positions on policy directly contradictory to those of the Presidential nominee. Interest groups and others influential in the convention are likely to remember Mark Hanna's plea in opposition to Theodore Roosevelt's nomination as running mate: "Don't any of you realize that there's only one life between this madman and the White House?"[12]

Changes in the role of conventions also are related to developments outside the party organizations. One of the most important of these has been the growth of pre-convention campaigning. Many decisions which once were made at the convention are now made before it meets. Until the advent of primaries and of the media of radio and television, most of the significant action occurred at the party conclave. Now candidates can be advanced, repulsed, and even eliminated or assured of nomination before the opening ceremonies.

Campaigning before the convention is of more benefit to some types of candidates than to others. Major candidates and acknowledged national leaders can gain from the increased emphasis on the preparatory period. Their candidacies are overt, nationwide, and sufficiently well-staffed to make use of the new techniques. Seeking an uncontested nomination or a quick convention victory, they have reason to seek all available support before the actual convention. Minor candidates or others hoping for lengthy deliberations,

[12] Malcom Moos and Stephen Hess, *Hats in the Ring* (New York: Random House, 1960), p. 153.

on the other hand, cannot benefit greatly from early campaigns. They wish most decisions to be delayed until the convention meets, until the party leaders gather in a "smoke-filled room." A vigorous preconvention campaign, however, may have eliminated some of these putative leaders, firmly committed the loyalties of others, and reduced the bargaining powers of the remainder. Willkie's nomination in 1940 showed that even a minor candidate, to be successful, must employ the tactics of preconvention campaigning.

Should an aspirant prove himself the popular favorite in pre-convention campaigning, he is now likely to gain the nomination even in the face of strong opposition from major factions of the party. Perhaps as many as a majority of the delegates present had personal preferences other than Eisenhower at the 1952 Republican convention or Kennedy at the 1960 Democratic conference. The basic decision, however, had been made earlier and outside the convention hall. The pre-convention period does not always reveal a clear popular preference. No such choice was apparent in the Democratic contest of 1952. In such a case, the convention again resembles the negotiating conference of legend—although its choice of candidates is more limited than in the past. When the public choice is clear, however, the nomination becomes basically the registration of a popular plebiscite.

Pre-convention campaigning has not been directly responsible for the diminution of convention choice for the Vice-Presidential nomination. There is little campaigning for the second-place nomination, and none among the general electorate. However, there has been an indirect effect. Because campaigning begins earlier, there is greater opportunity for the real strengths of all factions within the party to be measured and more likelihood that a firm alliance will be concluded. There is less likelihood, therefore, that an open conflict will occur over the choice of a running mate.

A final major influence resulting in decreased convention discretion has been the mass media of radio and television. One effect, as we have seen, has been to increase the importance of pre-convention campaigning and the influence of popular preferences. There have been other effects as well. Previously, parties were able to conduct their meetings in relative isolation, even though the press and some spectators attended the formal sessions. With radio and television present, however, millions of voters may be observing the convention. Insofar as the convention is a campaign rally, the larger audience is a great benefit. However, the presence of the media does not contribute to the function of the convention as a decision-making body.

For one thing, delegates cannot make decisions on a producer's timetable. If the object of the convention is to catch the maximum television audience, then the arguments, strategic maneuvers, and roll call votes necessary to reach decisions must be dispensed with, to hold that audience. On the other hand, if the delegates do engage in a factional battle, they must do so in view of millions whose support they will later ask in the election. In these circumstances, the tendency is to avoid a public display of intra-party differences so as to quell public doubt over the party's ability to govern. It is significant that the last lengthy convention came in 1924, the first year in which the conventions were reported by radio. Since 1952, the first election year in which television coverage was significant, party leaders have made further attempts to prevent public exposure of internal conflicts.

The coverage of conventions also makes it more difficult for party leaders to control the convention and to negotiate among themselves. Control is more difficult because practices which could once be carried out without mass attention are now likely to be observed by a vast audience. Thus, in 1912, the Taft faction of the Republican party was relatively free to employ the traditional "steamroller." Forty years later, Robert Taft's group was defeated when it attempted a similar strategy. In the later convention, the party also had to consider the effect of any decision on the national audience. This audience, perhaps incorrectly, had become convinced that Taft's group did not approve of "fair play." It could only be satisfied by a Taft defeat.

The recent difficulty in controlling conventions serves public interests by allowing more freedom to the party delegations. It is not clear that radio and television's effect in making negotiation more difficult has been equally beneficial. Negotiations and deals will continue to be necessary as long as there are disparate interests within the party which need to be reconciled. The increasing attention shown to the conventions by the mass media, however, may make it more difficult for these interests to find a location for their bargaining. In 1952, television crews gained access to the crucial meeting of the Republican credentials committee, and in 1960 cameras were admitted to the caucus of the Pennsylvania Democratic delegation. Such coverage satisfied public curiosity and may meet a legitimate public demand for information. Still, the privacy of convention diplomacy also deserves some respect.

> A political party is in many respects like an army preparing for battle; it is too much to ask a general or a party leader to debate in public his strategy, his choice of subordinate commanders, or his order of battle. And much of the business of a party is compromise, the finding of inclusive solutions, and the resolution of differences in a manner that will respect the reputation and preserve the political effectiveness of important political groups and interests. A combination of privacy and public debate seems indicated for the full discharge of these functions in a manner which is compatible with the right of the public to know what issues are being argued and what is being compromised.[13]

Undoubtedly deals will continue to be made. However, the difficulty in achieving privacy may change the content or at least the timing of agreements. More negotiations

[13] Charles A. Thomson, *Television and Presidential Politics* (Washington: The Brookings Institution, 1956), p. 105.

are likely to be carried out before the convention and away from the probings of radio and television. Because of the close coverage of all meetings, long and complex negotiations will prove difficult. The stimulus given to rumor by the mass media will have the same effect. The result of these developments, as of others previously discussed, will be to limit the chances of minor candidates and to enhance those of candidates who come to the convention with a large body of supporters.

In the future, we can expect the conventions of the party holding the White House to be increasingly under the control of the President and of other figures in the national organization. In the opposition party, either the acceptance of nationally prominent individuals or contests between major candidates are to be expected. The final decision will be made quickly and will be influenced greatly by the aspirants' popularity.

In the light of these past changes and possible future trends, questions arise as to the continued existence of the convention system. Is there a better way to choose the parties' and the nation's leaders? If not eliminated, how can the convention be changed to better fulfill its functions? These questions are the basis of the two concluding chapters.

Suggestions for Further Reading

Louis H. Bean, *How to Predict Elections* (New York: Knopf, 1948). A detailed statistical treatment of trends in American electoral behavior and predictions of future patterns.

Wilfred E. Binkley, *American Political Parties: Their Natural History,* 3rd ed. (New York: Knopf, 1958). The leading single-volume history of American parties, including great detail on conventions and nominating practices.

William G. Carleton, "The Revolution in the Presidential Nominating Convention," *Political Science Quarterly,* Vol. 72 (June, 1957), pp. 224-40. A well-reasoned prediction of the complete decline of the convention to mere ratifier of popular choices.

Robert A. Dahl and Charles E. Lindblom, *Politics, Economics and Welfare* (New York: Harper, 1953). A general theoretical investigation of decision-making models for the study of political life.

Henry Jones Ford, *The Rise and Growth of American Politics* (New York: Macmillan, 1898). A classic exposition of the growth of democracy and Presidential power and the effect of these changes on American political life.

Arthur N. Holcombe, *The New Party Politics* (New York: Norton, 1933). An early analysis of the basic changes bringing about more centralization and cohesion in the party system.

Charles A. McCoy, *Polk and the Presidency* (Austin: University of Texas Press, 1960). Biography of the first "dark-horse" candidate and President.

Robert Michels, *Political Parties* (New York: Collier Books, 1962). This landmark study, according to its subtitle is "a sociological study of the oligarchical tendencies of modern democracy," and particularly modern parties.

Nelson W. Polsby, "Decision-Making at the National Conventions," *Western Political Quarterly*, Vol. 13 (September, 1960), pp. 609-19. A series of logical propositions about convention behavior, designed to further a theoretical model of the institutiton.

Clinton L. Rossiter, *The American Presidency*, Rev. ed. (New York: Harcourt, Brace, 1960). In a lively style, this book demonstrates the growth and impact of the Presidency on the parties and other national institutions.

IX PROPOSALS FOR REFORM

"Politics," it is said, "is the art of the possible." Occasionally it also seems to border on the impossible, probably no more so than in the national nominating process. Through a combination of feverish primary contests in scattered and often unrepresentative states, the stimulation of the hysterical atmosphere of the convention and negotiations in smoke-filled rooms, Presidents of the caliber of Lincoln, Wilson, and Roosevelt have been chosen.

A common reaction to this situation has been a mixture of awe and incredulity. One writer is amazed at Lincoln's nomination. "Midnight conferences of liquor-stimulated politicians, deals for jobs, local leaders pulling wires to save their state tickets, petty malice, and personal jealousies —a strange compound, and the man of destiny emerges."[1]

[1] Eugene H. Roseboom, *A History of Presidential Elections* (New York: Macmillan, 1959), p. 180.

Ostrogorskii could only conclude that "God takes care of drunkards, of little children, and of the United States."[2]

Despite its absurdities, the system has remained. Clearly there must be some strength in the longest established system for the selection of party leaders in the world. Any proposed change in this process must take account of these strengths, and either retain them or substitute more vital qualities.

The Strengths of the System

One of the chief merits of the present system is the opportunity it provides for new personalities to rise quickly to the positions of party leader and President. The political parties and their convention delegates have been able to search widely for the men who serve as national leaders. Professional politicians have been preferred, as is to be expected, but the conventions have also been willing to choose men from the ranks of the military, business, the press, education, and public administration. Many paths of advancement have been available for able individuals, and the party conventions have sought and selected these individuals.

The convention system provides time and opportunity for agreement. Through it, a party is able to weigh alternatives, to consider and reconsider its decisions, and eventually to achieve a wide measure of consensus among its members. Because it possesses these characteristics, a convention is able to nominate an obscure "dark horse" or to draft a reluctant but attractive candidate. Through the convention system, candidates of the quality of Charles Evans Hughes, Woodrow Wilson, Wendell Willkie, and Adlai Stevenson have been advanced to the fore. All of these men were relative newcomers to politics or were reluctant to seek the Presidential nomination.

[2] M. Ostrogorskii, *Democracy and the Party System in the United States* (New York: Macmillan, 1910), p. 160.

In other nations, the means of advancement to party leadership are far fewer. In Great Britain, for example, an individual becomes a leader only after a long period of service in Parliament and in the Cabinet or "shadow" Cabinet. The opportunity for leadership is restricted to professional politicians who have demonstrated loyalty and service to the party. Certainly there is much to commend this system, which assures experience in government and promotes a high degree of party cohesion and responsibility. However, the British system does severely limit the party's alternatives, while also discouraging independence on the part of individual members. One may fairly claim, moreover, that the American method has produced leaders at least equal in ability to their British counterparts. While the United States has elected poorly qualified men such as Warren Harding to the Presidency, Great Britain has similarly chosen leaders of the character of Neville Chamberlain. The British selected Lloyd George and Winston Churchill in the great crises of war; the United States was led by Woodrow Wilson and Franklin Roosevelt. Individual comparisons do not prove the superiority of the American system, but they do indicate that it is not fatally defective.

Many critics of the conventions admit that able leaders have often been selected, particularly in crisis periods. They claim, however, that the results have occurred despite the system, not because of it. Thus, the English commentator Walter Bagehot declared the President is chosen "by processes which forbid the election of known men." Admitting that Lincoln, in particular, and other able leaders have been chosen by the conventions, he still dismissed the effectiveness of the method, concluding that "success in a lottery is no argument for lotteries."[3]

Actually, a great strength of the convention system is that its processes directly contribute to the selection of able leaders, although of course they do not guarantee their

[3] Walter Bagehot, *The English Constitution,* World Classics ed. (London: Oxford University Press, 1928), p. 28.

selection. In modern Presidential nominations, candidates are measured by two important criteria: popular appeal and political skill. Both of these are also relevant in considering the ability of a candidate as a prospective President.

Throughout his search for the nomination, an aspirant must demonstrate these qualities. Primary elections, opinion polls, and appearances on the mass media provide opportunities to demonstrate a public following. Without this following, his chances of success at the convention are considerably diminished. At the same time, he must show his political skill in dealing with other politicians and interest group leaders, as he seeks support at state party gatherings, interest group meetings, and the national convention itself.

To succeed as President, an individual needs many qualities. Some personal attributes of spirit and vision probably cannot be gauged by any nominating method. Administrative ability and experience are also important, and might be better appraised outside of a nominating convention. Among the most important qualities necessary to a President, however, are those which are crucial in the American system. Without popular appeal and political skill, a President will be unable to rally either public or governmental support for his programs. These attributes are necessary, if not sufficient, conditions for Presidential leadership.[4]

In securing a Presidential nomination, an individual is now demonstrating his ability not only to lead his party but to lead the nation. It is not true, as James Bryce contended, that "the merits of a President are one thing and those of a candidate another thing."[5] The two are closely related. Any suggested change in the method of Presidential nomination should preserve this relationship.

[4] See Richard Neustadt, *Presidential Power: The Politics of Leadership* (New York: Wiley, 1960).
[5] James Bryce, *The American Commonwealth*, 3rd rev. ed. (New York: Macmillan, 1914), Vol. I, p. 79.

Lincoln's nomination, which Bagehot regarded as a lucky accident, is in fact a demonstration of the strength of the convention. Lincoln was not an exception, but only the best example of the type of candidate preferred by the delegates—moderate, "available," popular, and politically skilled. His selection, wrote a disappointed Murat Halstead, was "a success of the ruder qualities of manhood and the more homely attributes of popularity over the arts of a consummate politician and the splendor of accomplished statesmanship."[6] Yet, Lincoln's selection was also certainly one of the glories of the American system.

The convention also provides a means of achieving party and national unity. The American government abounds in centrifugal forces from decentralized parties to the federal division of powers. Some unifying mechanisms are needed. The nominating process, culminating in the negotiations and decisions of the convention, is one of the most important of these mechanisms.

Through the compromises and deals concluded at the convention, thousands of state and local party organizations are temporarily drawn together for the Presidential campaign. To maintain its strength, a party must "seek bargains between the regions, the classes, and the other interest groups. It is intended to bring men and women of all beliefs, occupations, sections, and racial backgrounds, into a combination for the pursuit of power."[7] The convention provides an excellent locale for the reconciliation of these diverse groups.

Party unity is not simply desirable in itself, but as a contribution to the effective working of democracy. When each of two parties is reasonably united, the voters have a real and effective choice before them. The alternatives are

[6] Murat Halstead, *Three Against Lincoln*, ed. by William Hesseltine (Baton Rouge: Louisiana State University Press, 1960), pp. 176-77.
[7] Herbert Agar, *The Price of Union* (Boston: Houghton Mifflin, 1950), p. 689.

organized and the electorate does not have the impossible task of choosing its government from a multitude of candidates.

Many theorists now view the competition for leadership as the basic functional principle of democracy.[8] By promoting agreement among differing factions, the conventions provide a means by which this competition can be organized. The unity of American parties is delicate and fragile. Any changes in the nominating system which would further weaken the parties' cohesion must be closely examined. Clinton Rossiter has written, "No America without democracy, no democracy without politics, no politics without parties, no parties without compromise and moderation."[9] To this, one might only add, "no compromise and moderation without conventions."

A fourth advantage of the present system, centered on the conventions, is its flexibility. The conventions are encumbered by almost no legal restrictions. They make their own rules and can freely change them every four years. Over the years, they have exhibited great adaptability, and can quickly change to meet new popular demands or changed circumstances. Thus the conventions have responded to the direct primary, the advent of radio and television, and the increase in Presidential power. While the form has remained recognizable, the conventions today are far different from those of the nineteenth century.

The flexibility of conventions is shown by their ability to perform a multitude of functions. In a short period of time, a representative party body is able to nominate its leaders, declare its principles, settle questions of internal administration, and initiate a Presidential campaign. Since all of these vital tasks are performed by the same group, the decisions made tend to be consistent and to form a coherent

[8] See Joseph Schumpeter, *Capitalism, Socialism and Democracy*, 3rd ed. (New York: Harper, 1950), pp. 269-302.
[9] Clinton Rossiter, *Parties and Politics in America* (Ithaca: Cornell University Press, 1960), p. 1.

pattern. The party therefore is likely to present a clear image to the voter. On the other hand, some proposals to reform the convention system involve a separation of these functions. Implementing these changes would create the risk of incoherence in party policy and decisions.

The present system has the final advantage of tradition and legitimacy. The nominating process is well-known in the nation, and both the electorate and party politicians can plan their actions in accord with accepted procedures. The decisions of the convention are widely regarded as authoritative. All factions of the party are likely to accept these decisions and to follow the mandates given by the delegates. The authoritative character of the convention is symbolized by the customary motion to make unanimous the convention's choice of a Presidential nominee. This motion demonstrates the defeated aspirants' acceptance of the delegates' decision.

Although bitter contests have been frequent in party history, refusal to accept the convention's decision has been rare. Only twice, in 1860 and 1912, has a major faction refused to acknowledge the authority of the party conclave and gone on to form a third party. Other revolts have been limited to small minorities. Considering the feudal decentralization of American parties and the rivalry between their factions, this record is a remarkable testament to the legitimacy with which the nominating conventions have been invested.

Conventions are accepted as legitimate, among other reasons, because they operate on the democratic principle of majority rule. No candidate can be nominated unless he is supported by an absolute majority of the delegates. There is no possibility of a minority candidate winning by a plurality, as often occurs in the nomination and election of state and local officials.

In summary, the conventions are more than colorful and theatrical exercises or political lotteries. They also constitute a valuable and flexible institution which contributes to the search for new talent in government, measures candidates' political skill and personal appeal, and promotes party unity. Having explored their virtues, we may now examine proposed reforms and replacements.

Presidential Primaries

The most widespread proposals for reform of the Presidential nominating process are those to substitute a single national primary for the present mixed system of state primaries, state convocations, and a final national convention. The reform was first given wide currency by Woodrow Wilson in his first Presidential message to Congress in 1913. Although lacking Executive sponsorship since Wilson's time, the idea remains popular. In 1955 a Gallup poll found nearly three-fourths of a national sample in favor of the suggested change.[10]

The case for a national primary to choose Presidential candidates generally rests on two assertions. First, it is held that better candidates will be chosen through a popular election than by a conclave of party delegates. Second, selection through the primary is held to be more democratic. Since the voters already nominate candidates for most positions on the state and local level, it is said, the logic of democracy requires that the candidate for Chief Executive also be selected through a popular primary. Writing in 1860, Murat Halstead summarized the views which have continued to be held by opponents of the convention system:

> The lesson to the Nation ... is the necessity for the abolition of the Caucus System which, in whatever party organization operative, is a system of swindling, by which the people are defrauded out of the effective exercise of the right of suffrage. ... The revenues of King Caucus are corruption funds— ...

[10] U.S. Senate, Judiciary Committee, *Nomination and Election of President and Vice-President*, Hearings on S. J. Res. 3 and others, 84th Cong., 1st sess. (1955), p. 327.

his platforms of principles are elaborations of false
pretenses—his nominees are his obsequious viceroys
—and he is the power behind the chairs of our chief
magistrates, and under the tables of our cabinets,
far more potent than those who visibly assume
authority. If a Republican form of government is
to be preserved in our confederacy, the people
must make a bonfire of his throne.[11]

The quality of candidates, and their adequacy as
Presidents, cannot be fully discovered by any system. However, it would be difficult to prove that the candidates for
Chief Executive, on the whole, have been inferior men.
Many clearly superior individuals have been nominated by
the conventions. While others of quality, such as John Calhoun and Daniel Webster, were rejected by the delegates,
one can agree with Harold Laski that there were "powerful
reasons against their elevation in any representative democracy."[12]

In reviewing the party nominees defeated for the
Presidency, Irving Stone casts some doubt on the ability
of the electorate to choose superior individuals. Of 19 men
defeated up to the 1944 election, Stone considers nine as
more able than the successful candidate and three as equally
qualified. Only in a minority of seven cases does he find
that the electorate chose "the best man."[13] Of course, one
author's opinion is not conclusive, but it indicates that the
conventions may be as able to judge the quality of men as
the voters.

The second contention, that nomination through the
primary is more democratic, is not as obvious as it might
seem. Many would argue that democracy means more than

[11] Halstead, p. 279.
[12] Harold J. Laski, *The American Presidency* (New York: Harper,
1940), p. 49.
[13] Irving Stone, *They Also Ran* (Garden City: Doubleday, Doran,
1943), pp. 191, 367. Stone does not deal with candidates before 1824
or those both defeated and elected in different elections. I have reversed his listing of Hayes as the defeated candidate in 1876.

the casting of ballots. The voter must also be given some meaningful and organized choice of alternatives. To facilitate such a choice, at least two relatively united and cohesive parties are necessary. Primaries tend to disrupt this unity and cohesion by stimulating factional conflict. In primaries, moreover, the voter is less aware of the real choices involved than in a general election. Policy differences between primary contestants tend to be undeveloped and the candidates cannot be distinguished on the basis of their different party labels. Increased importance is given, as a result, to distorting factors such as personality, financial ability, and interest group support.

If instituted, a national presidential primary would undoubtedly produce effects which cannot be fully predicted. However, the history of state primary elections indicates that some of these results might be quite undesirable. In states with a competitive party system, interest in the primaries is low, with only from 25 to 35 per cent of the potential electorate taking part. If the same turnout occurred in a presidential primary, each party's candidates might be selected by as few as five per cent of the voters. The small vote in primaries, moreover, is unrepresentative of the party as a whole, in contrast to a convention. Rather, a disproportionate part of the primary vote is cast in those areas in which the party is particularly strong. Two results follow. First, nominations tend to be captured almost exclusively by aspirants from the party's areas of strength. Second, the party organizations in the weak areas tend to atrophy, as they are left without any function to perform and with little chance of gaining party nominations. The total effect is to make parties unrepresentative and limited in their appeal.[14]

In national politics the effect might be that all Republican nominations would be captured by candidates from the farm states, while Democratic designations would only

[14] V. O. Key, Jr., *American State Politics: An Introduction* (New York: Knopf, 1956), chaps. IV-VI.

go to Southerners. This would obviously complicate the parties' task of promoting consensus in the nation while limiting their opportunities to expand into areas of present weakness. The extension of a competitive party system to present one-party states would be hindered severely. To the extent that party competition is limited, democracy itself would be limited, and in a much more important way than by restrictions on the direct primary. These general defects of primary elections apply to all specific suggested changes.

The proposals for a national primary vary principally on the specific roles, if any, which they would retain for the convention. All of them, it may be said, lose most of the advantages of the convention system while also introducing new problems.

The simplest and most radical proposal was supported by the late Senator William Langer of North Dakota. Under this plan each party would hold a primary throughout the nation on a single day. Candidates would be placed on the ballot by obtaining a petition signed by one per cent of the party's national membership. The candidate receiving the most votes, even if only a plurality, would be the party's nominee for President.[15]

The Langer proposal presents a multitude of legal and practical defects typical of most plans for a national primary. It would require a Constitutional amendment and a national definition of party membership. Such changes would represent a significant weakening of state power in the federal system. Gathering and checking 300,000 petition signatures would represent a formidable task for any candidate, given the absence of formal organizations. The system would be obviously defective in allowing the choice of a minority of the party's members to be its Presidential candidate. In most cases, and certainly in the party out of power, there will be more than two serious candidates. This makes

[15] See Senate Hearings, pp. 1-10 for the details of the various proposals.

a minority choice not only possible, but likely. Even if these objections could be overcome, however, the intrinsic defects would remain.

The Langer proposal, like many others, would lose advantages of the convention system. One effect would be to greatly reduce the likelihood of quick advancement to the Presidency of new political leaders. Unable to judge the qualifications of relatively obscure individuals, the electorate would be confined to a choice among the most well-established personalities. A national primary, moreover, would necessarily be restricted to the active and announced candidates. Such restriction would end the tradition that "the office seeks the man." More importantly, it would eliminate those who are unwilling or unable to seek their party's nomination in open competition. The possibility of a draft would be completely eliminated. In 1952, for example, Adlai Stevenson would almost certainly have declined to enter a national primary, and Dwight Eisenhower might have refused as well. The result would have been a narrowing of the alternatives available to the parties. Leaving the 1952 case aside, the long-term effect of the narrowing of alternatives must be the selection of some candidates inferior to those not considered. In an extreme case, "fate may . . . decree that only the most egregious self-seekers and political charlatans shall be on the ballot."[16]

Another defect of a national primary would be its failings as a test of a candidate's skill in dealing with other politicians. Since the nomination would be decided directly by the party voters, there would be less need and opportunity for a candidate to demonstrate this kind of political ability. As a result, one of the qualities necessary for a President would be untested.

It is possible, of course, that the state and local organizations would remain active in the nomination of a President, even if they must exercise their influence in the pri-

[16] Paul T. David et al., Presidential Nominating Politics in 1952 (Baltimore: The Johns Hopkins University Press, 1954), Vol. I, p. 200.

mary rather than in the convention. In such a case, an aspirant would seek their support and thereby demonstrate his political skill. However, to the extent that party groups intervene in the primary, they destroy its original purpose: to transfer their control over nominations to the unorganized electorate.

If the parties do not intervene in the primaries, others will. Only in a simplistic theory of democracy do voters reach their decisions without any outside influences. If the parties are restricted, their place will be taken by agencies less responsive to broad public demands. In the absence of identifying party labels, the candidates will emphasize personality appeals. The mass media and public relations agencies, skilled in exploiting personality appeals, will increase in influence. Candidates will be deprived of the manpower and financial resources of the parties. They will be required to turn to individual contributors and interest groups for support. In fact, the interest groups may take the initiative, in an effort to guarantee "that qualified candidates satisfactory to them are on the primary election ballot."[17] It is difficult to see how either more qualified candidates or a more representative democracy would be furthered by such changes.

Rather than promoting democracy, a national Presidential primary might impair it, by damaging the unity and effectiveness of the parties. Engaged in a nationwide contest, the various factions of the party would draw apart. Repeated contests between the factions might result in the formal separation of the contending groups and the collapse of the two-party system. The task of unifying the parties would be further complicated by the likelihood that the primary victor would represent a particular faction, rather than a moderate compromise choice. The disunity created by the election competition itself would be increased by the result.

In the general election, the party would be handi-

[17] *Loc. cit.*

capped further by its choice of a more extreme, factional candidate. The nominee's appeal to independent and opposition voters would be severely restricted. Consequently, his and the party's chances of victory would be reduced. Of course, both parties might be at an equal disadvantage. In this case, however, the nation as a whole would suffer the divisive effects of a contest between two extreme factional leaders.

In a convention, these problems can be considered and in large measure resolved. Defeated factions can be conciliated. A moderate candidate and program able to unify the party can be discovered. The appeal of different individuals to the opposition and to independent voters can be brought to bear. In a national primary, these questions would be subordinated.

The proposal for a national presidential primary is also defective in its inflexibility. Senator Langer, in fact, would have written his plan into the Constitution itself. Once adopted, any minor future changes would require further formal amendments. The process would be cumbersome, if not ludicrous. Even if established by statute rather than by constitutional amendment, a national primary would mean a more stringent regulation of the nominating process than now exists. The easy adaptability of the conventions would be lost. A primary law written to deal with the situation of one year might be totally inapplicable at the next election. Such a law might well result in an unintended distortion of the voter's desires.

Particularly lacking in a national primary would be the ease with which conventions accomplish the non-nominating functions of the conventions: writing platforms, engendering campaign enthusiasm, and governing the party. Some provision undoubtedly would be made for the accomplishment of these other functions. However, no arrangement could be entirely satisfactory, for it would mean a separation of tasks that are inherently related. The result could be great differences between the policies of the party's candidate and those declared in the official platform, for example, or a campaign rally on behalf of a candidate opposed by a majority of the participants.

The Langer plan is particularly unsatisfactory in its provisions for the selection of a Vice-Presidential candidate. Under the plan, there would be a simultaneous choice of a running mate when the party leader was chosen. This proposal fails to meet all four standards suggested in Chapter VII. It would not promote party unity or increase the ticket's electoral appeal either to defeated party factions or to voters different from those favoring the presidential nominee. Public interests would also be neglected, for there would be the possibility of policy conflicts between the two running mates and the probability that the second spot would be occupied by an individual of too little prominence to be considered for President.

The defects of the Langer proposal are evident in other proposals for a national primary. One that retains more of the federal principle is that of Senator George Smathers of Florida. The party's nominee would not be chosen by direct vote. Instead, each state would have a number of "nominating votes," equal to its electoral votes. A candidate would receive nominating votes from each state in proportion to his popular primary vote in that state. If one candidate received a majority of the nominating votes throughout the nation, he would be the party's candidate. If none received a majority, a second primary would be held, limited to the two leading candidates.

The Smathers proposal would be little more effective than the Langer proposal in allowing the rapid advancement of new leaders. Nor would preserving a state role in Presidential nominations contribute to a testing of the political skill of the aspirants. It would certainly make campaigning even more difficult, however, as a candidate would have to concern himself with each individual nominating vote rather than the total national result.

This proposal has only one definite advantage over

the Langer plan: it might prevent the nomination of a candidate by a minority vote. It would do so, however, at the cost of distorting party structure and possibly shattering party unity. By disregarding geographical variations in party strength, the Smathers plan would revive the inequities characteristic of conventions before the reforms of the twentieth century. The few Republican voters of Mississippi would have as much influence over the choice of a candidate as the many party members in Kansas. A strongly Democratic state such as Rhode Island would have no more voice in the party's choice of a leader than the Republican stronghold of South Dakota. Furthermore, the provision for a second or "run-off" primary would encourage the multiplication of party factions and make their eventual unification for an election campaign unlikely. In the South, where the "run-off" primary is well established, its effect has almost universally been to disrupt and divide the party organizations into a number of discordant and unstable factions.

Despite the provision for a second primary, there is still no assurance that the candidate chosen will actually be the most popular choice. It might well be the case, for example, that a majority favors neither of the two leaders in the first primary, but that one could form in support of a third candidate. The mechanism of the primary does not allow the expression of such an order of preferences. The convention, on the other hand, does allow the switching of votes until a candidate has been found who is satisfactory to most of the party.

The Smathers proposal has no provision for a Vice-Presidential nomination and would presumably leave this decision to the parties. With the two leaders selected by different processes, however, the possibility of disagreement between them and of incoherence in the party's positions would be great. The proposal would also separate the Presidential nomination from all other aspects of party decision-making. Like the Langer plan, it is uncomfortably inflexible.

More of a role is granted to the party conventions by

Senator Estes Kefauver, who has had extensive experience with both primaries and conventions. One procedural element deserves commendation. Under the Kefauver plan, the Constitution would be amended simply to give Congress the power to provide for national primaries. Detailed regulations would be left to ordinary legislation. This procedure is certainly more flexible and desirable than that of other reformers.

If a Constitutional amendment were passed, Senator Kefauver would proceed with a national primary law, establishing a system similar to those proposed by Woodrow Wilson and by Louise Overacker, an early exponent of presidential primaries among political scientists.[18] Under this plan, the voters in each state would select pledged delegate slates to the national convention. Each state delegation would remain committed so long as its candidate received a tenth of the total convention vote. If a candidate won a majority of the delegates in the primary, he would obviously win the nomination on the first ballot. If no candidate won a majority, the convention would be required to choose its nominee from the three individuals placing highest in delegate votes.[19]

This plan has a number of advantages over both the Langer and Smathers proposals. It would be flexible and would leave the convention with some freedom, while promoting some congruence in its decision on candidates, platform and party government. By retaining the convention, it would retain a device for the measurement of aspirants' political skill. In addition, by allowing the convention to make the final decision when there is no clear popular preference, the Kefauver plan would provide an

[18] Louise Overacker, *The Presidential Primary* (New York: Macmillan, 1926), pp. 194-96. Both Wilson and Overacker would have eliminated the present method of selecting the delegates. Wilson would substitute a conference of some 600 public and party officials. Overacker suggested a conference of 150 persons, chosen by candidates for the nomination in proportion to their votes in the primary.
[19] Senate Hearings, pp. 110-14.

opportunity for the selection of new leaders.

However, the chances of new personalities would be severely limited by the restriction of the convention's choice to the top three contestants in the primary. Reluctant candidates and "dark horses" would be almost entirely eliminated under this proposal, since they are unlikely either to enter the primary or to place sufficiently high in the number of pledged delegates. There also remains some possibility that the successful candidate or candidates will represent extreme factions, making it difficult to unify the party and to appeal to non-party members in the general election.

The most serious defect of the plan is its destructive impact on party unity. Once delegations to the conventions were chosen, assuming no candidate had a majority, it is difficult to understand how any agreement could be reached. Each delegation would be committed both emotionally and legally to some candidate. Each would be loath to abandon its particular preference. The conciliatory functions of conventions would be hindered.

How then would party consensus be achieved? Presumably, sheer necessity would result in the nomination of some candidate. However, final agreement would be made even more difficult by the limitation of the field to the top three contenders. Party conferences are likely to become longer, perhaps approaching the length of those in the nineteenth century. In the process, major party figures most likely would veto one another, party dissension would increase, and the electorate would be confused. Some of the failings of past conventions were due to the limitations placed on delegates by previous instructions. In the 1920 Republican convention, for example, a decision could not be reached quickly because a large proportion of the delegates were bound to Wood, Lowden, or Johnson. In the end, it became necessary to nominate Harding. Four years later, in the marathon Democratic contest of 1924, pledged delegations were unable or unwilling to drop their previous commitments. Physical exhaustion alone forced a decision and the selection of Davis on the 103rd ballot. To make the convention system work, a comparatively large number of delegations must be free to maneuver, to bargain, and to transfer their votes. This would be impossible if the Kefauver plan were adopted.

In the Kefauver plan, the Vice-President would be chosen by the convention from the top three defeated Presidential aspirants. This plan has the advantage of allowing the convention sufficient freedom to promote coherence in the party's decisions on the two spots on the slate. By limiting the choice to three men, however, the plan may be too inflexible and may be thoroughly inapplicable in some years. Incidentally, under this plan, Senator Kefauver could not have been nominated for Vice-President in 1956.

A somewhat similar plan is that of Senator Paul Douglas. Its chief advantage is that it would not require any Constitutional amendment, but would employ federal grants-in-aid to the states to promote primary elections. A preference poll would be held on the same day in all participating states. Delegates could be chosen by any method, but they would be bound to support the leader in the poll in their districts or states until his vote fell below a tenth of the convention total. In return for adhering to federal standards, the state would receive up to 20 cents for every vote cast. No provision is made for the selection of the Vice-Presidential candidate.[20]

If the Douglas plan were widely adopted, its effect would be similar to the Kefauver scheme, and would be subject to the same criticisms. The plan has an additional, although less important, weakness in not providing for the election of delegates personally loyal to the primary victory. While these delegates will be bound to support the aspirant

[20] David, Vol. I, pp. 217-18.

on nominating ballots, there is no assurance that they will support him on other questions raised in the convention.

The Douglas plan has much merit, however, if considered simply as a reform within the present convention system, rather than a replacement of it. If this plan were adopted, it would introduce some desirable uniformity into the presently confused system of primaries. The results of those primaries would be more representative of national opinion and more valuable to the convention delegates as a guide to popular preferences.

One final plan involving a national primary is to hold it after the convention. Delegates would meet to make rules for the party, write its platform, and eliminate all but two aspirants for the Presidential nomination. Of these two, one would be designated the nominee in a later national primary. Alternatively, the national primary would be held only if the convention failed to make a choice on the first ballot by an absolute majority. In this way, it is held, the party organizations would retain an effective role, the electorate would be made aware of the issues and conflicts in the party, and the final choice would still be made in a democratic manner.[21]

An obvious defect of this plan is the possibility of public fatigue. With voters probably continuing to participate in primaries before as well as after the conventions, and presumably observing the conventions, the electorate may become too sated with politics to bother to vote on election day itself. More fundamentally, this plan would deprive the convention of its central reason for existence and would sever the relationship between the nomination and the other functions of the party body. The convention would determine the nomination only when there was no vigorous contest, when there was no need for a convention at all. The party meeting in other cases would be only "a prologue without a play."[22]

[21] See Overacker, pp. 187-93; David, Vol. 1, pp. 212-213.
[22] Bagehot, p. 19.

The Presidential nomination itself could be seriously affected. Party delegates would become irresponsible, since they would not bear the burden for a definitive choice. Only well-established leaders might be selected for the post-convention primary, with little attempt made to assess new talent. In such a case, the two final aspirants very likely would represent two extreme factions. Or, conversely, minority factions unable to agree on a candidate might combine to keep the most distinguished leaders from the primary ballot, leaving the electorate with a choice between unknowns. When the convention bears the final responsibility for a selection, it is unlikely to act so as to impair the public interest or its own chances of electoral success. When it is free of this responsibility, its behavior may be less salutary.

Once the final contestants were selected, furthermore, the party factions would be engaged in an exhausting and divisive campaign. After the primary, the defeated faction would be asked to support a candidate it had just opposed vigorously. Obviously this system would promote party disunity, and candidates unrepresentative of the entire party, rather than party unity and moderate candidates. Given the incohesive nature of American parties, the strain of such a contest might prove too great for the thin adhesive of party unity.

Under Charles Merriam's plan for pre-primary conventions, the Vice-Presidential choice would be the runner-up in the national Presidential primary. This plan would assure the nomination of prominent men for the second position, but it would not secure party unity, or a diversity of appeals to the electorate, nor would it guarantee basic policy agreement between the two designees. The parties might find themselves presented by the voters with some unusual tickets. Thus the 1952 Republican ticket would have consisted of Dwight Eisenhower and Robert Taft, probably in that order, while the Democratic slate might have been Estes Kefauver and Richard Russell. Of course, these combinations are only based on supposition, but they indicate the possible results of such a change.

Under any of these proposed primary systems, one may speculate that some of the most able Presidential candidates would never have been nominated. Lincoln and Wilson are among many brought to the fore by the conventions who might otherwise never have gained party leadership. Any of the primary systems suggested, on the other hand, probably would not have prevented the nomination of Ulysses S. Grant, George McClellan, or other war heroes whose qualifications for the Presidency were limited.

Generally, the supposition underlying the proposals for a national primary is that the conventions will reject the most popular and most qualified candidate in favor of some obscure but pliant party professional. Advocates of the system are symbolically seeking to reverse the outcome of the 1912 Republican convention. Such action is unlikely to be repeated. Aside from the delegates' patriotic interest in choosing the most able candidate, they also have a selfish interest in winning the election. When there is a definite popular favorite, they will nominate him. If the electorate clearly demands the best, the delegates will select him. The real need is not to abolish the convention, but to improve it, and the party system it epitomizes. "The problem of popular government is at bottom a problem of party government."[23]

Improvements within the Convention

The basic argument presented above is that the convention system should be retained. It is a useful instrument of representative democracy, one responsive to popular demands and able to contribute to the choice of leadership.

While many agree that the convention has real advantages, a number of changes within the system have been proposed.

[23] Key, p. 268.

One approach to internal reform of the convention is represented by the Committee on Political Parties of the American Political Science Association. In a 1950 report, the Committee sought a "more responsible two-party system." Its goal was parties more centralized and disciplined than now exist. Such a system would require "first, that the parties are able to bring forth programs to which they commit themselves and, second, that the parties possess sufficient internal cohesion to carry out these programs."[24]

As to the national party convention, the Committee assumed "its continuation as the principal representative and deliberative organ of the party," while also criticizing it as presently "unwieldy, unrepresentative and less than responsible." To correct these defects, a number of changes were proposed. It was suggested that the convention be reduced to some 500 to 600 delegates. Most of the delegates would be directly elected, and would be apportioned among the states in proportion to the party vote in each state. The convention would also include some 150 ex-officio delegates, including representatives in Congress and party officials.

Of major concern to the Committee was the formulation and implementation of the party platform. Established practices were criticized as "too hurried and too remote from the process by which actual decisions are made to command the respect of the whole party and the electorate." In the proposed reform, the platform would be prepared in advance with the participation of the party's legislative and executive leaders. The platform, to be considered binding, would be both proposed and interpreted by a party council of 50 members including members from all groups within the party.[25]

Obviously, these recommendations go far beyond the reform of the convention itself. They involve funda-

[24] American Political Science Association, Committee on Political Parties, *Toward a More Responsible Two-Party System* (New York: Rinehart, 1950), p. 1.
[25] *Ibid.*, pp. 28-56, *passim.*

mental changes in the American party system, and their desirability and feasibility has been widely disputed.[26] There are evident defects in the proposals affecting the convention. The Committee has concerned itself principally with the policy-making functions of the conventions, and has neglected their central purpose, nominations. However, these two cannot be separated. The manner in which the party leader is chosen will have a decisive influence on party policy, regardless of the procedure used for writing the platform. The aim of more disciplined parties could be thwarted by this neglect of the nominating process. Thus, if the proposal for direct election of most delegates were adopted, the effect would be similar to a national presidential primary. The centralized party leadership would always be subject to overthrow by a party maverick in the elections for delegates. No centralized party system could exist without control over the major nominations, but the Committee proposes only limited control.

It is also unclear whether the convention will have much of a policy role beyond approval of the proposals of the Party Council. The latter body will include the major leaders of the party and probably a large number of the Presidential aspirants. It would write and interpret the platform, establish internal party rules, and supervise Congressional nominations and party finance. The conventions would have little to do but ratify these actions and conduct a campaign rally—and even this would involve only a small proportion of the number of delegates who presently participate. The advantages of a large and representative body would be lost.

The defect of the political scientists' committee report is that it could reduce the convention to a position of only formal power. In contrast are proposals for giving the delegates increased independence and authority. John Lederle,

[26] Julius Turner, "Responsible Parties: A Dissent from the Floor," *American Political Science Review,* Vol. 45 (March, 1951), pp. 143-52.

for example, suggests that we adopt the procedures followed in Canadian nominating conventions. In that country, individuals are placed in contention for the position of party leader by a written notice to the convention. Each candidate is allowed two speakers on his behalf, and the aspirant himself addresses the delegates. The nomination is made by an absolute majority of individual, secret, written ballots. These procedures, it is claimed, create "an atmosphere of dignity and deliberation almost totally lacking in American party conventions." Moreover, according to Lederle, "Canadian parties . . . have given the delegate a chance to be independent if he so desires. . . . Convention procedures are peculiarly adapted to insure free self-expression . . . and at the same time avoid the irrational, emotional aberrations often associated with the convention process in this country."[27]

This argument is probably too critical of American conventions and too laudatory of Canadian practices. The irrational nature of American conventions has been grossly exaggerated, and a major theme of the preceding chapters has been the underlying logic and rationality of Presidential nominations. Lederle has certainly overstated the independence of the Canadian delegate. Politically conscious individuals will come to a convention with definite preferences and, if they are acting rationally, will use tactics and strategy to bring others to their view. To expect a truly autonomous decision on the part of each delegate is to ignore the reality of the political process. It is even more naive to expect to produce this result by some changes in formal procedures. American conventions could easily adopt speeches by the candidates, secret individual ballots and the like. It is difficult to believe that these changes alone would make much difference in the substantive results.

What is important about this view is not the pro-

[27] John. W. Lederle, "National Conventions: Canada Shows the Way," *Southwestern Social Science Quarterly*, Vol. 25 (September, 1944), pp. 130-38, *passim*.

cedural details but the underlying philosophy. Lederle favors a convention basically free of popular mandates, made up of delegates with "fairly open minds and uninstructed on the leadership issue."[28] In effect, he advocates a system of indirect election or aristocratic selection, whereby party representatives are given complete discretion in the choice of a party leader and, thereby, of the candidate for Prime Minister.

In the nineteenth century, the American convention system operated with such discretion. In modern times, devices have been evolved to introduce popular preferences. Presently, the convention system represents a balance between popular mandates and party discretion, and the strength of the system lies in this balance. Lederle would shift the balance toward increased discretion, while the advocates of a national presidential primary would increase the role of popular opinion. Both proposals are inadequate because they concentrate on only one aspect of the nominating process. If that process is to be improved, the claims of both popular choice and of party responsibility must be considered.

In contrast to the critics, the directors of the most extensive study of the nominating process are fundamentally satisfied with the present system. According to Richard S. Childs, the experience of 1952 shows "a pervasive decency and fair play in American politics even in the operation of diverse State systems which are wide open to perversion and corruption. Precinct caucuses and party conventions could have been packed but rarely were. . . . Factions that could easily have been suppressed were fairly counted in. Party governments untouched by law commonly respected parliamentary procedures."[29] In the national conventions, the authors observed that both parties chose the popular favorite among the aspirants, that the delegates were "remarkably representative," and that decisions were generally

[28] *Ibid.*, p. 124.
[29] Senate Hearings, p. 97.

made under conditions of due process and fairness, with little evidence of manipulation or "boss control." They concluded that the record of the 1952 conventions is "a tribute to the vitality of American political institutions."[30]

Impressed with the quality of the convention, they recommended a variety of procedural improvements to increase its efficiency as "a representative assembly of the party." In order to improve the deliberative atmosphere, they recommended the elimination of fractional votes, the seating of alternate delegates off the floor, and increased disciplinary powers for convention officers. To insure more responsible action, they suggested the publication of convention proceedings, some device such as an oath of individual responsibility, a prohibition of the acceptance of financial help from any candidate, and the provision of financial aid to delegates by the federal government.[31]

These suggestions are generally well-designed to improve the workings of the nominating process. None of them would hinder the operations of the convention or prevent it from fulfilling any of its functions. However, it is not possible to distinguish the truly significant proposals unless we are aware of the future of the convention and of the party system as a whole. If, for example, future conventions are unlikely to deliberate on party policy in any case, it is unnecessary to effect procedural reforms intended to increase their ability to deliberate. It is therefore necessary to venture into the prediction of future trends. This risky task is assumed in the next and final chapter.

Suggestions for Further Reading

American Political Science Association, Committee on Political Parties, *Toward a More Responsible Two-Party System* (New York: Rinehart, 1950). A far-reaching proposal to create more disciplined, programmatic parties, which has aroused controversy from the time of its publication to the present.

[30] David, Vol. I, pp. 234-36.
[31] *Ibid.*, pp. 244-47.

James M. Burns, *The Deadlock of Democracy* (Englewood Cliffs: Prentice-Hall, 1963). Analysis of the conflicts between Presidential and Congressional "parties," and a plea for greater party responsibility.

Thomas K. Finletter, *Can Representative Government Do the Job?* (New York: Reynal & Hitchcock, 1945). In the same tradition, this reform proposal concentrates on using political parties to bridge the gap created by the Constitutional separation of powers.

Edward J. Flynn, *You're the Boss* (New York: Viking, 1947). An expert practitioner's endorsement of traditional political practices, including nominating conventions.

Estes Kefauver, "Indictment of the Political Convention," *The New York Times Magazine* (March 16, 1952), pp. 9, 59-61, 63. A critique by a leading Presidential aspirant of the past, who has known victory in primaries and defeat in conventions.

V. O. Key, Jr., *American State Politics* (New York: Knopf, 1956). A critical examination of the direct primary and other aspects of state political practice, with obvious relevance to proposed reforms of national nominations.

Arthur Holcombe, *Our More Perfect Union* (Cambridge: Harvard University Press, 1950). Not specifically on conventions or nominations, but a general defense of present political arrangements, and a critique of suggested changes.

Sigmund Neumann (ed.), *Modern Political Parties* (Chicago: University of Chicago Press, 1956). A collection of generally excellent articles on parties and party systems throughout the world, which can provide much food for thought for changes here.

Louise Overacker, *The Presidential Primary* (New York: Macmillan, 1926). An early analysis and endorsement of state primaries to choose pledged delegates to the national conventions.

U. S. Senate, Judiciary Committee, *Nomination and Election of President and Vice-President*, Hearings on S. J. Res. 3 and others, 84th Cong., 1st sess. (1955). A discussion of many plans to change both the convention and Electoral College systems.

X OUTLOOK FOR THE FUTURE

It is easy to predict that American political parties of the future will show a marked resemblance to those of the present. Given the success of our system of government, drastic changes are unlikely. Yet innovations too can be expected. Particularly in Presidential elections, the parties will need to change some current practices in order to assure their own position.

The trend of future development is toward a national political system. In Presidential elections at least, the parties will evidence four shifts of emphasis. They will be more competitive and less sectional. They will be more concerned with policy and less ambiguous and similar in their programs. They will be more centralized and less unstable confederations of state organizations. They will include more national figures in their leadership and fewer purely local personalities. These are relative, not absolute changes, but the differences may be crucial.

These changes are primarily due to the increasing social and political unity of the nation as a whole. The general causes of this unity need only be mentioned to grasp their significance: rapid transportation and instantaneous communication, domination of the economy by national corporations rather than by local businesses, the concentration of population in metropolitian areas and the development of interstate urban complexes, the diminution of extreme differences in wealth between regions and between social classes, and—possibly most important—the active and persistent involvement of the United States in international affairs.

Other trends will have a similar and more direct effect on politics. With the ending of significant immigration, the effect of ethnic loyalties will decline substantially. As Negro migration to the North continues, the Negro vote and racial issues in general will become of national, rather than sectional, importance. Other issues will also be transformed from local and regional to national conflicts, as the federal government expands its power in areas formerly of only "local concern." Meanwhile, the Presidency will become even more the focus of American public life.

The trend, then, is toward a more unified nation and consequently toward a more simplified, more homogeneous politics. Certainly many local issues will persist; differences between states will not be completely obliterated. It is probably fortunate, as well as inevitable, that a distinction will still exist between Alabama and Minnesota. However, the distinctions will be less clear and the similarities much greater than they are now.

Party Competition and Party Policy

One effect of these social changes is to increase party competition throughout the nation. The foundations for electoral contests have been laid in all states, and interparty competition has increased rapidly. Democrats have been particularly successful in winning elections in areas previously considered safe Republican territory. One author, reviewing state contests from 1870 to 1950, classifies Illinois, Michigan, California, and Pennsylvania as G.O.P. bailiwicks.[1] By 1962, however, all of these states—and others of similar history—had elected Democratic governors and majorities in at least one house of the state legislature. Republican progress toward nationwide popularity has been slower, but still marked. The G.O.P. has invaded the erstwhile "Solid South" in three consecutive Presidential elections, and has gone on to win a Senate seat in Texas and a sprinkling of state legislative and Congressional seats throughout the region. Sectional loyalties have been partially displaced by national party ties.

The national trend can be seen by comparing the state-by-state result of the Presidential election of 1944, the last contested by Franklin Roosevelt, and that of 1960. When sectionalism is politically significant, the results in each state will vary considerably from the national result. Voters in different regions then cast their ballots in response to different issues. Party competition diminishes as each faction appeals to its particular sectional constituency. In a competitive system, the parties stress national questions, voters react to the same issues, and the state-by-state results come to parallel more closely the results in the entire country.[2]

As can be seen in the table below,[3] there was a marked decline in state divergencies from the national results in 1960, as compared to 1944. The greatest dis-

[1] Joseph A. Schlesinger, "A Two-Dimensional Scheme for Classifying States According to Degree of Inter-Party Competition," *American Political Science Review*, Vol. 49 (December, 1955), p. 1125.

[2] See E. E. Schattschneider, *The Struggle for Party Government* (College Park: University of Maryland, 1948) and "United States: The Functional Approach to Party Government," in Sigmund Neumann (ed.), *Modern Political Parties* (Chicago: University of Chicago Press, 1956), pp. 210-15, for a further discussion.

[3] The figures in this table for 1944 are from Louis H. Bean, *How to Predict Elections* (New York: Knopf, 1948), p. 183, and for 1960 from V. O. Key, "Interpreting the Election Results," in Paul T. David, (ed.), *The Presidential Election and Transition 1960-1961* (Washington: The Brookings Institution, 1961), p. 151.

crepancy in 1960 came in the case of Louisiana, which was 13.7% from the entire nation.[4] In 1944, however, nine states exceeded this figure. Of course, the election of 1960 was unusually close, but the point is that it was close in most states. The factors which affected the total vote also affected the voters in the several states to a fairly similar extent. In 1944, the voters did not respond as uniformly.

Competition between the parties is likely to increase still further. This in turn will probably lead to clearer

TABLE 10-1

SECTIONALISM AND THE PRESIDENTIAL VOTE

Deviation from National Democratic Percentage	Number of States 1944	1960
Less than 1%	6	10
1 to 1.9%	8	7
2 to 2.9%	4	6
3 to 4.9%	7	9
5 to 6.9%	7	6
7 to 9.9%	3	6
10 to 14.9%	5	6
15 to 19.9%	2	0
20% and over	6	0
National Democratic Percentage	53.8%	50.1%
Mean State Deviation	8.5%	4.4%
Median State Deviation	4.8%	3.5%

differences between party policies. The differences are not likely to be extreme, given the general moderation of American politics, nor will there be complete agreement within each party. However, "the development of a competitive two-party system in all parts of the United States makes it possible (and probably necessary) for the opposition party to develop an alternative national policy designed to appeal to a national constituency."[5] In an attempt to secure

[4] I have used the Democratic percentage of the two-party vote throughout, ignoring third parties, themselves an index of sectionalism. If the latter are included, the Democratic percentage in Louisiana becomes 50.4%, almost at the national average in 1960. Mississippi would then become the most deviant state, as the Democratic percentage would then be 36.3%, rather than 59.6% of the two-party vote. The general point would only be strengthened by such a change.

[5] Schattschneider, in Neumann, p. 210.

sufficient strength to become a majority, each party seeks to differentiate its policies from those of its rival. The appeals it makes are likely to be similar from one part of the country to another, although there will be regional differences in emphasis.

In the past, national elections were won by creating a coalition of separate sectional interests. Today, voters in all sections share many of the same interests. The parties cannot make different appeals to different areas, but must make one consistent appeal to a national electorate. Thus in the 1960 campaign, Henry Cabot Lodge could not promise in New York that a Negro would be appointed to the Cabinet of a Republican administration without causing an immediate reaction from the South. Nor could he retract the statement in the South later without incurring new dissent from Northern Negro voters. These tactics are even less likely to succeed in future elections. Issues such as foreign policy, civil rights, and federal welfare measures affect all voters, if not in precisely the same degree. Candidates will be required to seek a constituency extending beyond purely geographical boundaries. They and their parties will need to develop consistent and distinctive policies.[6]

Even at the present time, the major parties' policies are not merely two sides of the same coin. As we have seen in a discussion of the party platforms, there have been significant differences in their programs over long periods of time. Analysis of Congressional voting indicates that party affiliation is a significant index of a legislator's record, particularly when the influence of the President is brought to bear. In these circumstances, less than a fifth of the legislators desert their party colleagues.[7] Even greater differences be-

---

[6] The classic demonstration of the shift in American politics is that of Arthur Holcombe in *The Political Parties of Today* (New York: Harper, 1924) and *The New Party Politics* (New York: Norton, 1933).
[7] David B. Truman, *The Congressional Party* (New York: Wiley, 1959), *passim* and pp. 283-85.

tween the parties can be found if Southern Democrats are considered separately. An analysis of the 1957-59 Congress finds 97% of the Northern Democrats taking a liberal position on domestic social welfare issues, while nearly 80% of Republicans voted either for conservative or moderate policies.[8] As the South develops a competitive two-party system, it is likely that analogous party divisions will be evident there.

Changes in the parties' membership are increasing their interest in public policy. In the past, parties were largely staffed by members of local "machines," primarily interested in politics as a means of securing patronage or as a ladder of personal social mobility. Where not already dormant, the "machines" are being destroyed as the result of the assumption of welfare responsibilities by government, the growth of civil service, and the expansion of economic opportunities throughout the nation.

Parties now must rely more on individuals and groups interested in politics as a means to achieve certain governmental policies. Organized interest groups are now a crucial source of strength.[9] Labor unions now play an important, if subordinate, role in the Democratic party, contributing manpower, money, and organizational skills to the party's efforts.[10] Major corporations and groups such as the American Medical Association render equally valuable, if less publicized support to the Republicans.[11] In return for their

[8] Austin Ranney, "Republicans and Democrats: Principles and Perversities," in Alfred Junz, (ed.), *Present Trends in American National Government* (New York: Praeger, 1961), p. 52. I have combined Ranney's nine categories into three.

[9] See John Fenton, *Northern Politics*, a paper read at the American Political Science Association convention of September, 1960 in New York.

[10] See Fay Calkins, *The CIO and the Democratic Party* (Chicago: University of Chicago Press, 1952).

[11] See Alexander Heard, *The Costs of Democracy* (Chapel Hill: University of North Carolina Press, 1960), chap. 5, and Stanley Kelley, *Professional Public Relations and Political Power* (Baltimore: The Johns Hopkins Press, 1956), chap. 3.

help, interest groups expect the party to endorse, in relatively firm and specific terms, the governmental ends they seek.

A similar increased stress on public policy is likely to follow from the significant role in politics recently assumed by volunteers and "amateurs." Such groups as the Republican Assembly of California and the Democratic "reform" movement of New York City gain the loyalty of their members without reliance on political favors or patronage. Rather than personal advantages, these groups stress the party program and the policy issues involved in elections.[12] As the former incentives to political activity lose their effectiveness, the parties will find it necessary to rely more upon this type of grass-roots support. To maintain the allegiance of these workers, they will need to devote continuing attention to their public positions.

Changes in party leadership tend in the same direction. On the national level, the President is now securely established as the leader of his party. In this position, he is likely to make the party conscious of policy questions. The opposition party is similarly affected. In attacking the party in power, it must criticize the President as well, and thereby become involved in a discussion of public policy.

The President has been established as party leader for some time. More recently, public officials on the state and local level have assumed an analogous position in their constituencies. Governors and mayors are no longer distinct from, or subservient to, the party organization. More often, they are the recognized leaders of that organization. The public policy questions which face the elected official thereby become a major element in party operations and decisions. A public official, conscious of future elections cannot, for example, make appointments solely to meet patronage obligations. He must also be aware of the effects of his appointments on the administration of government

[12] See James Q. Wilson, *The Amateur Democrat* (Chicago: University of Chicago Press, 1962).

and, eventually, on his own standing with the voters. The difference between the old and the new politics is that between an old-time "boss" such as William Marcy Tweed and a new-style "leader" such as Richard Daley of Chicago. To the former, policy questions were basically irrelevant; to the latter, they are necessarily an integral part of political decisions.[13]

Future Party Leadership

The two trends in the national party system discussed above—greater competition and greater attention to policy—are supplemented by a third, increased centralization of the party organizations. Greater centralization is partially the result of more widespread competition. With fewer "safe" constituencies, the parties must seek to stimulate and maintain local organizations in all parts of the nation. When Democrats begin winning elections in Maine, for example, the Republicans in self-defense must attempt to penetrate the "Solid South." Both the Republican and Democratic national committees are therefore now involved in searches for candidates, campaign schools, registration drives, and nationwide fund-raising efforts.[14]

Increased attention to policy brings the same result. The parties seek not only the election of their candidates, but also the enactment of a limited party program. Dependent on the volatile support of a national constituency, the parties will seek more centralized power so as to fulfill their pledges to that constituency. American parties are still far from unified and disciplined organizations. The national organizations remain relatively weak, and party representatives in Congess are not subject to the command of

[13] For a further discussion, see V. O. Key, *Politics, Parties and Pressure Groups*, 4th ed. (New York: Crowell, 1958), pp. 375-78.
[14] See D. S. Broder, "Strategists for '62 and '64," *The New York Times Magazine* (October 15, 1961), p. 26.

a centralized leadership. However, some steps have already been taken toward greater unity.

This direction is indicated by the increased influence of the truly national party organs—the President and the National Committee. "The centralizing forces within the American parties and within American public life come to focus in the presidency. In other words, in as far as the presidency is magnified by the parties (making the president an effective national leader) the parties became centralized."[15]

The President can influence a wide range of party decisions. National party policy is now determined by him, and he can use many methods to gain the approval of this policy by Congress. Consultation between executive and legislative leaders is now normal practice. While the President lacks firm control, there are informal means available by which he can influence primary and local elections. Although restrained in his actions, President Kennedy intervened in 1962 Democratic primaries in Florida, Louisiana, New York, and Pennsylvania, and was generally successful. Presidential participation in mid-term elections, once criticized, is now accepted, and indeed expected.[16]

When a party has lost the Presidency, the National Committee is its only recognized national body. If there is to be any centralization of the parties, therefore, the National Committee is likely to evidence increased power. In recent years, there have been signs of such growth. This has been accomplished because it is in the interest of the "Presidential wing" of the party to provide for greater national power. The future demands of Presidential politics will probably lead to giving the National Committee further authority.

[15] E. E. Schattschneider, *Party Government* (New York: Rinehart, 1942), p. 151.
[16] Stephen K. Bailey, *The Condition of Our National Political Parties* (New York: Fund for the Republic, 1959), pp. 20-21.

The national committees have gained a more representative membership, greater resources, and a broadened role in policy making.[17] The national committees in the past gave equal representation to all state parties, regardless of their contribution to the electoral strength of the national ticket. Since 1952, the Republicans have provided a slight correction by allotting a third seat to states supporting the ticket.

The staffs of the committees have been enlarged. Permanent personnel did not exist until some thirty years ago. Now each party committee has up to a hundred regular employees, engaged in publication of a party journal, research, technical assistance to the state and local organizations, support of the party program and, occasionally, intervention in local organizations. The national parties have also become relatively richer. The demands of campaigning today result in increasing reliance on mass financing, rather than the contributions of a few wealthy families or the subventions of state organizations. If the parties succeed in building a popular financial base, or if government should provide subsidies, they would be freed from reliance on state and local groups. The other forces making for party centralization would then be less hindered.

Some centralization of finance has already been accomplished. For some time, the Republicans have concentrated much of their fund-raising activity in a National Finance Committee, and the Democrats adopted the same practice in 1960. In addition, the national groups have found new sources in small voluntary contributions, interest group efforts, and the donation of free time by radio and television stations. Before and after the last election, the Democrats took major steps which are likely to increase the National Committee's resources and, hence, its authority. State organizations failing to meet their financial quotas were punished, the quotas were substantially increased, and the National

[17] Much of the information for this section is from Hugh A. Bone, *Party Committees and National Politics* (Seattle: University of Washington Press, 1958), pp. 9-26.

Committee also sought to raise about one million dollars through a program of "national sustaining memberships," priced as $10 a year. In a final action, the Democrats merged the finances of the National Committee with those of its Senatorial and Congressional campaign committees.[18] This could be a first step toward merging of the party campaigns for all offices.

The National Committee has also come to have a role in making policy for the party. Its interest here is still limited, but there is a distinct change from the time when Democratic chairman Cordell Hull declared that the committee "has no authority, express or implied, to prescribe issues for the Democratic rank-and-file."[19] In the Republican party, the National Committee several times has taken the responsibility of developing campaign issues and a party platform before the national convention. Special committees were established for the 1920, 1940, 1944, and 1960 campaigns. The programs adopted by these groups served as the basis of the official platform and later party policy.[20]

The most ambitious attempt to give the National Committee a role in party policy-making was the Democratic Advisory Council, established after the party's defeat in 1956. Although boycotted by Congressional leaders, the Council came to be a recognized spokesman of the party's "Presidential wing." The membership of the group was never stabilized but included the more prominent members of the National Committee, titular leaders such as former President Harry Truman and Adlai Stevenson, and selected governors and mayors. Its widely-publicized policy statements were generally clear and specific, even when this necessitated criticism of Democratic office-holders, such as Governor Orval Faubus at the time of the Little Rock integration dispute.[21] The influence of the Council was acknowledged before the 1960 convention when some of the candi-

[18] Herbert Alexander, "Financing the Parties and Campaigns," in David, particularly pp. 133-44.
[19] *Democratic Manual*, cited by Bone, p. 21.
[20] Bone, pp. 225-33.
[21] *Ibid.*, pp. 219-25.

dates for the Presidential nomination, including Senator Kennedy, accepted membership on it.

After the Democrats' victory in 1960, the Council was abolished in recognition of the new President's role as policy leader of the party. Certainly there was less, if any, need for the Council after the Democrats occupied the White House. In the party out of power, however, the Presidential wing of the party lacks a recognized forum. Recognizing this lack, and despite the hostility of Congressional leaders, the Republicans have recently created an "All Republican Conference" and a "National Republicans Citizens Committee."[22] Like the Democratic Advisory Council, these bodies will give a voice to the areas and groups under-represented in Congress. Whatever their names or composition, such bodies will continue to be created to represent the "Presidential party" between elections and to provide a means of expression for the parties' national constituencies. Due to its institutional obstacles, Congress cannot provide leadership for these constituencies. Future, improved models of the Democratic Advisory Council are more likely to meet the need.

The increased power of the National Committee and central party organs are part of a movement toward a more nationalized leadership of the parties. Presidential candidates are less likely than in the past to be "dark horses" or men who have established a reputation simply in state government. They are more apt to be men who have gained prominence in federal affairs, who can appeal to a nation-wide constituency, and who can gain support among national interest and party groups.

As we have previously noted, the emphasis on national personalities will be spurred by the influence on nominations of popular opinion and the mass media. These candidates are likely to do best in state primaries and public opinion polls. Television and the other media tend to con-

[22] See Meg Greenfield, "Charles A. Halleck and the Restless Republicans," *Reporter*, Vol. 26 (March 29, 1962), pp. 27-30.

centrate on the most prominent candidates, and thereby to limit the possible advance of more obscure individuals. Moreover, the increased and immense powers of the Presidency make it less likely that untried individuals will be entrusted with nominations for the position.

An emphasis on national leadership does not necessarily imply a monopolization of party control by a few individuals, or "that the national party leaders will nominate one of their own number for the presidency, adopt him as their *permanent candidate,* and continuously build the program and propaganda of the party around him."[23] To accomplish this change, there would need to be far more unification of the nation and reduction of institutional barriers between President and Congress than can now be forseen. For the immediate future, the centralization of the parties will be most notable in Presidential politics. The Congressional parties will follow, not lead, the development. There will be some narrowing of the paths of advancement to national leadership, but a number of channels will remain open. Future nominations may go to cabinet officers, legislators, members of the National Committee or its advisory council, unusually prominent governors, or interest group spokesmen. All would be alike in their national prominence and their national appeal.

Senators and representatives will be nominated more frequently. However, those chosen will not necessarily be the most conspicuous leaders of Congress. The political demands upon the executive and legislative branches are likely to remain different for some time. So long as they do, party leaders will become Presidential candidates or Congressional spokesmen. Only rarely will one individual play both roles.

The American party system is in a period of change. The parties will not be simply "loose, supple, overlapping, decentralized, undisciplined, interest-directed, and principle-shunning enterprises in group diplomacy that are encircled

[23] Schattschneider, *Struggle for Party Government,* p. 43.

and penetrated by a vigorous array of interest groups."[24] Nor will either party become "a disciplined authoritarian machine, able to impose its will from the top."[25] Many divisive forces still exist in American parties. Third parties were established as late as 1948, and the threat of defections from both parties remains evident. Racial, religious, and class differences are real, and often acrimonious. Moreover, American institutions do not contribute to centralization. The traditions and strengths of local organizations, the federal structure, the barriers between Congress, the President, and the parties, and the intricacies of election laws will delay the result. The new party system will not be established quickly. However, the gross trends of American development do lead in the same direction.

When these innovations are accomplished, they will be more evident in those elements of the parties most interested in Presidential elections. Prescription and prediction lead to the same conclusion. Changes should be made in the politics of choosing a President, for the Chief Executive can now decide ultimate questions of life and death for the entire nation. Changes most likely will be made here for the Presidency is now our most responsive national institution. Until now, modifications in national politics have been limited. Yet, there is reason to believe "that our traditional party system, like a vast glacier, may now have reached the edge of the sea."[26]

The Role of the Conventions

As we have seen, the national party conventions have been useful, indeed necessary, institutions in the past. They can continue to fulfill a vital role. For the forseeable future, there will be a need for a large representative insti-

[24] Clinton Rossiter, *Parties and Politics in Amercia* (Ithaca: Cornell University Press, 1960), p. 164.
[25] Herbert Agar, *The Price of Union* (Boston: Houghton Mifflin 1950), p. 347.
[26] Bailey, p. 6.

tution to decide on party policy, government and leadership. Under the pressures of nationwide competition, the parties will need to marshal every available resource in order to obtain the electoral majority which they seek. By providing an opportunity for compromise and consolidation, the conventions will continue to justify their existence.

However, the party conclaves cannot remain the same. Changes will be needed to meet new conditions. If a national party system is being developed, as argued above, then the conventions must adopt themselves to the new conditions of Presidential contests. The nominating process must be adjusted to the new competitive situation of the parties. With active contests for the electoral vote of more states, the parties must revise their fundamental strategy. Emphasis should be placed on the national voting constituency and on the competitive states which largely encompass this constituency. The parties should no longer provide rewards for state organizations which contribute only marginally to a national majority.

The convention, and all other party organs, must be made more representative. The apportionment of delegates should no longer be based simply on states, but on the electoral support given to the party in each state. At the present time apportionment unduly benefits one-party states. In the 1960 conventions, for example, Mississippi had one delegate for about 6,300 Democratic voters of 1956, and one for 4,000 Republican voters. In contrast, a competitive state like New York had only one delegate for 24,000 Democrats and one for 45,500 Republicans. Convention decisions should be designed to appeal to the most competitive states. This would be best accomplished if apportionment were based simply on the party vote in each state in the last Presidential election. An indirect but important result of this system could be to increase Negro voting in the South. State organizations would now have a distinct incentive to increase total turnout, and therefore to allow voting by minority groups.

The change in representation could easily be accomplished. Representation on the basis of the electoral vote of the state alone, as well as the crazy quilt system of bonus votes, should be eliminated. Instead, each party should determine in advance the total number of votes in its convention, perhaps 1500. On the basis of the 1960 election, each state group would then have one delegate for approximately every 22,750 votes cast for the party. The party voters in each state would be represented equally, and the convention would be suitably constituted to appeal to the most competitive areas of the nation.

If the scheme were in effect for the 1964 conventions, for example, Mississippi's Democratic representation would fall from 23 to 5 (or to 10 if votes cast for "independent electors" were included in the party total) and from 15 to 3 in the Republican convention. New York would have 168 Democratic delegates, instead of 114, and 152 Republican, rather than 96. These are drastic changes, to be sure, but they are necessary if the parties are to appeal to the national constituency which will decide future elections.

Similar, if less extreme, changes should be made in the National Committee. While each state certainly must be given some representation, each need not be given equal representation. Those areas contributing most to the party's national success should be accorded additional power. To accomplish this change, the states could be divided into three groups according to the number of party voters. The 17 states with the most voters would each have three seats on the National Committee, the 17 with the least voters would have one seat each, and the others would have two seats. The total membership of the Committee would then be 100, about at the limit for an active decision-making body.

These measures obviously would give an advantage to states of large population and in which party competition is prevalent. This advantage is justified, since it is precisely these states which are crucial for the success of the national party and its Presidential candidate.

As the parties become competitive, they will obviously have an interest in deterring sectional and dissident movements. Basing convention representation on the party vote will contribute to this result, as state parties will be penalized for deserting the national ticket. More stringent sanctions may be required in the future. The "loyalty oath" now imposed on Democratic national committeemen is a first step in this direction. At the present time, however, American parties are too decentralized to make such sanctions effective.

The attempt to impose a "loyalty oath" on Democratic convention delegates failed in 1952. This indicates the continuing absence of centralized disciplinary power within the parties. It is significant, however, that the national party has been successful in requiring all state parties to cooperate in placing the national nominees on local ballots, and in somewhat deterring third-party movements.[27] More effective than formal sanctions will be the spread of party competition itself. Faced by a strong opposition, state organizations will hesitate before abandoning the protection and assistance of the national ticket. What cannot presently be accomplished through national coercion will eventually be reached through the voluntary actions of the local parties.

Competitive parties also must seek to increase popular participation in internal party processes. Selection of all convention delegates through primaries is not necessary. However, the system should be made more open, more subject to legal safeguards for minority factions, and more regular. The choice of delegates through informal meetings and private caucuses does not usually contribute to widespread participation and popular interest. Rather, selection

[27] See Allan P. Sindler, "The Unsolid South: A Challenge to the Democratic Party," in Alan F. Westin, (ed.), *The Uses of Power* (New York: Harcourt, Brace and World, 1962), pp. 229-81.

should be made either through direct primaries or by state convention members who are themselves directly elected. The time for party elections should also be moved closer to that of the national convention, to increase the relevance of these elections to the eventual decisions of the national party.

As parties will be competing for the allegiance of a national constituency, they must attempt to bring the demands of that constituency to bear on convention deliberations. This will be done partially through the changes in state apportionment already suggested, through the direct involvement of interest groups in the parties, and through party platforms. Provision could also be made for the direct representation of organized and unorganized interests which make up the national constituency of each party, such as Negroes, business, and organized labor. For the most part, the parties are already providing seats for these groups through internal and informal processes. It does not now seem necessary to prescribe such representation, as is the case in Canadian conventions.[28] However, a reasonable proportion of the delegates from each state should be chosen at-large to allow for the allocation of seats to important interests within the party.

Competition will require alterations in the conventions. Other changes will be necessitated by the parties' increased attention to public policy. If issues are to become more central to the national parties, they must receive longer and more deliberate consideration than that possible at the convention itself or the week preceding it. In the future, parties would be well advised to follow the practices of 1960, when both organizations began the preparation of their platforms months before the convention. Through large and representative groups, nationwide public hearings and consultation with experts, the parties eventually were

[28] See John W. Lederle, "National Conventions: Canada Shows the Way," *Southwestern Social Science Quarterly*, Vol. 25 (September, 1944), pp. 121-24.

able to draft reasonably articulate programs which expressed a wide measure of consensus in each party.

Party programs can be made more meaningful not only by longer preparation, but also by changes in the composition of the platform drafting committee. With equal representation from each state, the committee is not representative of the party's true areas of strength. Given the large size of the conventions, it is increasingly likely that the platform committee will make final decisions on party policy. To make it truly representative and responsible, the committee should be revised so that the delegates from each state cast the same vote in the smaller group as the state holds in the entire convention.

Committee decisions will also be more meaningful if the members of the group are public office-holders with the actual responsibility and power to change party pledges into governmental policy. State delegations are increasingly adopting the practice of assigning legislators to the platform committee. This practice should be continued, and extended to include state officials and interest group leaders.

The policy decisions of the national party would be further highlighted if conventions were held in years in which no Presidential nomination and election was scheduled. Unless there is some meeting of the entire party, policy comes to be dominated by the legislative leadership, which is unlikely to be representative of the party's total national constituency. A midterm convention would allow the other elements of the party to bring their strength to bear, while also providing a means of revitalizing the national organization.

A mid-term convention would be particularly important for the party out of power, as it would be given a chance to publicize itself and its leadership. However, the party in power would also benefit. Through the public attention generated by an off-year conclave, the President's party might avoid the usual loss of Congressional representation in a non-Presidential election. In the second term of a President, moreover, his party would also gain from the publicity given to would-be heirs.[29]

If these changes were made, the role of the entire convention in policy decisions would be decreased. With more frequent meetings and with the platform committee more representative and more expert, there would be fewer occasions for policy decisions by the entire body of delegates. The role of the convention in policy would be reduced to that of an appeals court and a safety valve. When party factions cannot reconcile their differences through negotiation in the platform committee, the convention would make the final decisions. Minority factions which were defeated in the committee and on the convention floor would retain the satisfaction of airing their grievances before the entire convention membership and the national audience.

To fulfill its role on these occasions, the conventions must limit their size and streamline their procedures. There is great pressure on the parties to increase the number of delegates in order to widen the sense of participation and to kindle the enthusiasm of partisans. It is clearly impossible now to limit the conventions to the five or six hundred delegates recommended by the American Political Science Association. However, the four thousand present at the Democratic 1960 convention is certainly excessive. The parties should set an upper limit of about 1,500 on the total number of delegates. Even this number is far too large to allow open debate, but it is probably the minimum acceptable to the parties. Realistically, the goal cannot be rational debate and autonomy for individual delegates. Limiting the size of the convention, however, can contribute to more rational decisions within the state delegations and to more careful bargaining between these delegations.

Party loyalty can be rewarded by naming a large number of alternates, to be seated off the main floor. The

[29] Similar suggestions on platforms are made in Paul T. David *et al.*, *The Politics of National Party Conventions* (Washington: The Brookings Institution, 1960), pp. 497-98.

public galleries can, if necessary, be used for these alternates. Distribution of tickets to the galleries has become subject to much abuse and seats frequently are not used in any case. The public's interest in open conventions can probably be better satisfied by television and newspaper coverage.

Whatever the size of the conventions, their procedures will need to be more tightly controlled. Increased size and the demands of the mass media will provide the necessity for greater discipline; the more centralized national organizations will provide the means. "Interminable demonstrations or harmonica solos by sons of important local politicians make little sense on nationwide television. The goal will be short speeches, relevant and dramatic; a minimum of byplay and horseplay and sharp, clear movement toward the important decisions."[30]

In order to keep the convention under control, longer preparation will be necessary. In the drafting of platforms, this can be done through permanent advisory councils or through the early selection of a convention platform group. The same preparation is necessary in the case of convention decisions on officers, rules and credentials. It would be impractical to appoint all of these committees long before the convention. In most cases, the National Committee can be entrusted with these preliminary decisions, particularly if representation on the Committee is changed to represent the party's areas of strength more equitably.

The National Committee, or its executive body, should also assume responsibility for the scheduling of convention events, the allocation of time for debate, and similar procedural decisions. In the crowded and emotional atmosphere of a convention there is some possibility that minority rights will be ignored and that presiding officers will be able to make and enforce arbitrary rulings. This possibility will be reduced greatly if there is prior agreement on the rules of the game.

[30] Charles A. Thomson, *Television and Presidential Politics* (Washington: The Brookings Institution, 1956), p. 145.

The certification of delegates may continue to be a problem. There probably will be fewer disputes if more regular procedures for selection of delegates are adopted in those states now using informal methods. The spread of party competition will also help to stabilize these methods. New problems of certification may arise, however, from increased party centralization. If a loyalty test of any sort is imposed, the parties may become involved in disruptive internal investigations.

The parties will need to proceed cautiously in imposing standards of loyalty. When credentials disputes do arise, they can continue to be settled under the same procedure as now followed. The credentials committee, however, should be reconstituted to reflect the voting power of each state. As in the platform committee, each state should have the same voting power in the smaller body as it has in the entire convention. Decisions would also probably be more deliberate, equitable, and acceptable if the committee met a week or two before the entire convention.

Reforms in Nominations

Procedure could be streamlined most easily by reducing the number of speeches and formalities and by placing more controls on the nominating speeches and demonstrations. The former will be easily accomplished once the party managers, and their public relations advisers, are convinced of the need. Curtailing the nominations, however, must overcome the objections of potential nominees, their state parties and backers, and those excited by an atmosphere resembling that of New Year's Eve.

Actually, the defect is not the nominating speeches and demonstrations themselves, which provide a harmless outlet for great emotions. The fault is the number of speeches and of demonstrations, which can quickly become boring. This fault can be remedied by making a distinction between major and minor candidates. Major candidates would be those who present a petition to the presiding officer, or a convention nominating committee, signed by a significant number of delegates. An appropriate figure might be five per cent, including no more than four per cent from one state. These candidates would be entitled to a traditional formal nominating speech, a demonstration, and a severely limited number of seconding speeches. A minor candidate would be nominated simply by one delegate presenting his name to the presiding officer or nominating committee. At the end of the nominations for major candidates a list of these other aspirants would be read by a convention officer, together with a short biography or campaign statement. Under this procedure, time-consuming nominations of frivolous and purely "favorite-son" candidates would be eliminated, but the name of any potential "dark horse" would still be before the convention if it chose to disregard the major candidates. Major candidates would benefit from the petition process. The number of signatures could be used as an index of their strength, rather than the length of their demonstrations. Demands for recognition by the candidates' backers could be satisfied by asking them to sign the petition. The candidates would thus be partially relieved of the agonizing task of trying to satisfy the conflicting requests of delegates.

In the 1960 Democratic convention, under this procedure, John Kennedy, Lyndon Johnson, Stuart Symington, and Adlai Stevenson would have been nominated as major candidates. The convention could easily have endured four nominating speeches and demonstrations. It would have been spared the boredom of repeating the process for five others who were not serious aspirants. In the last contested Republican convention, in 1952, three candidates would have been formally nominated—Dwight Eisenhower, Robert Taft, and Earl Warren. These were in fact the only real contenders. The others may have been more embarrassed than gratified by the feeble response to their nominations.

Restricting the nominating process would be in accord

with the increased centralization of the parties. It would also be a recognition of the emergence of a group of national leaders in the parties. A further step in this direction would be the establishment of permanent advisory councils, particularly in the party out of power. This would provide a training ground for potential future Presidential candidates. These councils cannot be expected to have a strong power over party policy, Congressional nominations, and internal discipline, as recommended by the American Political Science Association.[31] They can, however, provide a means of expression for those areas under-represented in Congress, as well as a forum for the leaders of these constituencies. The membership of the councils should be institutionalized to some extent. Automatic representation might be accorded to party governors of the largest states, as well as the National Committee's executive committee. A small number of seats might be filled separately by the party's legislators, while Congressional leaders, if amenable, would be seated ex-officio. Additional members could be co-opted by the full committee, such as prominent former office-holders, leaders of interest groups or persons of individual distinction.

In selecting the Presidential nominee, the convention is likely to be limited to a choice among national leaders. The nominating process should be revised so that popular choices can be made manifest during the pre-convention period, while leaving to the delegates the final selection when no clear popular choice is presented. A single, binding national primary would be inadequate, for the reasons discussed in the last chapter. State primaries can still be useful guides to public sentiment. It is necessary, however, that there be some degree of uniformity in the primaries, that their decisions be binding, and that potential candidates have an incentive to participate.

Uniformity could be achieved through federal legislation. A constitutional amendment would not be necessary

[31] American Political Science Association, Committee on Political Parties, *Toward a More Responsible Two-Party System* (New York: Rinehart, 1950), pp. 41-43.

if Senator Paul Douglas' suggestion were adopted. Under this plan, federal grants-in-aid would be made to states holding primaries conforming to federal practice. The undesirable and constricting effects of a national primary could be avoided by limiting the number of states eligible for federal grants. A maximum of eight states might be admitted into the program, each representing a different region of the nation with approximately the same number of electoral votes. If more than one state in a region wished to participate, a choice might be made on the principle of rotation, with a different state from the region participating in each presidential year.

A popular preference could be heard in this way, without creating the possibility of a deadlocked convention or a minority nomination. If one candidate won all primaries, he would undoubtedly be formally nominated by the convention on its first ballot. If the contests showed no clear favorite, however, the convention would then be in a position to choose among the remaining contenders for the party leadership. With a majority of the delegates not bound by the results of the federally-aided primaries, there would be sufficient opportunity for negotiation and conciliation.

Under this plan, the demands of both popular rule and party responsibility would be met. The importance of pre-convention campaigning by national personalities and publicity by mass media would be recognized. Yet the possibility of compromise and "dark horse" nominations also would be preserved. Candidates might be entered in primaries without their consent or could still be advanced by delegates from non-participating states.

The mechanics of such a primary could largely follow the system developed by Paul David for use in Florida.[32]

[32] David, 1960, pp. 535-37. In state primaries, David himself now seems to prefer the New York system, which does not allow delegates to be officially pledged—*ibid.*, pp. 491-94. This plan is obviously irrelevant to any plan for federally-aided primaries. A small number of ex-officio seats might be provided to assure state party leaders that they will not be excluded from the delegation, a problem which occurred in Florida in 1956—*ibid.*, p. 537.

Candidates could be placed on the ballot by a petition signed by a small number of voters, perhaps 1,000, in each of the participating states. This would probably eliminate most frivolous or purely sectional candidacies. Each petition would list a full slate of candidates from each participating state, running both at-large and in the individual Congressional districts. In the case of competing slates, the Presidential candidate would have the right to designate the single list supporting his nomination. The election would be held on the same day in all states, no more than two months before the meeting of the national convention, and would be limited to enrolled members of the party. Finally, candidates should not be allowed to remove themselves from the ballot. By not allowing declinations, the way is left open for the draft of an unwilling candidate or a spontaneous expression of popular preference.

A federally-aided system of representative state primaries would provide for popular participation in the nominating process. There would then be less need for the remaining primaries. More states could then use state conventions for the selection of their delegates. If states wish to continue their own primaries, however, a few changes should be instituted. For one, preference polls should be eliminated. Divorced from the selection of delegates, they are basically unfair. They cause a candidate to invest his time, energy, and money without bringing him any certain reward if he is successful.[33] In elections to choose delegates, uninstructed or "no-preference" slates should be allowed, in order to preserve some freedom for state party organizations at the national convention. If federally-aided primaries were adopted, candidates should be allowed to withdraw from additional state contests. It might well be physically impossible for one to participate in all these elections. There will be sufficient opportunity in the federally-aided pri-

[33] This was first suggested by Louise Overacker, *The Presidential Primary* (New York: Macmillan, 1926), pp. 84-85.

maries and state conventions for the consideration of reluctant candidates.[34]

With these changes, some of the worst defects of the
primary system should be alleviated while a large measure
of popular control would be preserved. Through simple and
uniform filing requirements, the setting of a date close to
the convention, and the holding of the election on a single
day, the expenses and rigors of a pre-convention campaign
would be limited. By restricting the primaries to a small
number of states, the divisive effects of primaries would be
limited. By providing opportunities for compromise candidacies, the parties are not forced to choose between undesirable alternatives. Thus, this system preserves the role
of the party as the chief instrument of American politics.

The nomination of the Vice-President is best left to
the convention, the Presidential candidate, and other party
leaders. With the increased responsibilities of the office,
prominent and able men are increasingly likely to seek the
office. The spread of national party competition will also
serve to encourage the choice of attractive and competent
running mates. What is needed, however, are better means
of insuring that the party leadership soberly considers the
choice of a Vice-President. There is danger, to the parties
as well as to the nation, in having the selection made by a
handful of men. Hurried conferences in a room behind the
speaker's platform, as in the 1952 Democratic convention,
are an inadequate means of choosing a candidate who may
become the President.

Two procedural changes can promote this closer consultation. First, the parties should provide for mandatory
discussions between the Presidential candidate and the in-
coming National Committee or other recognized leaders of
the state delegations. This method, used by Richard Nixon

[34] For the thoughts of the National Municipal League, see U. S. Senate, Judiciary Committee, *Nomination and Election of President and
Vice-President,* Hearings on S. J. Res. 3 and others (1955), pp. 706-09.

at the 1960 Republican conclave, will at least assure that differing viewpoints are heard, that the choice of a candidate is justifiable in some measure, and that party conciliation is furthered by this choice.

Secondly, more attention and consideration would be given to the second nomination if all major unsuccessful candidates for the Presidency were automatically considered for the Vice-Presidency. Convention rules could easily prescribe, for example, that any individual receiving five per cent of the convention's total vote for President be placed in nomination for the second position. Such a procedure would overcome the understandable reluctance of defeated aspirants to enter another contest. Moreover, this method would force the party leaders to consider the most prominent individuals. They would still be free to reject these individuals, who in turn would probably be willing to withdraw their candidacies for Vice-President if they were not approved by the leaders. However, like the first method, this plan would result in freer expression of minority views and require that the designation of a running mate be explained to the delegates and indirectly to the national electorate.

Of course these changes would not guarantee the selection of able Vice-Presidential nominees. No purely institutional change could achieve such a guarantee. These changes would provide, however, for more deliberate decisions and greater public scrutiny, while preserving the necessary autonomy of the parties. Thus they provide a measure of security for national interests within a free political system.

❊   ❊   ❊

It seems clear that conventions in the future will not be mere duplications of the autonomous, free-wheeling party conclaves of the past. The development of a national party system will lead to more centralization and more popular influence. The demands for unity within the parties and the influence of external pressures will result in reduced freedom for the delegates. Yet the conventions can still retain a vital role; they need not be reduced simply to giant campaign rallies, as some predict and others fear.[35] Given the immensity of America and the diversity of its politics, there is still a need for a representative institution to decide upon and sanction party rules, policy, and leadership.

If the conventions still serve a useful purpose, however, the need for change also is evident. The older methods of unorganized and unprincipled parties are inadequate. Today, "the overriding issue is the new necessity for what might be termed a 'national state'—for a government strong enough to define and enforce the national interest in a world in which atomic war constantly threatens."[36]

The newer type of party politics is already emerging. Calculated action by the political parties can make the changes more rapid and more adequate to the needs of the United States today. The President in particular can guide this development. In command of his national party, and with the resources and prestige of his office at hand, he can act to better prepare the American political system for its future challenges. An act of will is necessary to make use of the present opportunity and to meet the present need. We might well conclude with Machiavelli's plea to an earlier executive:[37]

> Having now considered all the things we have spoken of, and thought within myself whether at present the time was not propitious ... and if there was not a state of things which offered an opportunity to a prudent and capable man to introduce a new system that would do honour to himself and good to the mass of the people, it seems to me that so many things concur ... that I do not know of any time more fitting for such an enterprise.

[35] See David, 1960, pp. 495-97 and William G. Carleton, "The Revolution in the Presidential Nominating Convention," *Political Science Quarterly*, Vol. 72 (June, 1957), pp. 224-37.
[36] Samuel Lubell, *The Future of American Politics*, rev. ed. (Garden City: Doubleday Anchor, 1956), p. 262.
[37] Niccolo Machiavelli, *The Prince and the Discourses* (New York: Modern Library, 1940), pp. 94-95.

Suggestions for Further Reading

Stephen K. Bailey, *The Condition of Our National Political Parties* (New York: Fund for the Republic, 1959). Prediction and endorsement of a more centralized, "responsible" party system for the United States in future years.

Angus Campbell *et al., The American Voter* (New York: Wiley, 1960). The most complete analysis of American voting behavior, a necessary part and limit of any changes in the political parties.

Paul T. David, "The Changing Party Pattern," *Antioch Review,* Vol. 16 (Fall, 1956), pp. 333-50. Describes many of the basic underlying changes now occurring within and between America's major parties.

Anthony Downs, *An Economic Theory of Democracy* (New York: Harper, 1957). A fascinating attempt to apply economic logic to the theory of democracy, with a heavy reliance on the role of the political party in a democratic system.

Alexander Heard, *A Two Party South?* (Chapel Hill: University of North Carolina Press, 1952). The prospects for increased competition in the nation's largest one-party area are carefully examined in an analysis still valid despite the passage of time.

Austin Ranney, *The Doctrine of Responsible Party Government* (Urbana: University of Illinois Press, 1954). A critical and incisive examination of the men who have championed responsible party government, and of their general theory.

Clinton Rossiter, *Parties and Politics in America* (Ithaca: Cornell University Press, 1960). A generally satisfied and generally convincing study of American politics.

E. E. Schattschneider, *Party Government* (New York: Rinehart, 1942). The original and carefully-reasoned analysis of American parties by the leading exponent of responsible parties.

Florence Weston, *The Presidential Election of 1828* (Washington: Catholic University, 1938). A scholarly study of the election which marked the beginning of mass democracy in national politics, providing comparisons to the present and thoughts on future trends.

James Q. Wilson, *The Amateur Democrat* (Chicago: University of Chicago Press, 1962). Critical description and analysis of the new-style volunteer politician and his preference for issue-based, internally democratic party organizations.

Appendix A CHRONOLOGY
OF PARTY NOMINATIONS

1789. No parties existed, and no nominations were made.

1792. Party lines began to be distinguished. Washington was unopposed for President but Federalist and Republican leaders informally advanced John Adams and George Clinton, respectively, for Vice-President.

1796. An informal caucus of Republicans in Congress chose Thomas Jefferson and Aaron Burr. John Adams was acknowledged as the Federalist candidate for President and Thomas Pinckney was named for Vice-President. The lack of complete party unity among Federalist electors made Jefferson the Vice-President.

1800. The Congressional caucus was now established in both parties. Adams was nominated for a second term, and Charles C. Pinckney was named as running mate. Republicans again chose Jefferson and Burr. The two Republican candidates received identical electoral votes, necessitating election of Jefferson by the House of Representatives.

1804. Republicans renominated Jefferson in caucus without controversy, but a formal vote was necessary before George Clinton was named for Vice-President. This was the first real contest for a party nomination. Through caucuses, the Federalists chose a ticket of Charles C. Pinckney and Rufus King.

1808. Republicans again met in caucus. Over the objections of representatives from New England, New York, and other areas, James Madison was named to succeed Jefferson. Clinton, defeated for President, was renominated as the running mate. Federalist representation in Congress was too small to provide for a meaningful caucus. Instead, party leaders met in a secret, unrepresentative and primitive convention in New York, the first national political convention. The 1804 ticket was named again.

1812. Opposition to Madison's renomination was strong but unsuccessful in the Congressional caucus. The defeated faction, principally from New York, bolted the party and supported DeWitt Clinton. The Federalists again met in a closed convention and also nominated Clinton in an expression of opposition to the newly-begun War of 1812. The Republican caucus of this year took the first step toward a national party organization by naming a committee of correspondence, consisting of one member from each state. Republicans named Elbridge Gerry for Vice-President and the Federalists selected Jared Ingersoll.

1816. In the most sharply contested nomination to this time, James Monroe was selected over William Crawford by a 65–54 vote in the Republican caucus. Many refused to attend, and the authority of the caucus was widely disputed. Daniel Tompkins was named as running mate. Two years earlier, the Federalists had established many precedents for later practice at the Hartford Convention. By 1816, however, the Federalists were too weak to contest the election seriously. Rufus King was accepted as the

Federalist candidate for President without the convening of either a caucus or convention. No nomination was made for Vice-President.

1820. In the atmosphere of the "Era of Good Feelings," no formal nominations were necessary. The Republican ticket of 1816 was again presented to the country and was re-elected by an almost unanimous electoral vote.

1824. In the last Congressional nominating caucus, Crawford was selected by a minority of the Republican members. Four other candidates were named by the legislatures of their home and other states—John Quincy Adams, John C. Calhoun, Henry Clay, and Andrew Jackson. Calhoun soon dropped out of the race, but the other four divided the electoral vote. Adams, second in both the popular and electoral vote, was named by the House. Proposals were made for a national nominating convention in this year, but the only results were local caucuses and a state convention in Pennsylvania. Of six candidates for Vice-President, Calhoun was elected.

1828. The campaign began soon after Adams' inauguration in 1825. Jackson was nominated by the legislature of Tennessee and later by legislatures and conventions in other states. Adams was the obvious candidate of those supporting the Administration and was formally renominated by various legislatures and conventions in the Eastern states. Calhoun now ran on the Jackson ticket, while Richard Rush became Adams' Vice-Presidential choice.

1832. The first national convention was held in 1831 by the short-lived, sectional Anti-Masonic party, which designated William Wirt for President. Later in the same year most of the opponents of Jackson joined in the only convention of the National Republican party. Procedures and credentials were haphazard, but all present agreed on the nomination of Henry Clay for President and John Sergeant for Vice-President. An "address to the people," a forerunner of party platforms, attacked the record of Jackson and his party, now known as the Democratic-Republicans. The latter held their own initial convention in 1832. Jackson himself had already been renominated by state legislatures. The convention's principal job was to nominate Jackson's choice, Martin Van Buren, for Vice-President. Rules adopted at this convention and maintained in the future provided for apportionment on the basis of the electoral vote of the states, the casting of votes by state delegations, and the necessity of a two-thirds vote for nomination for either place on the party ticket.

1836. Opposition to Jackson had not been consolidated into a national party organization and no convention of the nascent Whig party was held. Instead, three different opposition candidates—William Henry Harrison, Daniel Webster, and Hugh White—were named by conventions and legislatures in, respectively, the West, East, and South. In the Democratic convention, Van Buren was unanimously chosen as the Presidential candidate, but disagreement arose over the two-thirds rule and the Vice-Presidential nomination. In the end, the rule was retained and Richard Johnson was selected as running mate.

1840. The Democrats, as they now came to be called, renominated Van Buren unanimously. Opposition to the incumbent Vice-President, however, resulted in the convention not designating any candidate for the second place—the only occasion on which a major convention failed to present a complete slate. The Democrats wrote the first true platform in this year, consisting of nine short resolutions. The Whig convention also represented some new departures. For the first time, the Presidential nomination was in dispute. The responsibility for naming a candidate was given to a committee of delegation leaders, casting the unit vote of each state. Clay, the early favorite, was defeated by the crucial support given by New York and Pennsylvania leaders to Harrison. The Vice-Presidential nomination was then given to a Democrat, John Tyler, later to become the first "accidental" President.

1844. After his earlier convention defeat, Clay engaged in an extensive campaign and won the Whig nomination by acclamation. In three ballots, Theodore Frelinghuysen was chosen for Vice-President. The Whigs also adopted their first platform. Among the Democrats, there was less harmony. Van Buren, seeking a third nomination, had a clear majority from the beginning but his opposition to the annexation of Texas lost him the necessary two-thirds vote. In a compromise move, the party named James Polk, the first successful "dark-horse," an avowed candidate only for Vice-President. Silas Wright was selected to complete the slate, but declined, and was replaced by George Dallas.

1848. Democrats nominated Lewis Cass, a leading candidate acceptable to all sections, for President, and William Butler for Vice-President. At the conclusion of the convention, one member from each state was named to a national committee, the first to be established. In the Whig meeting, Clay was again defeated as the delegates chose a ticket of Mexican War hero Zachary Taylor and Millard Fillmore.

1852. Fillmore became President on the death of Taylor, but did not have enough strength in his party to win renomination. He was able to remain in contention, however, until the 53rd ballot, when Winfield Scott was nominated. Later, William Graham was named for Vice-President. For the first time, the platform was adopted before designations were made. The Democratic convention, too, engaged in long balloting, as both parties felt the increasing strains of the slavery controversy. A long conflict between Cass and James Buchanan was finally resolved by the compromise nomination of Franklin Pierce on the 49th tally. William King was chosen as running mate.

1856. As one result of the conflicts aroused by the slavery issue, Pierce was unable to win renomination. After 17 ballots, Buchanan finally won a Presidential nomination, with John Breckinridge named as Vice-President. More significant in this year was the first convention of the Republican party, which had replaced the Whigs. Its platform opposed the extension of slavery. John C. Fremont won a majority of the delegates' votes on an informal ballot and was then formally designated. William Dayton was chosen for the second place by the same method.

1860. On the eve of the Civil War, the Republicans cast aside their leading candidate, William Seward, and instead looked for a more moderate leader who could bring victory in crucial states. On the third ballot, after many caucuses, Abraham Lincoln was nominated. Party leaders then chose Hannibal Hamlin to complete the ticket. The Democrats found it impossible to reconcile their differences on the issue of slavery. Northern delegations favoring Stephen Douglas and moderation on the extension of slavery controlled a majority of the convention but lacked the necessary two-thirds vote to nominate. After the adoption of the platform, many Southern delegations left the convention. When no nomination was made after 57 ballots, a six-week recess was called. At the reconvened meeting, new Southern delegations were admitted and new defections occurred. By this time, more than a third of the delegates were absent and it was impossible for any candidate to win two-thirds of the entire vote. After two more ballots, Douglas was declared the winner of a now worthless nomination. Benjamin Fitzpatrick was chosen for Vice-President, but later declined, to be replaced by Herschel Johnson. Two other parties entered the election, further guaranteeing a Republican victory.

1864. Early opposition to Lincoln's renomination was dissipated by Northern military victories. To emphasize their national appeal, the Republicans changed their name to the Union party and named a War Democrat, Andrew Johnson, for Vice-President. The Democratic party presented a divided front. After adopting a platform calling for negotiations to end the Civil War, it named an exponent of strong military action, George McClellan, for President. The General later complicated matters still further by interpreting his designation as supporting vigorous prosecution of the war. The Peace Democrats then named George Pendleton for Vice-President.

1868. In the wake of the Civil War, Republicans had the ideal candidate in General Ulysses Grant, who was nominated unanimously. Controversy on the Vice-Presidency was settled after five ballots by the selection of Schuyler Colfax. The Democrats had more difficulty finding an acceptable candidate. On the 22nd ballot, a movement toward Horatio Seymour, presiding officer of the convention, began and succeeded. While this occurred, Seymour left the hall in protest against the first genuine draft in convention history. Francis Blair was easily chosen for Vice-President.

1872. Grant was unanimously renominated by the Republicans, but a new Vice-Presidential candidate, Henry Wilson, was selected. Those dissatisfied with the corruption of the Administration had already seceded to form the Liberal Republican party, which called for reform in government, and nominated Horace Greeley and B. Gratz Brown. The Democrats, devoid of original ideas or their own candidates, meekly accepted both the Liberal Republican platform and candidates.

1876. The Democrats had now revived and had an attractive reform candidate in Samuel Tilden, who conducted a vigorous pre-convention campaign that brought his nomination on the second ballot. Thomas Hendricks, a defeated candidate for the party leadership, was named to second place on the ticket. The Republicans were divided among many factions. James G. Blaine, the early leader, was unacceptable to a majority, which finally chose a ticket of Rutherford Hayes and William Wheeler.

1880. Hayes was removed from contention by the circumstances of his earlier election and by own inclinations. Republicans were divided among those favoring a third term for Grant and those supporting Blaine and John Sherman. Those opposed to Grant won a decisive victory when they prevented the imposition of a unit rule on all state delegations. After prolonged voting, these groups united to draft James Garfield, Sherman's floor manager. Chester Arthur was accepted as Vice-President. In the Democratic convention, General Winfield Scott Hancock, a perennial aspirant, and William English were quickly selected.

1884. Arthur succeeded to the Presidency on the death of Garfield, but could not win renomination. He was the last President denied a second term by his party. Instead, Blaine was finally allowed to test his national appeal, while John Logan was named for the Vice-Presidency. The Democrats considered many familiar names and a new contestant, Grover Cleveland. Aided by adoption of the unit rule, which gave him the unwilling votes of Tammany Hall, Cleveland received the party designation on the second ballot. Hendricks was named for Vice-President again over the objections of his own state delegation.

1888. Cleveland dominated the Democratic convention, winning renomination by acclamation and an endorsement of his low tariff policy in the platform. Allen Thurman was easily nominated as the running mate. Republicans, seeking new candidates with which to regain control of the White House, turned to Benjamin Harrison, the last of the Civil War military heroes, and Levi Morton. Control of the convention by state leaders and interest groups was notable.

1892. In control of the party organization, particularly in the South, Harrison was able to win renomination despite opposition centered particularly around Blaine. Whitelaw Reid was substituted for Morton for the second place. Despite his defeat in the last election, Cleveland was able to win a third nomination and to have his tariff views again incorporated in the platform. Adlai Stevenson was named for Vice-President.

1896. Nominations were made under the influence of great popular agitation, manifested in the growth of third parties, demands for a national policy of bimetalism and labor disputes which often resulted in violence. The Democrats reacted by repudiating the Cleveland Administration and adopting a policy of free coinage of silver, under the prodding of William Jennings Bryan's emotional "Cross of Gold" speech. Many delegates favoring a gold policy then bolted the convention. The search for a candidate to run on this platform ended with the nomination of Bryan himself on the fifth ballot. In a free Vice-Presidential contest, Arthur Sewall was named, also on the fifth tally. The Republican convention was dominated by Mark Hanna, who had lined up the Southern delegates in favor of William McKinley. The convention adopted a platform calling for a gold standard and protective tariff, and then overwhelmingly voted for McKinley and Garret Hobart. A small group of Silver Republicans left the party.

1900. McKinley was unanimously renominated in a convention notable only for the nomination of Theodore Roosevelt for Vice-President. This choice was the result of both the enthusiasm of the delegates and the desire of party leaders to put Roosevelt in an office of comfortable obscurity. Bryan was also renominated unanimously, this time on a platform condemning imperialism, and Stevenson was again named for Vice-President.

1904. Roosevelt, upon succeeding to the Presidency, gained complete control of his party. He dominated the convention, and was renominated unanimously. His self-selected running mate, Charles Fairbanks, was chosen by acclamation. The Democrats took a conservative turn, omitting any mention of the silver question from the platform and nominating a Gold Democrat, Alton Parker, for President. Parker accepted the nomination only after re-stating his position on the money question and forcing the convention to acknowledge this stand. Henry Davis was named for Vice-President, largely in the hope that his great wealth would be employed for the Democratic cause.

1908. For the first time, some delegates were chosen in state primary elections. Contests were muted in both parties. Having declined to run again, Roosevelt was able to achieve the Republican nomination of William Howard Taft over scattered opposition. James Sherman was similarly chosen for Vice-President. Wisconsin delegates, elected in the primaries, unsuccessfully advanced a number of progressive ideas for inclusion in the platform. Bryan easily won his third Democratic nomination on a relatively progressive platform and John Kern was named as running mate by acclamation.

1912. Primary elections were now of great importance. In the Republican party, Roosevelt came out of retirement to seek a third term. Although winning most primaries, he was overwhelmed by Taft's control of the state party organizations and the convention machinery. An Administration platform was adopted, after which Taft and Sherman were renominated. Sherman's renomination was the first of a Vice-Presidential candidate in two successive elections. Supporters of Roosevelt and Robert LaFollette bolted to form the Progressive party. The Democratic convention featured a contest between Champ Clark and Woodrow Wilson. Clark reached an absolute majority but was prevented from gaining the necessary two-thirds vote by the opposition of Bryan. With the support of many organization leaders, Wilson was nominated on the 46th ballot. Acknowledging this help, Thomas Marshall was selected for the Vice-Presidential place.

1916. Despite opposition to a second term expressed in the last Democratic platform, Wilson and Marshall were renominated by acclamation. The rift in the Republican party was healed by Roosevelt's return to party loyalty, an ambiguous platform and selection of a compromise candidate, Charles Evans Hughes. Fairbanks was again named for Vice-President. Unrepresentative apportionment, which had caused much difficulty in 1912 and in other past conventions, was partially corrected by alloting "bonus" votes to states providing significant support for the G.O.P. Southern representation was sharply reduced as a result.

1920. Extensive pre-convention campaigns were conducted in both parties, but were unsuccessful. Leonard Wood and Frank Lowden contended for the Republican nomination, but neither won majority support. When deadlock developed, party leaders met in the most famous "smoke-filled room" in history and chose Warren Harding. The delegates were allowed to name Calvin Coolidge for Vice-President. In the Democratic party, a contest between William McAdoo and A. Mitchell Palmer was resolved by naming James Cox on the 44th ballot. Young Franklin Roosevelt was acclaimed as Vice-Presidential nominee.

1924. Coolidge was able to overcome opposition within the Republican party and was easily renominated. The delegates then chose Lowden for Vice-President, but he reiterated his earlier refusal to run and the convention was then forced to vote again, naming Charles Dawes. Defeated liberals, led by LaFollette, later formed the Progressive party. Conflict was far more marked at the Democratic convention, which was split into two major factions. One—rural, dry, and conservative—was committed to McAdoo; the other—urban, wet, and liberal—was led by Alfred Smith. The division was marked on a minority platform plank condemning the Ku Klux Klan, which was defeated by only 4/5 of a vote. Selection of a nominee was complicated by the two-thirds rule, the unit rule, the stubborn loyalties of delegations, and the great antagonisms aroused before and during the convention itself. As the third week began, delegates finally accepted John Davis as a compromise on the 103rd ballot. Charles Bryan was named for Vice-President as the longest convention in history drew to a close.

1928. Decisions were made much faster in this year. Herbert Hoover, after a long pre-convention campaign and with the tacit endorsement of the Administration, held a substantial lead and was easily nominated after Lowden, his major opponent, withdrew. Charles Curtis was selected as running mate with no real opposition. In the Democratic party, Smith won a number of primaries and was able to win nomination on the first ballot. Joseph Robinson was chosen for the Vice-Presidency. The nominations of the two parties were notable in this year for the inclusion of a Californian and a Southerner, indicating changes in the balance of party and electoral strength.

1932. Despite the Depression and opposition in the primaries, Hoover was in complete control of the Republican convention and was easily renominated, as was Curtis, although he faced much greater opposition. In the Democratic party, Franklin Roosevelt entered the convention with a majority of the delegates' votes, but faced the combined forces of Smith and John Nance Garner. Before the fourth ballot, a deal was concluded, and a ticket of Roosevelt and Garner was quickly nominated. The Presidential candidate broke precedent by flying to the convention to address the delegates.

1936. The Democratic convention had little to do. The platform consisted of complete praise for the New Deal, and Roosevelt and Garner were renominated unanimously. Most significant historically was the abolition of the two-thirds rule. As compensation to the South, a system of bonus delegates to strongly Democratic states was promised for 1940. The Republicans were equally harmonious, nominating Alfred Landon and Frank Knox. Landon accepted the nomination on the understanding that the party endorsed his position on certain issues, such as wage and hour protection for women and children.

1940. Various factions in the Democratic party opposed a third term for Roosevelt. However, the President's control of the party and popular appeal were too great to withstand, and he further weakened any opposition by refusing to take a definite position on another nomination. In a simulated "draft," he was easily designated. More potent dissent developed to the President's choice of a running mate, but the delegates eventually succumbed and nominated Henry Wallace. The Republicans found themselves bereft of well-known aspirants. The search for a new personality was stimulated by the pressure of important party financiers and an unprecedented popular campaign. On the sixth ballot, the delegates named Wendell Willkie, a political novice. Charles McNary was chosen to balance the ticket.

1944. Willkie was eliminated from possible renomination by defeat in the primaries. By the time the convention met, Thomas Dewey was assured of all-but-unanimous nomination. This was followed by John Bricker's uncontested designation for running mate. Roosevelt had no difficulty in winning a fourth nomination in the middle of war, but the opposition to Wallace was now too strong to overcome, particularly in view of doubts about the President's health. After much involved maneuvering and two ballots, Harry Truman was named for the Vice-Presidency.

1948. Truman faced opposition from both the left and right wings of his party, but his detractors could not find an acceptable leader. Truman's forces first won endorsement of his liberal civil rights program and then achieved his nomination by a heavy first ballot vote. Alben Barkley was chosen to complete the ticket. Dissidents from the Democratic party went on to form two new and short-lived parties —the Progressives and States Righters. Republicans, confident of victory, engaged in a sharp contest between Dewey, Robert Taft, and Harold Stassen. Primary victories and organizational skill combined to give Dewey victory on the third ballot, after which Earl Warren was nominated for Vice-President.

1952. For the first time since 1928, the incumbent President was not a candidate, leading to open conventions in both parties. The Republican contest was a two-man battle between Taft and Dwight Eisenhower. Primary victories, supplemented by the aid of important interests and convention leaders, gave Eisenhower a narrow first ballot victory. Party leaders then chose Richard Nixon for Vice-President. The Democrats were in search of a candidate. The primary winner, Estes Kefauver, was unacceptable to major factions. Despite his personal hesitancy, Adlai Stevenson was nominated on the third ballot, with the aid of major delegation leaders, Truman and some spirited "amateurs." A loyalty oath was first imposed on the delegates and then removed, in an unsuccessful attempt to prevent Southern defections. John Sparkman was chosen as running mate.

1956. Eisenhower and Nixon were renominated unanimously, after flurries of opposition to Nixon were quelled. Adlai Stevenson won his second Democratic nomination after a long preconvention and primary campaign, and despite the opposition of Truman. The convention was allowed to choose the Vice-Presidential candidate in open balloting. Amid much confusion, Kefauver won the designation. A liberal minority platform plank on civil rights was rejected.

1960. Even before the Republican convention opened, Nixon had won control of his party. Opposition to some liberal platform provisions by various factions was soon settled, and the delegates then ratified the nominations of Nixon and Henry Cabot Lodge. Conflict in the Democratic party centered on the Presidential nomination. After a four-year effort, climaxed by a series of primary victories, John Kennedy won the nomination on a close first ballot vote. Lyndon Johnson was then designated as Vice-President by the party leaders and approved by the convention.

INDEX

Adams, John, 15, 156f, 267
Adams, John Quincy, 20f, 269
Adams, Sherman, 98n
Agar, Herbert, 22n, 29n, 39, 213n, 250n
Alexander, Herbert, 247n
American Political Science Association, 231, 235, 256, 260
Angle, Paul M., 31n
Anti-Masonic party, 269
Apportionment of convention votes, 24, 28, 49, 270; and bonus votes, 50, 276, 278; in Democratic party, 1960, 50-52, *Table*, 52; reform proposals, 51-53, 224, 231, 251-3; in Southern Republican party, 49f, 152; *see also* Credentials committee; National party committees
Arthur, Chester, 25, 183, 274

Availability, 113, 122-33, 203, 213; and conventions of 1960, 124; criteria, 123f; and Presidential elections, 128f, *Table*, 128; and Presidential nominations, 126f, *Table*, 127; and "prominence, 129-33; *see also* Candidates; Political recruitment.

Bagehot, Walter, 64, 211, 213, 228n
Bailey, John, 133n
Bailey, Stephen K., 245n, 250n, 266
Bain, Richard C., 4n, 25n, 39, 80n, 82n, 88n, 102n, 126n, 147n, 185n
Baker, Russell, 153
Barkley, Alben, 173, 180; as Presidential candidate, 97, 104,

281

Liberal Republican party, 273
Liberty League, 37
Lincoln, Abraham: and convention qualities, 211, 213, 230; renomination, 96, 164; and Republican convention of 1860, 31, 146, 149f, 209, 272; and site of convention, 48, 152
Lindbloom, Charles E., 89n, 207
Lockard, Duane, 65
Lodge, Henry Cabot, 160, 173, 177, 241, 280
Logan, John, 172, 274
Lowden, Frank, 44, 151f, 172, 173n, 227, 277
Lubell, Samuel, 36n, 40, 265n

McAdoo, William, 277
MacArthur, Douglas, 179
McClellan, George, 75, 80, 230, 272
McCloskey, Herbert, 91
McCoy, Charles A., 208
Machiavelli, Niccolo, 265
McKee, Thomas H., 18n, 23n, 30n, 67n, 69n, 75n, 79n, 201n
McKenzie, Robert T., 5n
McKinley, William, 102, 165, 275
MacMahon, Arthur, 6n, 65
McNary, Charles, 161, 279
Madison, James, 17, 268
Marshall, Thomas, 276
Martin, Joseph, 34n, 65, 161
Mass Media: and convention program, 85, 257; and negotiations, 63, 205-7; and nominations, 26, 62f, 105, 120, 153, 201, 212, 221, 248; and political system, 11, 246; and preconvention campaigns, 106, 109, 131, 203f, 261; and site of convention, 49; *see also* Candidates; Conventions, national party, Parties in the United States; Political recruitment; Technology
Mazo, Earl, 167n
Melnik, Constantin, 154

Mencken, Henry L., 124, 125n
Merriam, Charles E., 193n, 229
Meyner, Robert, 110n, 116, 119n
Michels, Robert, 208
Middleton, Lamar, 181
Miles, Samuel, 15
Moley, Raymond, 37n
Monroe, James, 17, 268
Moos, Malcolm, 83n, 150n, 158n, 175n, 197n, 203n
Morison, S. E., 17n
Morse, John T., 156n
Morse, Wayne, 118
Morton, Levi, 274

National party committees: chairman, 100; composition, 48, 87, 246, 252; and delegate selection, 49, 152; origins, 17, 21, 23, 268, 271; powers, 24, 48f, 53, 87f, 244-47, 257
National Republican party, 22, 28f, 184, 269
Negroes, 103, 254; as candidates, 163; in Democratic conventions, 37f, 70, 118, 125, 141; as voters, 238, 241, 251; *see also* Civil rights issue
Neumann, Sigmund, 6n, 236, 239-40n
Neustadt, Richard, 212n
Nevins, Allan, 31-33n
New Deal, 36-39, 67, 75, 179, 278
Nichols, Roy, 32-33n, 91
Nixon, Richard, 100, 180; and policy positions, 139-41, 149; as Presidential candidate, 60, 98, 108n, 115, 125, 160f, 184, 263, 280; as Vice-President, 169-71, 173f; as Vice-Presidential candidate, 160, 162f, 166f, 279f
Nominating system: characteristics, 5f; majority rule in, 215, 219f, 224; merits, 9, 11, 210-16; and political recruitment, 9, 210-13; *see also* Conven-

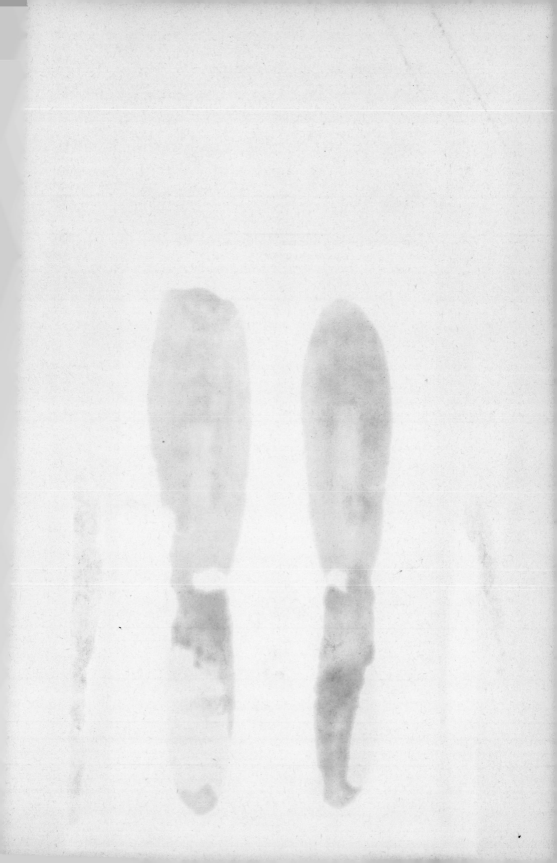